HIGH PERFORMANCE HOSPITALITY

Sustainable Hotel Case Studies

By

Michele L. Diener

Amisha Parekh

Jaclyn Pitera

©March 2008

With a Foreword by Andrew J. Hoffman

All greenhouse gas emissions generated from air and road travel associated with the development of this report have been offset through carbonfund.org. This handbook has been printed on 30% post-consumer recycled paper with vegetable-based ink.

Table of Contents

Foreword

Let us eliminate the phrase "green construction" from our lexicon. Let us talk instead of "smart building," "high efficiency building," "high-performance building," or simply "the future of building." Certainly, that is not going to happen immediately. The term "green" remains far too ubiquitous and salient, even in 2008. However, the future of the construction industry is clear. It is the creation of buildings that use less energy and less water, and are healthier places to work, play, live and rest. But, do not think of green building as a moral or even an environmental issue. Think of it as a market shift.

The signals of this market shift are clear. Energy prices are steadily increasing – more than $100 per barrel of oil, and a price for carbon soon to add to that staggering figure. Water price increases also are looming on the horizon – the American Southwest has lived with this burden for years and the Southeast is now learning about the fragility of a so-called secure water source. The fact is that buildings use 71% of this country's electricity, 39% of its overall energy, and 12% of its water. And yet, our building codes have not kept pace with the reality that we need to use these resources more efficiently. For every unit of gross domestic product (GDP) we create in the United States, we use 50% more energy than the European Union and Japan use for the same GDP unit. While that is due, in part, to the sheer size of our country and to the costs required to ship materials across it, it is also an indication of how badly we build our buildings.

This does not mean that the opportunity does not exist for companies to reap benefits in the absence of regulation. When Andreas Schlaepfer, head of Internal Environmental Management at Swiss Re, was charged with the task of making his company's buildings more energy efficient, he was surprised to find that, "If you've never focused on energy efficiency before, achieving a 30 percent reduction is simple."

And the market is responding.

- **Customers** want green buildings. While single family housing starts fell 14.7%, and sales of lumber and construction materials fell 12% between December 2005 and December 2006, makers of green building products reported increasing sales. According to a 2007 study by Forrester Research, 12% of American consumers would pay extra for consumer electronics that use less energy or come from a company that is environmentally friendly.

- **Employees** want green buildings. According to another 2007 study, 80% of young professionals are interested in securing a job that has a positive impact on the environment, and 92% give preference to working for a company that is environmentally friendly. Among MBA students, 75% from top schools are willing to accept a salary that is lower by between 10% and 20% to work for a "responsible" company.

- **Financial markets** want green buildings. Goldman Sachs, Bank of America, and Citigroup are just three of the many companies that have announced multi-million dollar set asides for investments in green buildings and energy-efficient technologies. In 2006, the total United States venture capital investment devoted to clean energy companies reached $2.4 billion, over 9% of all venture capital spending.

- And, the **construction industry** wants green buildings. The nation's largest green building conference, Green-Build, has witnessed a steady increase in attendance that reflects its growing importance: from 4,000 in 2002 to 22,000 in 2007. What used to be a conference of smaller companies offering hard-to-find products is now populated by major corporations such as Siemens, General Electric, Turner, Trane, and Skanska. These companies are drawn by market returns. The reality here is that if you are in the construction industry, you have to be in the green building segment.

This means that, whether you are an engineer, architect, contractor, designer, or owner; or whether you are in the home building, hospital, commercial, retail, manufacturing, or hospitality sectors, you have to do it, too. The economics of the market signal are here. The market demand is here. The future of green construction is now.

This report focuses on the hospitality market segment. Not an insignificant piece, the hospitality industry is the third largest retail industry (after automobiles and food) in the United States, generating annual revenues of $133 billion in 2006 and spending $3.7 billion in energy to do it. But, the hospitality industry is not immune to the demands of the green market shift. Nor is it denied the opportunities to be gained by embracing that shift. As this report shows, there are financial benefits in green buildings, both in construction and operations. Among these pages, you will find evidence that energy-efficient hotel lighting alone could save $133 to $777 million annually. Opportunities in water management could yield additional savings of 25% to 30% over business as it is currently operated. And using less toxic materials in both construction and operations creates a healthy indoor environment that customers and employees will find attractive.

If you are a hotel operator, owner, or developer, and you do not recognize these benefits, you are leaving money on the table. Your customers are beginning to ask for it. Your workers will have more allegiance if you do it. And most of all, your competitors will steal your market-share if they do it before you do.

This report lays out a solid case that dispels any preconceptions about the costs and benefits of high performance buildings. However, it is not just another advocate's plea. Based on real case studies, this report is a solid analysis, from a business perspective, of the financial rationale for thinking differently about the infrastructure and operations of the hotel industry. It is grounded work. Industry readers should use it as a guidepost en route to where the future of the hospitality industry is going. If you do not, your competitors will.

Andrew J. Hoffman
Holcim (US) Professor of Sustainable Enterprise
University of Michigan

Acknowledgements

We would like to thank our faculty advisor Andy Hoffman for his encouragement and guidance. We also would like to thank Elsie Orb, Jackie DiGiovanni, and Fred Wessells, our editors, and Tish Holbrook, our graphic designer, for their technical assistance and enthusiasm. For their generous financial support, we would like thank our sponsors: American Hotel & Lodging Educational Foundation, Graham Environmental Sustainability Institute, Interface, Inc., Knoll, Inc., Frederick A. and Barbara M. Erb Institute for Global Sustainable Enterprise, Sustainable Conservation, and the University of Michigan School of Natural Resources and Environment.

We would like to thank the following people for assistance in developing the case studies: Benjamin Birge, Kevin Carter, Gina Clatterbuck, Paul Clevenger, Jennifer Dekkers, Oliver Dibble, Ranie Fukumoto, Lori Grant, Melinda Hinkley, Robert Hoonan, Lee Kirby, Jean LaChance, Rhonda Leach, Gerry Link, Carlos Lopez, Milet D. Lukey, Linda Lyons, Jeslyne Madamba, Kristina Malcolm, Chris Marsh-Demers, Kurt Matsumoto, Mike McCarthy, John Mitchell, Stefan Mühle, Shaun O'Bryan, Jessica Patrick, Riley Saito, Evelyn Saludares-Monje, Tedd Saunders, Paul Savarino, Marty Schenk, Beth Scher, Mark Sheldon, Jen Singer, Tom Terrill, George Trujillo, Michelle White, Jackie Williams, and Omar Zenon. Your help was invaluable and your accomplishments exemplary.

We would also like to thank the following people for their support of our project: Chris Balfe, Kimo Bertram, Ashley Boren, Kass Bradley, Bill Browning, Jim Burba, Ray Burger, Javier Carey, Kit Cassingham, Cyndy Cleveland, Sarah Connick, Susan Corlett, Cox Family Fund, Peter deBrine, Lyndall deMarco, Jeffrey Diener, Sushma Dhulipala, Tim Eaton, Heather Furmidge, Chris Garvin, George Glazer, Dave Good, Bjorn Hanson, Sara Harding, Aaron Harris, Glenn Hasek, Elliot Helman, Rina Horiuchi, Drew Horning, Alex Karolyi, Ashley Katz, Jennifer Kelly, John Lembo, Corey Limbach, Mimi Limerez, JD Lindeberg, Charles Lockwood, Bryan Magnus, Kevin Maher, Michelle Moore, Matt Ouimet, Michael Pace, Janak Parekh, Audrey Paskel, Michael Petrone, Steve Pinetti, Michelle Poinelli, Naomi Porat, Rhonda Ratcliff, Maurice Robinson, Dan Ruben, Max Saffell, Matt Salazar, Corey Seeman, Amy Spatrisano, Emma Stewart, David Stipanuk, Jason Stone, Brian Swett, Brian Talbot, Lyle Thompson, Bob Tierney, Jeff Vahle, Melissa Vernon, Austin Whitman, and Katherine Wood. Your insights were indispensable.

Michele L. Diener
Amisha Parekh
Jaclyn Pitera
University of Michigan

Executive Summary

At the beginning of this century, the high performance building movement began to gain nationwide attention and momentum, starting with institutional and commercial development and, more recently, with hospitality development. Membership in the United States Green Building Council (USGBC), a national non-profit organization committed to expanding sustainable building practices, has grown dramatically. The Council's Leadership in Energy and Environmental Design (LEED®) rating system has been adopted nationally and internationally as the *de facto* high performance building standard.

High performance hotels, especially those that are designed, constructed, *and* operated sustainably, use energy, water, materials, and land much more efficiently and effectively than hotel buildings that are simply built to code. High performance hotels capitalize on the opportunity to enhance efficiency in the hotel market – a market that traditionally has not been concerned with its environmental impact. High performance hotel developers, owners, and managers create healthier working, playing, and resting environments with more natural light and cleaner air. These buildings improve occupant health, comfort, and productivity. When developers build in an environmentally sustainable manner, they increase profit margins and create a differentiated product that is increasing in demand. Hotel owners and managers save money by reducing the costs of operations and maintenance and by increasing employee productivity.

Nevertheless, across North America, misconceptions about high performance building abound. Many people still believe that high performance hotels are not financially feasible and that there is no consumer demand for them. Others believe that specific hotels can not achieve high performance because of those buildings' geographic location, prevailing climate, or corporate brand. There are still others who believe that high performance practices will have a negative effect on the guest experience. And, some believe that high performance practices can not be successful when developers, owners, and management companies are distinct entities.

This report dispels these misperceptions. The case studies alone demonstrate how high performance hotels can be financially feasible. The report features examples from across the North American continent and demonstrates how different companies and organizations can benefit from the design, construction, and operations of environmentally sustainable hotels. The hotel case studies reveal a variety of high performance financial and environmental benefits, as well as the concerns of developers, owners, and managers for their employees and for society at large. The key finding in this report is that a hotel's financial drivers, property oversight, location, brand, and size are not inhibitors of successful high performance practices, and that wide application is feasible. The case studies in this report affirm that high performance hotels are thriving in North America and that those hotels are experiencing a positive consumer response to environmentally friendly features.

Case Study Matrix

		MID RATE		CONVENTION CENTER			LUXURY		
		San Francisco, CA	Revere, MA	Adelphi, MD	Airlie, Virginia	Vancouver, WA	Kohala Coast, HI	Banff, Alberta, CANADA	San Francisco, CA
	Page Number	33	53	73	89	107	127	145	161
Key Topics	Site – Brownfield Redevelopment		●						
	Site – Historic Landmark Preservation				●			●	●
	Site – Stormwater Management			●		●			
	Materials and Resources	●	●	●		●			
	Waste Management	●	●		●	●		●	●
	Energy Efficiency	●	●	●		●	●		●
	Water Efficiency	●	●	●	●		●		
	Indoor Environmental Quality	●	●	●	●	●		●	●
Advantages of Green Development	Lower Operating Costs	●	●	●	●	●	●	●	●
	Less Negative Environmental Impact	●	●	●	●	●	●	●	●
	Product Differentiation	●			●	●			
	Education	●	●		●	●	●	●	●
Initial Implementation Phase	Design Phase	●	●	●		●			
	Construction Phase	●	●	●		●			
	Operations	●	●		●	●	●	●	●
Certification	LEED	●		●		●			
	Green Seal – Certified and Pending	●			●	●			
High Performance Champion	Developer		●			●			
	Owner		●	●	●		●		
	Management Company	●	●					●	●
Rating	Two Diamond		●	●					
	Three Diamond	●			●	●			
	Four Diamond						●	●	
	Five Diamond								●
Location	Urban	●				●			●
	Rural				●		●	●	
	Suburban		●	●					
Size	1–300 Rooms	●	●	●	●	●			
	301–600 Rooms						●		●
	601–900 Rooms							●	

User Guide

This report is a starting point to help interested parties learn more about environmentally friendly construction and operations for hotels. While each individual case study in this report may not be directly applicable to all new hotel projects, the key "lessons learned" in each case are widely applicable. One objective of this report is to evoke serious thought and discussion regarding the advantages and disadvantages of sustainability within the hotel industry. We hope that such discussions will lead to more environmentally friendly hotel construction and renovation projects, and business operations practices in the future.

The hotels featured in this report were selected because their cases successfully demonstrate high performance construction and/or operations. Additionally, the cases show that high performance sustainable development can be both practical and achievable. This report can be a tool for the hotel developer or owner who is designing and building a hotel from the ground up, just as it can be a tool for the hotel manager who is operating an existing hotel.

To summarize, this report can be used as a guide to learn why some practitioners have created sustainable hotels, understand how sustainable hotels achieve success, and gain insight into what features and practices are feasible. It is not a comprehensive report on all sustainable hotels, nor does it assess whether hospitality or tourism is or can be sustainable. The report does, however, assume that hotels will continue to be built, renovated, and operated.

The report is divided into four complementary sections:

Research Background – This section details the following elements: current hospitality industry trends; definition of high performance hotels; the existing market for high performance hotels; perceived barriers to high performance; and research goals and methodology. The information in this section is based on a review of high performance hotel literature available at the time of publication and on interviews with industry professionals.

Key Findings – This section presents the key findings from our research regarding high performance hotel best practices, the business case for high performance hotels, lessons learned from high performance hotel practitioners, and opportunities for industry improvement.

Case Studies – This section shares the unique story behind each high performance hotel. The detailed cases describe stakeholder advantages and practical applications of high performance hotel design, construction, and operations. The case studies are grouped by category – mid rate, conference center, and luxury – to help the reader find the cases most relevant to his or her situation. A standard design template is used in all of the cases, facilitating the identification of areas of interest and points of comparison.

Resources and Contact Information – We intend for this report to assist in the expansion of a high performance development resources network. Wherever possible, we provide resource and contact information for high performance features and for the developers, owners, managers, architects, and contractors of the projects covered. In the fourth section, the Appendices contain additional resource information, including a summary of certification programs for high performance hotels, a checklist of metrics and key performance indicators, a summary of the advantages of high performance hotel construction and operations, and a glossary.

SECTION 1:
Research Background

Hospitality Industry Overview

Hospitality comprises the third largest retail industry in the United States. In 2006, the American hospitality industry employed over seven million people directly, and more than that indirectly. For example, a waitress in a restaurant in Palm Springs, California, has her job because Palm Springs is a tourist destination. The hospitality industry indirectly employs wait-staff, accountants, nurses, salespeople, lifeguards, park rangers, street cleaners, car rental agents, blackjack dealers, caterers, cruise directors, the actress in the Snow White costume, the clerk selling t-shirts, the tennis pro, and the golf course groundskeeper.[1]

Hotels in the United States offer more than four million guest rooms and, in 2006, generated revenues of $133.4 billion. The average occupancy rate was 63%.[2] The industry includes a mix of large chains (e.g., Marriott, Hilton, and Starwood) and smaller independent hotels and motels.

The negative environmental impact of an individual hotel is significant. A hotel's operations require and generate inputs and outputs that involve water, energy, chemicals, food, sewage, and solid waste.

> The US hospitality industry spends $3.7 billion a year on energy. Electricity use accounts for 60–70 percent of the utility costs of a typical hotel. Guest lighting accounts for 30–40 percent of hotels' electricity consumption. Typical hotels use 218 gallons of water per day per occupied room.
>
> *Building Design+Construction*[3]

Given the size of the hospitality industry, the collective environmental impact is enormous. Rising energy costs in the United States have propelled large and small hotel developers, owners, and management companies to consider energy efficiency and resource conservation initiatives to help reduce operational expenses. Some hotels have implemented small measures such as towel and linen reuse programs and compact fluorescent lighting retrofits. However, a vast number of opportunities for expanding sustainability efforts still exists across the entire hotel industry.

What Is a High Performance Hotel?

Since the beginning of this century, the high performance real estate development movement in North America has gained significant national attention and momentum, originally with institutional and commercial development, and now with hospitality. Membership in the United States Green Building Council (USGBC), an American non-profit organization committed to expanding sustainable building practices, has grown dramatically. Its Leadership in Energy and Environmental Design (LEED®) rating system has been adopted nationally and internationally as the *de facto* high performance building standard.

The terms and phrases *high performance*, *sustainable*, *environmentally friendly*, and *green* are used interchangeably throughout this report and, when applied to hotel development, define projects of any scale integrating environmental and social goals with financial considerations. Analogous to these terms is the Triple Bottom Line, focusing on "economic prosperity, environmental quality, and social justice," [4] along with the "3 P's" (People, Planet, and Profits) and the "3 E's" (Equity, Ecology, and Economy).

What constitutes a green hotel is not defined consistently across the hotel industry. For some, a green hotel is one that incorporates building structure efficiencies, such as a well insulated building envelope and a reflective roof. Others consider a hotel to be green if it has incorporated energy and water-efficient fixtures, such as compact fluorescent light bulbs (CFLs) and low-flow toilets. And there are still others in the hotel industry who consider a green hotel to be one that has implemented operational environmental services, such as a towel and linen reuse program. This report uses the designation *high performance* to describe hotels that have implemented green features in building design and construction, in the hotel's operations, or in both.

Three key hospitality stakeholder groups can influence the existence of high performance hotels in the market. The first set of stakeholders includes developers, owners, and managers of hotel properties. We refer to this group by the designation "Property Oversight" throughout the

[1] http://www.wetfeet.com accessed on August 30, 2007.

[2] http://www.ahla.com/products_info_center_lip_2007.asp accessed on December 10, 2007.

[3] *Building Design+Construction*. 2006. "Green Buildings and the Bottom Line." White Paper. Pages 24–25. November.

[4] Elkington, John. 1998. *Cannibals with Forks: The Triple Bottom Line of 21st Century Business.* Gabriola Island, BC, Canada and Stony Creek, CT, U.S.A.: New Society Publishers.

report. The second group consists of large corporations, government agencies, and travel management companies that set business contracts. The third group comprises the individual travelers who make decisions regarding leisure and personal business travel. These latter hotel guests, like the corporate and government customers, may travel for business, but the assumption is that they have less negotiating power in the decision-making process because they are not initiating business contracts.

Table 1-1 below outlines the influence each stakeholder group has over the existence of high performance hotels in the market. The property oversight group directly influences high performance hotel existence by choosing to construct and/or operate a hotel sustainably and to sell their product to consumers. Corporate and government clients influence high performance hotel existence if their organizational policy dictates they select only environmentally friendly vendors. Individual travelers who care about environmental features increase the prevalence of high performance hotels.

Table 1-1 Stakeholders Influence on Hotel Design & Construction

Stakeholder	Influence In High Performance Hotel Existence
Property Oversight: Developers, Owners, Managers	• Decision makers for property development and management practices. • Responsible for communicating property features to customers and consumers.
Corporate and Government Customers	• Represented 44% of lodging business in 2006.[5] • Most large companies have preferred-vendor agreements with hotel companies.
Individual Travelers	• Represented 56% of lodging business in 2006.[6] • Make decisions based on personal preference.

Growing Interest in High Performance Hospitality

From 2006 to 2007 the market for high performance hotels across North America showed a noticeable increase. Influential groups in hotel development – developers, owners, managers, corporate customers, government customers, and individual travelers – recognized the value of high performance properties.

A 2007 study in *Building Design+Construction* emphasized the fact that over 51% of the survey's hotel business respondents had incorporated green building concepts in recent construction or renovation projects. Another 33% indicated they planned to do so in the near future. Sixty-five percent of the businesses surveyed identified consumer demand as the driver for incorporating sustainability concepts.[7]

This research on consumer demand aligns with *TripAdvisor*'s 2006 global survey which revealed that 34% of today's travelers would be willing to pay more to stay at an environmentally friendly hotel. Twenty-five percent would be willing to pay a 5% to 10% premium, and 12% would pay a 10% to 20% premium.[8]

According to *Building Design+Construction*'s 2006 survey on green building trends, the majority of consumer respondents willing to pay more to stay at a green hotel focused on the health benefits associated with better indoor air quality. In addition, there are 43 million travelers who say they prefer to do business with companies that share their concerns about environmental issues. Large hotel chains that rely significantly on corporate customers (e.g., Marriott) are now fielding questions about environmental practices in their responses to requests for proposals (RFPs) for corporate contracts. According to *Building Design+Construction*, green hotels also are included in website presentations that recommend lodging destinations for traveling government employees.[9]

Despite these positive trends in the high performance market segment, there is still some uncertainty among industry practitioners regarding the long-term consumer demand for high performance hotels. And, there is a continuing misconception that high performance hotels cost more to construct. What is apparent is that a few industry leaders have experimented with integrated high performance hotels while the larger hospitality community is waiting for legislated government regulations or the adoption of a standardized certification process.[10]

[5] http://www.ahla.com/products_info_center_lip_2007.asp accessed on December 10, 2007.

[6] http://www.ahla.com/products_info_center_lip_2007.asp accessed on December 10, 2007.

[7] *Building Design+Construction*. 2007. "Green Buildings and the Bottom Line." White Paper. Pages 44–45. October

[8] http://www.hotel-online.com/News/PR2007_2nd/Apr07_TripAdvisorGreen.html accessed on December 10, 2007.

[9] *Building Design+Construction*. 2006. "Green Buildings and the Bottom Line." White Paper. Pages 24–25. November

[10] Ibid.

Figure 1-1 Location of High Performance Case Study Hotels

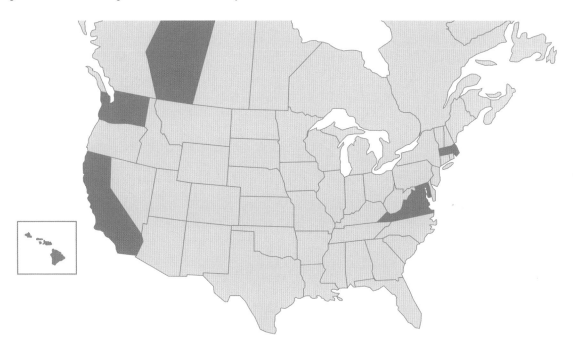

Perceived Barriers

Four main barriers to high performance hotel design, construction, and operations emerged through literature reviews and industry expert interviews at the beginning of the project. These perceived barriers helped to shape the structure of the project research and served as the starting point of our data analysis. The perceived barriers include:

1. **Business Case:** Lack of financial drivers to build and operate high performance hotels. Perception that green costs more.

2. **Consumer:** Lack of demand. Perception that green features will harm guest satisfaction.

3. **Property Oversight:** Difficulty of implementing procedural changes if the developer, owner, and manager are distinct entities. Each entity has different financial drivers.

4. **Hotel Characteristics:** Location, climate, size, and brand are variables that limit and restrict successful high performance hotel design, construction, and operations.

Research Goals and Methodology

The goal of this report is two-fold. The first objective is to understand the business case for high performance construction and operations while validating or invalidating perceived barriers to high performance hotels. The second objective of this report is to disseminate information on best practices in high performance building design, construction, and operations across the North American hospitality industry. We accomplish these objectives by presenting reliable data about environmentally sustainable hotel practices and the associated stakeholder costs and benefits.

The research for this report was conducted between the summer of 2006 and the summer of 2007. It involved interviewing nine hotel organizations across the United States and Canada, as seen in Figure 1-1.

Table 1-2 High Performance Hotel Case Studies

Mid Rate Hotels	• Orchard Garden Hotel, San Francisco, California • Comfort Inn & Suites Boston/ Airport, Revere, Massachusetts
Conference Centers	• The Inn and Conference Center, University of Maryland University College, Adelphi, Maryland • Airlie Center, Airlie, Virginia • Hilton Vancouver Washington, Vancouver, Washington
Luxury Hotels	• Mauna Lani Resort, Kohala Coast, Hawaii • The Fairmont Banff Springs, Alberta, Canada • The Ritz-Carlton, San Francisco, California

Hotel Selection Criteria: The research team developed both quantitative and qualitative hotel selection criteria. Initially, the team conducted an extensive review of the existing literature (academic publications, news articles, and business magazines) and interviewed industry professionals and experts to develop a comprehensive list of hotels representing successful high performance design, construction, and operations. The hotels were then categorized as mid rate facilities, conference centers, and luxury hotels. These were further broken down into branded (e.g., Marriott and Hilton) or independent (e.g., Orchard Garden and Mauna Lani) properties, as well as big or small and rural or urban hotels.

The final selection criteria were based on a hotel's level of commitment to environmentally sustainable practices. Under design and construction, these practices were classified as site development, energy consumption, water consumption, materials and resources, indoor air quality, and other innovations. Under hotel operations, practices were classified as front-of-house marketing, community outreach, and guest amenities and as back-of-house utility consumption, indoor air quality, janitorial/ maintenance, measures/instruments, and staff training and compensation. For hotel building design and construction, the LEED rating system is used as a base to measure the extent of high performance practices achieved. For hotel operations, the combination of hotel certifications listed in Appendix C is used as the base. In addition, both construction and operations are measured against the research team's industry knowledge.

Using the criteria described above, the team selected nine hotels, including two mid rate hotels, three conference centers, and four luxury hotels that are located across the United States and Canada and represent small, large, branded, and independent hotels. One property prefers to remain anonymous, so we present eight detailed case studies (listed in Table 1-2), while aggregate data and statements include the ninth property.

The Case Study Matrix on page 10 further describes the diverse aspects of each hotel beyond its assigned category, and includes data on high performance features, stakeholder advantages, when it "went green," high performance implementation leadership, and whether or not the hotel achieved LEED or Green Seal certification. (Green Seal is one of the certifications for high performance hotel operations. Additional detail is found in Appendix C.)

Data Collection: We collected our case study data through on-site, in-person interviews of hotel management teams. These teams always included the general manager and often the director of engineering, housekeeping, food and beverage, sales/marketing, front desk personnel, and the hotel owner. We also interviewed members of the project team, including the hotel contractor and the architect, whenever possible.

SECTION 2:
Key Findings

The project research produced the following significant results:

1. **Business Case:** Each hotel pursued high performance design and construction and/or operations with different objectives, but these were always supported by a strong financial rationale.

2. **Consumer:** Most of the high performance hotels benefited from increased media attention but only some hotels could link it to increased consumer demand. On the other hand, high performance hotels did not find that high performance features compromised the guest experience.

3. **Property Oversight:** High performance success was independent of the hotel's oversight structure. The research found that members of the property oversight team collaborated to achieve success for sustainable hotel projects.

4. **Hotel Characteristics:** Each hotel among the case study samples had implemented different, yet successful, high performance programs, regardless of location, climate, size, and brand.

The research also indicates that all of the case study hotels have been successful in implementing high performance design and construction and/or operations. The case studies in Section 3 provide the detail for these activities.

High Performance Hotel Best Practices

As mentioned in the key findings, all of the hotels interviewed successfully implemented high performance design and construction and/or operations, but did so in diverse ways. This section presents the green features that were most commonly implemented across the case studies, as well as those features that were innovative. The green features are construction elements or operational practices that are classified according to site, materials and resources, waste management, energy efficiency, water efficiency, and indoor environmental quality. In addition to construction and operations components, we also reviewed the high performance educational practices at each hotel.

The research team assessed whether the construction, operations, and educational components were common or distinct occurrences, and whether the complexity and cost of implementation was low, medium, or high. We also evaluated guest perceptions of these components. Our assessments were based on the research results as well as on interviews with industry experts.

In Table 2-1, on the next page, complexity is displayed from low to high in the columns and financial cost is displayed from low to high in the rows. The third dimension, guest response to green features, is found in the colored text. Table 2-1 reveals that most of the hotel's green features produced either a neutral or a positive guest response, indicated by black text.

Common Construction and Operations Features:
The most common green features incorporated by the case study hotels are generally low to medium in cost and complexity. Today, many of these practices are common across the hotel industry. They make good business sense and are not too complex or difficult to implement.

Site – A hotel's site location is unique, so trends are less apparent for this feature. Hotel transportation, however, is one-site related activity that has potential for industry-wide incorporation. Forty-four percent of the studied hotels are accessible to public transportation, and the same percentage use environmentally friendly on-site vehicles. Another common site-related practice is minimizing the heat island impact through installation of a reflective roof and/or reflective pedestrian hardscapes.

Energy Efficiency– Among the studied hotels, the most common energy-efficient feature is compact fluorescent lighting (CFL). All the case hotels utilize compact fluorescents and CFLs have been accepted as cost effective for the hotel industry. Other prevalent energy-efficient features, utilized by two-thirds of the case study hotels, include occupancy sensors, hydronic heating and cooling systems, and low-emittance windows that reflect radiant heat, thus lowering the total heat flow through the window. All of these features have the potential to become mainstream hotel practice. Occupancy sensors, however, have produced some negative guest response, and are more controversial for luxury hotels where guests expect

Table 2-1 Cost, Complexity, and Guest Perception of Common High Performance Construction and Operations Features

COST	COMPLEXITY — LOW	MEDIUM	HIGH
LOW	**SITE** Public Transportation Accessible Minimize Heat Island Impact – Roof & Hardscapes **MATERIALS & RESOURCES** Fly Ash in Concrete FSC Certified Wood EPP Paper Products Minimize Water Bottles On Site **WASTE MANAGEMENT** Back-of-house Recycling **ENERGY EFFICIENCY** Occupancy Sensors **WATER EFFICIENCY** **Low-Flow Hardware** Linen and Towel Reuse Program Washable Drapery and Linen **INDOOR ENVIRONMENTAL QUALITY** Low VOC Adhesives Low VOC Paint Operable Windows CO_2 Sensors **Smoke-Free Environment** **EDUCATION** In-House Guests Prospective Customers Local Community Members Staff/Employees	**SITE** Minimize Construction Site Disturbance Minimize Light Pollution **MATERIALS & RESOURCES** Locally Extracted Materials Locally Manufactured Materials Recycled Content for Construction Natural and Rapidly Renewable Chlorine-Free Pool Cleaning Process **WASTE MANAGEMENT** Guest Room Recycling Common/Public Area Recycling On-Site Composting **WATER EFFICIENCY** Washing – Environmentally Friendly Drycleaning – Environmentally Friendly Irrigation – Environmentally Friendly Drought Tolerant/Indigenous Plantings Brackish Water **INDOOR ENVIRONMENTAL QUALITY** Green Cleaning Supplies HCFC/CFC Free/No Ozone Depleting Substances **EDUCATION** Shareholders/Investors/Owners Government/Regulators	
MEDIUM	**ENERGY EFFICIENCY** Low e (energy-efficient) Glazing (windows) Compact Fluorescent Light Bulbs Energy Star Equipment **WATER EFFICIENCY** Dual-Flush Toilets	**SITE** Alternative Fuel House Vehicles **ENERGY EFFICIENCY** Commissioning Energy Recovery Units Hydronic HVAC LED Light Bulbs **INDOOR ENVIRONMENTAL QUALITY** Daylighting Natural Ventilation	**SITE** Storm Water Treatment Restored Native Vegetation Wildlife Protection **WATER EFFICIENCY** Recirculated Water
HIGH	Guest Room Key Cards	**SITE** Underground Parking	**SITE** Urban Infill Development Historic Site Preservation **Brownfield** **ENERGY EFFICIENCY** On-Site Cogeneration Photovoltaic Solar Panels **WATER EFFICIENCY** On-Site Sewage Treatment

Legend
Neutral-Positive Guest Perception — Neutral-Negative Guest Perception — **Negative Guest Perception** — **Mixed Guest Opinion**

their rooms to be at a certain temperature when entered. Energy Star equipment and light emitting diode (LED) lighting are common in more than half of the hotels studied.

Water Efficiency – Water-efficient irrigation is common in the hotel industry and was found at all of the hotels included in this study. Drought tolerant landscaping, in combination with efficient irrigation, improves overall water efficiency. Two-thirds of the studied hotels use this kind of landscaping. Two-thirds of the hotels also offer linen and towel reuse programs. Water-efficient low-flow bathroom fixtures are a cost saving technology implemented at two-thirds of the hotels, even though some guests view low flowing water as less than luxurious.

Materials and Resources – Currently, materials and resources are not the strongest environmental focus in the hotel industry. The most prevalent trend is the use of recycled content materials for office paper, brochures, toilet paper, and other paper products. For the future, the industry seems to be moving toward locally extracted and manufactured materials and an on-site ban of bottled water.

Waste Management – Waste management is an area on which hotel management groups have focused for a long time. All of the hotels in this study perform back-of-house recycling and use old linens and towels as rags–common industry practices that have proven to be cost effective. Many of the case hotels are now adding food composting and public area recycling to their waste management programs. These are cost effective practices and can facilitate the achievement of Green Seal certification.

Indoor Environmental Quality – In the arena of indoor environmental quality, certain programs already exist, including smoke-free environments, heating and cooling equipment that is free of ozone depleting substances (now required by regulation for new construction), and programmable thermostats. The no smoking policy trend is seen across other building types. At hotels, the guest response is completely mixed on this issue. Programmable thermostats have become a hotel industry norm and are now classified as environmentally friendly. Seventy-eight percent of the studied hotels have operable windows, which is not a common feature in the hotel industry. The use of low volatile organic compound (VOC) paints and adhesives in building construction and renovation, as well as green cleaning supplies, is increasingly common and will most likely become the industry standards.

Innovative Construction and Operations Features: As mentioned in the section on common features, most of the hotels interviewed have incorporated high performance features that require low financial investment and are fairly simple to implement. However, each of the hotels also has implemented fairly expensive and complex features. Several hotels have used creative financing techniques or have retrofitted existing systems to meet their objectives.

For example, one case study hotel wanted to implement a key card system to control guest room lighting and electricity consumption. The cost of the key card system went beyond the hotel's budget, so the management decided to install a simple circuit breaker in each guest room. This in-house system is not as sophisticated as the advanced technology option, but it meets the hotel's goal of reducing energy consumption and expense. Many of the other more complex and expensive green features, such as co-generation plants and photovoltaic systems, have been implemented with creative financing techniques. These include partnering either with suppliers or with a local bank to reduce initial capital investment.

Table 2-2, on the next page, describes some of the innovations implemented by the nine hotels and the rationale behind the decisions.

High Performance Hotel Education: The most common educational trend across all hotel categories is educating the hotel's employees regarding green construction design and/or green operational practices. The second most prevalent educational trend is that of engaging local community members in a hotel's environmental efforts. Please see Table 2-3 on page 23.

Green Teams – Over half of the studied hotels have a staff green team for researching and implementing environmental initiatives. These green teams consistently have been volunteer efforts and have proven to increase staff morale. We predict that green teams will become standard for hotels pursuing sustainability goals.

Table 2-2 Rationale for Innovative High Performance Construction and Operations Features

Green Feature	How Did They Make It Work?
Site	
Urban Infill Development	• The project received the construction permit allowing the developer to begin work immediately and that reduced the overall project time.
Historic Site Preservation	• The hotel's historic site was key to the guest experience and a significant reason the guest selected the hotel.
Brownfield	• The project obtained the land at a low market cost, which reduced the total project cost. • The selected brownfield site required minimal clean-up. • The project made use of an Alternate Use License and purchased insurance against any liability claims. • The hotel has not received any negative feedback from guests.
Underground Parking	• The parking area is also used as an exhibition hall for large conventions.
Stormwater Treatment	• The new construction shared a retention pond with an existing building on site. • The project installed stormwater retention tanks on site, which also counted as LEED credits.
Restored Native Vegetation	• Drought-tolerant native vegetation requires minimal maintenance, and thereby reduces overall operational costs.
Wildlife Protection	• Wildlife on site became a tourist attraction and may help increase occupancy rates. • Improved relations with environmental groups may pre-empt resistance to further development.
Energy Efficiency	
On-site Cogeneration	• Leveraged federal and state tax rebates. • Leveraged subsidies offered by local utilities. • Captured excess heat, generated by heating and cooling air or water, and reduced overall energy consumption.
Photovoltaic Solar Panels	• Leveraged federal and state tax rebates. • Leveraged subsidies offered by local utilities.
Water Efficiency	
Recirculated Water	• Reduced potable water consumption and the associated sewage fees.
On-site Sewage Treatment	• Used reclaimed water for landscape irrigation instead of using potable water. • Used reclaimed water to control construction dust. • May allow the developer to continue expansion by not exceeding the usage cap on county water and sewage systems.

Business Case

Each of the nine hotels had a strong business case for constructing and operating a high performance hotel. This section highlights the key financial drivers for considering high performance features, the market response, and how each stakeholder group benefited from implementing high performance features.

Drivers for Constructing and Operating Sustainable Hotels: The financial drivers for pursuing sustainable hotel design, construction, and operations are diverse. In addition, the timing of feature implementation is different for those hotels ranking higher in the sustainable design and construction spectrum when compared to those ranking higher in sustainable operations. Lastly, among the hotels studied, the person leading the green charge varies from owner to architect to governor. (Please see Table 2-4.)

Operations – Many of the hotels studied did not decide to pursue sustainability goals until the hotels already were in operation. This is possibly due to the fact that these hotels were operating before the beginning of the 21st century, at a time when high performance construction was not yet a part of the industry's mainstream agenda.

Construction – Hotels pursuing more substantial environmentally sustainable construction goals initiated the process during the facility's original construction, in contrast to hotels that primarily were undergoing renovations. A key finding from this analysis is that all the hotels pursuing green construction have indicated market differentiation and/or public relations value as a leading financial driver for achieving sustainability.

The University of Maryland Inn and Conference Center by Marriott is an exception to the findings about green construction. The hotel was built sustainably as a result of a government mandate. In 2001, at the time of the project's design, the cost premium for a LEED building was 15% because of the lack of product options. The State of Maryland mandated the decision to pursue LEED certification during the design phase of the project.

In Washington state, the Hilton Vancouver Washington pursued LEED certification with a 0.29% premium because it would allow the hotel to achieve market differentiation. At San Francisco's Orchard Garden Hotel, the general manager led the agenda and pursued high performance at a premium of 0.17%, primarily to gain market differentiation. This finding is consistent with an overall industry trend that appears to require high performance construction to achieve differentiation in the marketplace. High performance operations traditionally have been the hotel industry's focus if any high performance practices are implemented. As a result, high performance operations are viewed as more common and less innovative than high performance design and construction.

Table 2-3 Audiences for High Performance Hotel Education among Hotel Types

EDUCATION	TOTAL	Mid Rate	Conference Center	Luxury/ Resort
In-house Guests	67%	100%	67%	50%
Prospective Customers	56%	50%	67%	50%
Shareholders/Investors/Owners	56%	100%	67%	25%
Local Community Members	78%	100%	67%	75%
Staff/Employees	89%	100%	67%	100%
Government/Regulators	56%	50%	33%	75%

Table 2-4 Drivers for High Performance Hotel Design and Construction

		FINANCIAL DRIVERS	OTHER DRIVERS	TIMING	WHO LEAD THE CHARGE
MID RATE	San Francisco, CA	Market differentiation	Owner – Healthy building passion	When GM was already working with contractors, first learned about LEED. Had owner's passion prior.	General manager with aid of general contractor
MID RATE	Revere, MA	Long-term business commitment	Family values	During construction design phase	One of the owners
CONFERENCE CENTER	Adelphi, MD	Government mandate	NA	During conceptual design	Governor of Maryland
CONFERENCE CENTER	Airlie, VA	Market differentiation	Mission alignment	During hotel operation	Hotel executive team
CONFERENCE CENTER	Vancouver, WA	Market differentiation	City revitalization	During construction design phase (GC on board)	Architects (and developer on board)
LUXURY/RESORT	Kohala Coast, HI	Reducing expenses	Owner philosophy	During hotel operation	The president of Tokyu Corporation of Japan
LUXURY/RESORT	Banff, Alberta	Brand standards	Park regulations	During hotel operation	Fairmont corporate leadership
LUXURY/RESORT	San Francisco, CA	Reducing expenses	Local expectations	During hotel operation	Engineering department

Market Response: The consumer response from the case study hotels indicates that high performance features do not compromise the guest experience. Six out of the nine studied hotels have received free media attention for their high performance activities. Over half the hotels have begun to receive inquiries from individual guests and corporate clients regarding efforts to reduce the hotel's environmental footprint. This public attention reduces marketing costs for some hotels, but it is hard to translate those savings into increased occupancy rates. In general, hotel managers still believe that guests will choose a hotel for its location, price, amenities, and special features. However, convention hotels are noticing an increase in occupancy rates and customer interest related to high performance activities. (Please see Table 2-5.)

Table 2-5 Consumer Response of High Performance Hotel Design and Construction Activities

	Mid Rate	Convention	Luxury
Did the hotel receive free media attention for high performance activities?	100%	67%	50%
Are guests inquiring about high performance activities?	100%	67%	50%
Are corporate or government customers inquiring about high performance activities?	50%	67%	50%
Can the hotel attribute high performance activities to higher occupancy rates?	0%	67%	0%

Stakeholder Advantages: Property oversight, hotel category, size, location, climate, and whether the hotel was branded or independent did not negatively affect the success of the hotel case studies. The developer, owner and manager comprise the hotel property oversight. The research team found that the property oversight structure was irrelevant to the overall success of a high performance strategy and that the property oversight structure varies greatly among hotels (as seen in Table 2-6).

Table 2-6 Number of Hotels with Similar Property Oversight Structure

	Number of Hotels
Developer, Owner, and Manager all different entities	4
Developer, Owner, and Manager same entity	3
Developer, Owner same entity (Manager different)	2

An important finding of the property oversight structure analysis is that, regardless of the type of structure, the nine studied hotels have been successful because they had a collaborative property oversight group and a collaborative project team (including the architect and contractor). The hotels stated that this was an essential component of their success and was more cost effective in the long run than conventional isolated practices. In the cases of the Orchard Garden Hotel and the Inn and Conference Center at the University of Maryland University College, for example, the owner depends on the management company to implement environmentally sustainable operational practices, and to realize additional cost savings in excess of what is produced by high performance construction. The Hilton Vancouver Washington is an example of a public/private partnership where distinct entities (FaulknerUSA, the City of Vancouver, and Hilton Hotels Corporation) work together to revitalize the local community and the environment.

Additionally, independent *versus* branded is not a key criterion in determining the success of environmentally sustainable projects, nor is a mid rate, conference center, or luxury category. All nine hotels, covering the entire criteria spectrum, have implemented successful environmentally sustainable initiatives, regardless of these differences.

This section digs deeper into the financial drivers of each hotel case study by looking at the advantages to each property oversight stakeholder, that is, the developer, owner, and manager.

For the Developer: Developers derive multiple benefits from high performance construction. Green construction practices can be implemented at minimal additional cost, which allows developers to create a differentiated product and potentially earn a higher profit when they sell the property. This scenario is evident both when the developer and owner are the same entity and when they are not. However, the benefit is greater for hotels pursuing a high level of sustainable construction.

A second advantage for developers derives from choosing a location with a beautiful natural site. Industry trends indicate that consumers still care most about a hotel's location and price. This trend is evident at the Airlie Center, where the property oversight is performed by a single entity, and at the Mauna Lani Resort, where the property oversight is performed by multiple entities.

A few among the nine hotels were unique in their developer advantages. The developer of the Hilton Vancouver Washington benefited by obtaining LEED project experience. The developers of The Ritz-Carlton, San Francisco benefited from building on a historic site in a premier location that created a highly attractive consumer product.

For the Owner and Manager: If the hotel manager and owner are the same entity, or if the manager is paid a fee based on profit, then the most common high performance benefit is reduced cost. Managers whose pay is based on revenue are more likely to focus on methods that boost sales, such as public relations and an enhanced guest experience. Typical cost savings occur for utilities, public relations, and/or employee productivity. Utility cost savings are the only quantifiable measure, but this data is difficult to collect from hotels. Where possible, we have presented a detailed analysis in the hotel case studies. The public relations and employee measures also defy quantification and are based mainly on qualitative data.

Utility cost savings originate in a wide variety of efficient technologies and resource conservation practices. Implemented energy and water programs achieve the largest savings, and these are described in more detail in the section on High Performance Features.

Hotel owners and management companies achieve public relations savings when they differentiate their hotels by marketing their green features. This is the case with the Orchard Garden Hotel, Comfort Inn & Suites Boston/ Airport, The Inn and Conference Center at the University of Maryland University College, the Hilton Vancouver Washington, Mauna Lani Resort, and The Ritz-Carlton, San Francisco.

Employee-related savings result from decreased staff turnover, increased productivity, and increased morale. The research also revealed that green cleaning products improve employee productivity and that green teams or other staff environmental programs boost employee morale and reduce turnover.

Lessons Learned

This section highlights, through anecdotes, the lessons learned by property oversight or project teams while they were implementing environmentally sustainable design, construction, and operations programs at the eight case study hotels. (Please see Table 2-7.) This is not meant to be a thorough "how-to" guide of high performance practices. The lessons are either strategic or practical in nature and include examples from the individual hotels. The strategic advice falls under team management, communication, project management, general strategy, and procurement, and the practical advice includes marketing and consumer response, operations, materials and resources, waste management, and performance measurement. For more information on measuring performance, see Appendix B.

Table 2-7 Highlights of Strategic and Practical Lessons Learned by High Performance Hotels

Strategic	Lesson Learned	Example
Team Management	• If pursuing environmentally sensitive design and construction (and/or a USGBC LEED certified building), hire the general contractor early in the process; it may appear to cost more, but it saves money during the project and over the life of the building. • Hire an experienced LEED Accredited Professional to facilitate the USGBC LEED certified building process and paperwork. • Leverage external experts to keep abreast of trends. • Establish performance-based contracts with building system providers and third-party consultants to guarantee operational savings. • Establish solid relationships with local utility and municipal representatives and create symbiotic public/private partnerships that may reduce permit approval time and potentially create tax incentives and rebate programs. • Seek out other groups and companies to collaborate in sharing new knowledge and celebrating successes. • Provide guests with information explaining how they can support the hotel's environmental initiatives. • Consider incentive programs that make employees partners in developing a hotel's sustainability initiative.	A mid rate hotel depended on their architect and general contractor teams for guidance and leadership throughout the project. A luxury hotel hired an external consultant with a performance-based contract to perform an energy audit.
Communication	• Keep senior management informed, but realize that management focuses on payback; they are not technology experts. Encourage management to make decisions using lifecycle evaluations. Senior management should champion environmentally sustainable programs through consistent messages, especially if the effort is not led by senior management. • Continually inspire the staff to suggest innovative green initiatives. Employee awareness is the "lowest hanging fruit." • Explain to employees how energy savings benefit hotel operations as well as lower the cost of running their homes. Employees take the lessons learned at work and apply them at home.	A conference center hotel initially took time to educate its general manager to facilitate the processing of all future lifecycle analysis proposals.
Project Management	• If pursuing a USGBC LEED certified building, make the commitment early so you can track construction and demolition waste hauling. Do not wait until the end of the project to calculate recycling rates for LEED certification. • Consider multi-phase projects; it may be cost effective to implement programs in steps rather than all at once.	A luxury hotel had more than five phases to install photovoltaic solar panels that now generate more than half a megawatt of energy from the sun's radiation.
Procurement	• Study new technology and consider a trial and error strategy. Work with prototypes and investigate new products. No product is as good or bad as it initially appears. Similarly, what worked yesterday may not work tomorrow, so be aware of the products and trends that are in the pipeline. • Leverage the research of Green Seal, Co-op America, and other third-party experts when evaluating alternative products to minimize internal time and resources allocated for similar activities. • Leverage parent company and/or corporate resources and buying power to improve the hotel's return on investment by taking advantage of bulk purchases and economies of scale.	Employees at a conference hotel took home and tested a number of low-flow shower heads before selecting a product.
General Strategy	• Challenge conventional wisdom. • When evaluating new initiatives, consider opportunities that reduce expenses and/or have the potential to increase revenues. Energy conservation is more than reducing expenses if it also generates more business. • Never lose sight of the core business. Even if the philosophy is green, ensure that all programs and initiatives are appropriate for the hotel and its locale. • It does not have to cost more to build an environmentally sustainable LEED certified building.	At the time of a conference hotel's proposal for a new building, it cost approximately 15% more to build green, but now it is getting closer to nothing, currently 2–5%.

Table 2-7 Highlights of Strategic and Practical Lessons Learned by High Performance Hotels (continued)

Practical	Lesson Learned	Example
Marketing and Consumer Response	• Leverage consumer databases to gauge sustainability preferences to develop relevant customer-facing programs. • Start learning about LEED early and then educate the staff; help everyone respond appropriately to guests' questions. • Help consumers see that green operations do not equal poor aesthetics or compromised services. • It is critical to train front desk staff and prepare them with responses to guest questions and concerns related to the on-site green programs. • Some people take advantage of green claims and use it solely as a marketing tool and not as a way to do business. This discredits the efforts of others. One way to mitigate this is to educate people. • Continue to be a showpiece; work to educate guests and staff and to promote green awareness for the industry.	A luxury hotel is putting together an environmental response "cheat sheet" to communicate a consistent message to guests.
Operations	• Understand your building systems! • Plan solar collection from photovoltaic solar panels in the design phase of a new or renovation project. The financial impact of retrofits as well as legacy building systems may prohibit modification. • Twenty percent of the achieved energy savings come from implementing a good preventive maintenance program.	A conference hotel is pursuing Green Seal certification to validate its ongoing operations and preventive maintenance program.
Materials and Resources, and Waste Management	• Water-based wood stains should be tested for use in high traffic areas. • There are now aesthetically and environmentally preferred products on the market, so aesthetics can drive environmental decisions in a positive direction.	A luxury hotel has changed its room standard from vinyl wall-covering to low VOC paint.
Measuring Performance	• If you can't measure it, you can't improve it. • Benchmark and learn from the industry leaders who have paved the way. • Best practices can be replicated at other properties, so sharing information is key. • Before considering any project, understand the purpose (environmental and economic benefits) and the associated financial implications. Generic case studies and comparison data without exact numbers are acceptable. Since every hotel situation is different, rough orders of magnitude should suffice. Use the framework and overlay your own business conditions to make the business case based on your locale. • Periodically audit supply chain and business partner practices to make sure they are acting on their commitments.	A mid rate hotel shares its best green practices with other properties in the brand portfolio. A conference hotel followed its recyclables hauler only to find the materials were being sent to the landfill.

Opportunities for Industry Improvement

Table 2-8 summarizes some of the gaps that currently exist in environmentally sustainable design, construction, and operations as indicated anecdotally by the nine studied hotels. We believe these deficiencies regarding management, materials and resources, waste management, energy, and indoor environmental quality represent opportunities that can move the hospitality industry toward more environmentally sustainable practices, and that an entrepreneurial supplier will have a sympathetic audience.

Table 2-8 Opportunities for Industry Improvement by Business Area

Business Area	Need
Management	• Provide a service or a framework to help hotels evaluate and prioritize projects using the following criteria: financial impact (initial cost and cost over the expected life), environmental impact, consumer impact. • Create the de facto green hotel certification program, a single point of reference for the industry, and reduce the cost of the certification process.
Materials and Resources, and Waste Management	• Improve the recycling infrastructure throughout North America and identify uses for recyclable materials. • Find someone who can recycle telephone books. • Provide carpeting style options that are durable and conservative; sustainable options seem to be limited in design and are primarily edgy and modern. • Improve the durability of rapidly renewable flooring products. • Improve the options for recycled content toilet paper and other paper products.
Energy	• Create special nightlights and CFL bulbs that are difficult to remove from the guest rooms. • Create more cost effective light bulbs.
Indoor Environmental Quality	• Create organic weed killers that perform as well as the traditional chemical products.

MID RATE HOTELS

Property	Orchard Garden Hotel, 466 Bush Street, San Francisco, California 94108
Contact Information	http://www.theorchardgardenhotel.com
	(415) 399-9807
Category	Independent, Mid Rate
	Expected to achieve Three Diamond AAA Rating
Property Oversight	Developer: Mrs. S. C. Huang
	Owner: Mrs. S. C. Huang
	Management Company: Portfolio Hotels and Resorts
Gross Square Feet (GSF)	55,751 GSF
	Ten stories above grade
	One basement below grade
Number of Guest Rooms	86 @ 648 GSF per room
Construction Type	New construction
Date Completed	December 2006
Project Cost	$21 million (excluding restaurant costs)
	• Innovative technology: Key card energy system: $35 thousand
	$377/SF (excluding land and associated fees)
	$6 million additional for land and associated fees
High Performance	• Site
	• Materials and Waste Management
	• Energy
	• Water
	• Indoor Environmental Quality
	• Education
Awards and Certifications	• 2007 Certified Green Small Business Award
	• "Best Places to Work" in the Bay Area
	• Condé Nast Traveler's "138 Top New Hotels in the World" for 2007
	• "Green" Hotels Association, member
	• Green Seal certification (audit completed, certification pending)
	• LEED New Construction version 2.1 basic certification

San Francisco, California

Orchard Garden Hotel

Opened in November 2006, the Orchard Garden Hotel is California's first LEED (U.S. Green Building Council Leadership in Energy and Environmental Design) certified hotel. This effort is a result of the developer's commitment to healthy interiors, the general manager's interest in sustainable design, and the general contractor's knowledge of the subject. The hotel project team was able to achieve third-party certification with an approximately $35,000 premium (0.17% premium) added to the construction budget. The third-party certification allows the hotel to realize reduced marketing expenses and create a differentiated product. The hotel's efficient building and sustainable features pay dividends in multiple ways, including significantly lower utility bills and positive consumer and employee responses. As a result, the Orchard Garden Hotel offers an exemplary case study in effective team collaboration and high performance construction.

Background

Mrs. S. C. Huang was born in Shanghai, China. Mrs. Huang has been a hotelier since 1958, when she and her husband opened the original Orchard Hotel in Singapore. The couple sold that hotel in 1983 and subsequently built a new Orchard Hotel in Perth, Australia. After her husband's death in 1993, Mrs. Huang spent several years developing plans to build and operate another Orchard Hotel in San Francisco. The San Francisco property opened at 655 Bush Street in the year 2000.

The Orchard Garden Hotel rises ten stories high at 466 Bush Street in San Francisco. Although it is a sister property to the award-winning Orchard Hotel at 655 Bush Street, the Orchard Garden has its own story to tell. Opened at the end of 2006, the Orchard Garden Hotel is San Francisco's first LEED (U.S. Green Building Council Leadership in Energy and Environmental Design) certified hotel (see the LEED scorecard in Figure 2). After the untimely cancer-related deaths of three of her family members, Mrs. Huang has become passionate about clean environments and has devoted herself to creating an environmentally safe hotel.

Mrs. Huang has partnered with Stefan Mühle, the general manager for both San Francisco properties, and with Architecture International and Swinerton Builders. This team has been able to design and construct a simple, elegant, and comfortable hotel. The Orchard Garden has applied for a Three Diamond rating to ensure that the hotel exceeds consumer expectations by providing a Four Diamond guest experience. It is a conventional hotel where the environmental features are not obvious to the guest. If you did not know about the environmental features, you would not be able to see the majority of attributes. As a result, the Orchard Garden Hotel offers an exemplary case study in effective team collaboration and high performance construction.

Organization

Project Team

The project team consists of the property oversight group – the developer/owner and the management company – as well as the general contractor and architect.

Contact Information

Below is contact information for the project team.

Developer/Owner	Mrs. S. C. Huang
General Manager	Stefan Mühle Portfolio Hotels and Resorts www.portfoliohotels.com smühle@theorchardhotel.com
General Contractor	Oliver Dibble Swinerton Builders www.swinertongreen.com odibble@swinerton.com
Architect	Sherry Caplan Architecture International www.arch-intl.com scaplan@arch-intl.com

> *This is the future of construction. There is no way we can build the way we built for the last 100 years for the next 100 years. We won't have the materials available.*
>
> OLIVER DIBBLE, *General Contractor/Senior Project Manager,* Orchard Garden Hotel

Owner/Developer: Mrs. S. C. Huang

High Performance Qualifications: Mrs. Huang had no specific experience with high performance buildings, but did have a passion for healthy hotels.

General Manager: Stefan Mühle

High Performance Qualifications: Mr. Mühle was aware of high performance construction practices because of his European background. However, prior to his work with the Orchard Garden Hotel, he did not have direct experience with the U.S. LEED rating system.

General Contractor/Senior Project Manager: Oliver Dibble

High Performance Qualifications: Mr. Dibble worked for Swinerton Builders and had direct experience with several LEED projects. He was a LEED accredited professional (AP), but was not the LEED AP for this project. Swinerton Builders is committed to high performance practices and provided the LEED AP and commissioning agent for the Orchard Garden project.

Architect/Designer: Sherry Caplan

High Performance Qualifications: Ms. Caplan had limited exposure to LEED projects, but was supportive of and interested in high performance architecture and design.

Managerial Structure

There is one labor pool for both the Orchard and Orchard Garden Hotels. Depending on the level of occupancy, the number of employees on average is 120 overall, with 65 at the Orchard Hotel and 55 at the Orchard Garden Hotel. The diagram below in Figure 1 outlines the reporting structure for the administrative and managerial positions at the Orchard Garden Hotel.

Figure 1: Managerial Structure

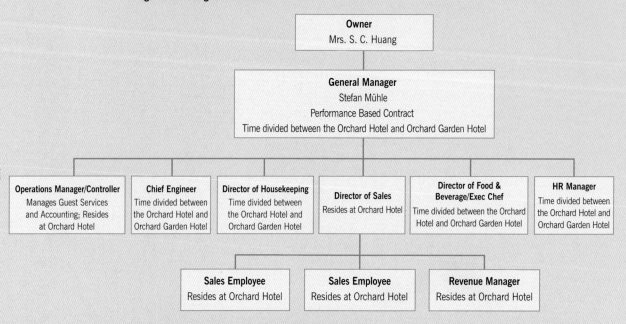

Staff Training and Compensation

The Orchard Garden general manger educated his staff and gained their acceptance of environmentally friendly cleaning products. When Orchard Garden first introduced fruit acid–based natural cleaning products, the house-keeping staff (trained in the use of traditional chemical-based products) was skeptical of alternative cleaning methods. They believed it would impact the quality of their work and might require additional cleaning time. To counter this belief, the management team, along with the natural cleaning product company Sierra Environmental Technologies, conducted a six-week trial during which half the staff used the traditional chemical products and the other half used natural products. Management surveyed the housekeeping staff every few days for results, and then the cohorts were switched in order to gain buy-in from all staff members. The housekeeping staff now acknowledges that natural cleaning products clean just as well as bleach, and that natural products help to eliminate health issues (such as dry skin and respiratory difficulties) associated with chemical-based cleaning products. New housekeeping staff are trained to use fruit acid–based cleaners through a buddy system in which they are paired with current staff to ensure consistency of performance.

In the hospitality industry, it is common to pay hotel management companies a fixed rate based on revenue. At the Orchard Garden Hotel, the compensation paid to the general manager and senior staff is a base salary plus an incentive program based on gross operating profit. This has made it easy to convince the hotel manage-ment team of the rationale for a high efficiency hotel. Staff bonuses are based on gross operating profit, which includes occupancy, room rate, and the cost of labor. All of these factors combine to ensure that the management company is not compromising the customer experience by cutting costs.

Community Outreach and Education

The Orchard Garden Hotel offers educational tours for students interested in high performance design and operations, and it hopes to promote a new generation of environmentally conscious professionals. In addition, hotel visitors can read about the hotel's sustainable initiatives in the documentation provided at the front desk or online. The terrace and the art exhibits in the hotel are open daily to the general public, from 9:00 a.m. to 5:00 p.m., in compliance with San Francisco public space laws.

Construction and Operations

The Orchard Garden has incorporated more high performance construction elements than operational practices, with the operational practices focused on a healthy indoor environment and resource conservation. Table 1 summarizes the most prominent among the high performance features of the Orchard Garden Hotel's construction and operations.

Table 1 HIGH PERFORMANCE CONSTRUCTION AND OPERATIONS HIGHLIGHTS	
1. Site	• The location is characterized by dense urban infill development close to public transportation, following smart growth principles. • During the construction of Orchard Garden, actions were taken to reduce the amount of soil erosion, sedimentation in waterways, and dust.
2. Material and Resources, and Waste Management	• The total amount of recycled materials in the building construction is over 10% (based on cost). • The building's construction specifies fly ash in the concrete to avoid landfill disposal, to conserve natural resources, and to reduce thermal cracking effects. • 55% of the materials were extracted locally, and 22% of the materials were manufactured locally. • Out of the total new wood in the facility, the hotel uses 50% Forest Steward Council (FSC) certified maple from Minnesota for most of the furniture and trim. • Every guest room provides in-room recycling for plastic bottles, metal cans, and paper, and the hotel offers used-battery collection for guests.
3. Energy	• Daylighting is incorporated in 82% of Orchard Garden's occupied areas. • A high albedo roof coating on the hotel decreases heat island effect and saves energy. • The property employs a guest room key card energy conservation system that is projected to lower electricity consumption by 20%. • The building's central hydronic heating and cooling system is more efficient than a fan coil system. • Through commissioning, the team solved problems in advance, and reduced energy consumption by ensuring systems operated as designed.
4. Water	• Laundry practices, including bulk washing and less frequent washing, conserve resources. • Faucet aerators and low-flow bathroom toilets and showers help conserve water. • No outside irrigation system is needed.
5. Indoor Environmental Quality	• The hotel's central hydronic heating and cooling system requires no ozone-depleting substances (CFCs, HCFCs, or halons). • Housekeeping staff use non-toxic, fruit-based cleaning products. • Adhesives, paints, carpet systems, furniture, and fixtures have low volatile organic compound (VOC) emissions.

1. Site

The Orchard Garden Hotel is located between the downtown financial district and the Chinatown cultural neighborhood, just down the street from its sister property the Orchard Hotel. The Orchard Garden's dense urban location on a previously developed site demonstrates environmentally responsible land use and follows smart growth principles. The hotel's density is 381,800 square feet (SF) per acre and the density of the surrounding buildings is 207,912 square feet per acre (according to LEED calculations). Transportation alternatives are inherently encouraged because the hotel offers only valet parking and there are many public transit options nearby.

While beneficial in other respects, the building's small footprint (roughly 5,600 square feet) does limit the amount of available space for outdoor landscaping, green areas, and public use. A small patio is located on the hotel's roof, where guests can enjoy premier views of the city. The heating, ventilating, and air conditioning (HVAC) equipment, as well as the elevator shaft space (a building code requirement), are hidden. However, with these technical features and an outdoor patio all occupying an already small roof, there is no extra space for alternative energy sources like solar photovoltaic cells or wind turbines.

Construction

During the construction of the Orchard Garden Hotel, Swinerton Builders implemented an erosion and sedimentation plan. This plan controlled soil erosion on site, sedimentation of waterways off site, and the release of airborne dust into the atmosphere.

2. Materials and Resources, and Waste Management

The design and execution of the Orchard Garden Hotel project emphasizes resource conservation throughout. Table 2 gives an example of the hotel's materials, which reveals that many construction and interior decorating materials are made with recycled content.

Table 2 **MATERIALS AND RESOURCES**	
Building Core and Shell	• 25% recycled content in the window glass • 25% recycled content in the steel • 30% recycled content in the acoustical ceiling tile • Armstrong Optima and Cortega ceiling systems in the basement • Skim-coated concrete ceilings in the guestrooms
Concrete	• 30% fly ash concrete in the foundation mat slab that covers the entire building footprint • 19% fly ash in the walls • 15% fly ash in the concrete floor slabs
Carpeting	• 100% recycled content in the carpet backing and double back padding for sound attenuation • Carpet that can be recycled at the end of its useful life through the manufacturer's take-back program (e.g., Antron nylon fibers that are down-cycled into padding and other flooring products) • Embassy 32 carpet pad, manufactured by Reliance Carpet Cushion Co. in Garden, California, made of 100% post-consumer recycled content, and registered as a low-emission indoor material • Bentley Prince Street broadloom carpet products manufactured in Southern California and contributing to the LEED point criteria for manufacturing within a 500-mile radius of the project site
Other Flooring	• Granite and limestone flooring in the lobby • Terrace flooring is not set apart to enable water runoff
Fabrics	• 53% recycled polyester in the drapes • 86% recycled polyester in the shower curtains • 49% recycled polyester in the bed coverlets • Guestroom fabrics (drapery, coverlets, and shower curtains) developed by Luna Textiles, a local Northern California–based design firm • Fire rated and machine washable fabrics that do not require treatment with harsh dry cleaning chemicals • Washable bed "linens" made with high thread count Egyptian cotton (but not organic because of durability requirements)

Construction

Although specifying fly ash in the concrete does not have a particular visual appeal, increasing the amount of fly ash in construction materials does have significant environmental benefits. These include avoiding landfill disposal of the product and conserving the natural resources that would otherwise be used in the concrete mixture. Additionally, fly ash helps to reduce the damaging effects of thermal cracking of concrete while it is curing, which is a problem particularly in thicker pours. According to an article authored by Swinerton Builders, typical concrete specifications limit fly ash content to 25% by weight. However, by working closely with the concrete supplier, Swinerton Builders was able to use 30% fly ash content in the hotel's 42-inch-thick concrete mat slab for the building foundation.

The construction team also used a Pioneer 100% biodegradable product made of recycled sawdust for day-to-day cleanup, and they partnered with Golden Gate Disposal to recycle over 75% of the construction debris. The total amount of recycled materials in the building construction is over 10% (based on cost) and the percentage can be largely attributed to the concrete and steel structure.

Swinerton's dedication to a sustainable job site extended to the materials and furnishings used at the job site's office. All office furniture was either salvaged from another site or bought used from Hertz Equipment, both of which reduced waste and saved money. The Orchard Garden team also used 100% recycled paper for the project and, whenever possible, sent digital documents instead of faxes.

Interior Design

At the Orchard Garden Hotel, the wall covering is primarily vinyl and the wood paneling is a photo plastic laminate (P-Lam) on top of recycled-content particle boards. Vinyl is not an environmentally sound product, but is still used by many in the hotel industry because of its durability. Orchard Garden, however, uses low VOC adhesives for the vinyl as well as for the P-Lam. Most of the hotel's carpet is Bentley Prince Street, which is made with its new non-adhesive technology for the carpet. The team also used recycled content for the carpet backing and pads.

The project team selected Forest Steward Council (FSC) certified maple wood from Minnesota for 50% of the project need, including most of the hotel's furniture (primarily guest room desks, headboards, sliding bathroom doors, night stands, side tables, and recycling bins), as well as for trim pieces. In lieu of purchasing chairs with FSC wood, the Orchard Garden Hotel was able to procure locally manufactured chairs with faux leather for durability and ease of maintenance. Chemicals are not required for cleaning these chairs. Other seating items, as well as the remaining doors, are not made with FSC wood because of market limitations.

The Orchard Garden Hotel was able to incorporate local materials such as the Bentley Prince Street carpet, tile, flashing, sheet metal, plaster, and different concrete mixtures into the hotel's design. Fifty-five percent of these materials were extracted within 500 miles of the hotel, and 22% of those same materials were manufactured locally (based on cost).

Operations

The sales and marketing team for both the Orchard Garden and the Orchard Hotel uses recycled-content paper products for stationery and soy-based inks for published brochures. In addition, the hotel toilet paper (Renature brand) has 100% recycled content, as does the copy paper (30% post-consumer). Office staff also participate in printer toner return programs and receive discounts on new toner purchases.

The Orchard Garden Hotel uses recycled paper for all back office operations. Recycled paper traditionally costs more than conventional printing paper, but the Orchard Garden has been able to make the cost neutral by selecting a more gray color.

The housekeeping staff recycles old linens for use as rags, and they provide for in-room recycling by placing a sorting bin for plastic bottles, metal cans, and paper in every guest room. The maid carts have the same recycling divisions to facilitate sorting, and the hotel offers used-battery collection for guests. Members of the Orchard Garden Hotel staff periodically drop off the collected batteries at a nearby Walgreen's drug store for proper disposal.

3. Energy

The Orchard Garden is an energy-efficient hotel, due in large part to its small footprint and effective building envelope and core system. The building envelope helps reduce energy consumption through its high albedo roof coating, well insulated exterior walls, and effective use of daylighting. The roof coating has an emissivity of at least 0.9 and complies with Energy Star label requirements. This technology reduces the heat island effect, which lowers the amount of energy needed to cool the building. The hotel has daylighting (with a daylight factor of at least 2%) in more than 82% of the occupied areas.

The hotel also realizes energy savings through its core building hydronic heating and cooling system. This system is demand-responsive and enables room-specific zoning. The digital Building Management System works with the hydronic system by monitoring heating and cooling needs and adjusting the system accordingly. Additionally, the Orchard Garden commissioned their HVAC, hot water heating, electrical, and life safety systems to ensure that they performed as designed. This proactively fixed future problems and saved future energy consumption.

The Orchard Garden installed an innovative guest room key card system that is predicted to decrease the hotel's electricity consumption by 20%, based on EPA projections of future occupancy. After entering a guest room, the customer inserts the key card into a wall unit that activates the room's lighting, and heating and cooling systems. Once the card is removed from the unit, those features automatically turn off. This energy efficient system is much more common in Europe and Asia than in the United States. The Orchard Garden is the first hotel in San Francisco to utilize this technology. Compact fluorescent lighting and liquid crystal display (LCD) televisions are two other technologies that also reduce guest room energy use.

As noted above, the building design incorporated natural daylight. However, this was a challenge, because the hotel is bordered on three sides by other buildings and has very limited roof space of its own. The project team compensated for these limitations by choosing a building design with a tiered façade, allowing for the addition of natural light through light wells.

Another project limitation was the lack of access to alternative energy sources. There is no space available at the Orchard Garden for on-site energy production, and the hotel is not conveniently located near other energy sources (e.g., steam). Unlike the Orchard Hotel, the Orchard Garden has no steam conduits in the vicinity, and it has not been cost effective to install them under Bush Street.

4. Water

The Orchard Garden's project team members did not confine themselves to energy when they designed the hotel's resource conservation features. They also introduced and implemented operational water conservation equipment and procedures. Mr. Mühle, who continually challenges operational practices in order to be more efficient, currently has only staff laundry facilities on-site. Small rags and robes are washed on-site in small Energy Star washers. The bed linen and towel laundry goes to a local company, Royal Laundry, in South San Francisco. The vendor processes the laundry in bulk, promoting both resource conservation and energy efficiency, and uses peroxide instead of bleach. Advantages of using peroxide include less allergens and a longer life span of the fabric. The hotel achieves additional water conservation by using restaurant tablecloths only in the evening. The guest room linens are changed every three days unless a guest leaves earlier. (The average guest stay is currently 2.3 days.) Mr. Mühle is researching the possibility of offering shorter-length robes for guests, so that more robes can be washed at one time.

The Orchard Garden's project team designed for water conservation by installing low-flow equipment in the guest bathrooms. The toilets allow water flow at a rate of 1.6 gallons per minute. Sink aerators in other hotel areas result in additional savings. Mr. Mühle is testing new showerheads with a water flow rate of 1.5 gallons per minute. Outside, the hotel achieves water conservation because it does not use an irrigation system for the planters.

The project team's decisions regarding water conservation were based primarily on four considerations: the construction budget; what the San Francisco building codes and planning commission would allow; space considerations; and what the team determined would provide a positive customer experience. For example, the project budget, complicated building codes, and a lack of space prohibited installation of a water recycling or treatment system. Also, less traditional water conservation equipment items (e.g., dual-flush toilets) were rejected because the hotel team felt customers were not familiar with such equipment and that the guest experience could be compromised.

5. Indoor Environmental Quality

Construction

The Orchard Garden project team ensured that the hotel would maintain excellent indoor environmental quality, both during construction and during occupancy, by implementing an indoor air quality (IAQ) plan to reduce the amount of indoor air pollutants. Part of that plan was the prohibition of smoking during the building construction phase and throughout occupancy, and avoiding the absorption of pollutants in the permanent building fixtures. The IAQ plan was developed in accordance with SMACNA (Sheet Metal and Air Conditioning Contractors' National Association) IAQ guidelines for occupied buildings under construction. No permanent air handlers were used during the construction of the Orchard Garden Hotel, and this helped to improve the indoor air quality. The hotel also added floor mats to the entrances of the building to eliminate the indoor spread of pollutants. And, the areas where chemicals were to be stored were constructed to maintain negative pressure. The ventila-tion of the building meets American Society of Heating, Refrigerating and Air-Conditioning Engineers (ASHRAE) 62-1999 requirements.

Additionally, the Orchard Garden's design included HVAC&R (R meaning refrigerating) systems that did not use CFCs, HCFCs, or halons, which benefit the employees, the guests, and the atmosphere. Utilizing HVAC&R equipment without CFCs, HCFCs, or halons benefits human health and the health of the planet. Those chemical substances lead to the depletion of ozone and an increase in greenhouse gas levels in the atmosphere.

Operations

Mr. Mühle makes it a priority for his guests and his staff to have a healthy and comfortable indoor environmental experience. To this end, he promotes the use of environmentally friendly cleaning products for his housekeeping staff, and low VOC furniture and fixtures for both his employees and his customers. The cleaning products are non-toxic fruit acids from Sierra Environmental Technologies and Method. The products from Sierra Environmental Technologies are the bulk environmental products and can be purchased from the California company, whereas the products from Method are Method Home Surface Cleaners and are sold at most Target retail outlets. The Method products are used mainly in the office space. According to Mr. Mühle, when the employees switched to the new, healthier products, the respiratory issues and dry hands caused by chemical cleaners disappeared. "Our housekeepers were skeptical at first but we let them make the decision. Once you let [the staff] participate, it instills a great deal of pride and makes them a much better team." It took approximately six months to phase out the traditional bleach-based cleaning supplies.

Mr. Mühle selected hotel furniture and fixtures that would limit the amount of harmful substances released into the indoor air. The hotel carpet is a Bentley Prince Street broadloom variety that uses innovative non-adhesive technology and eliminates the VOC emissions of traditional adhesives. The wood used in the dining area furniture is made locally and does not contain adhesives. The furniture's durable faux leather also eliminates the need for chemical cleaning.

At the Orchard Garden Hotel, guests have the ability to control the temperature of the air in their own rooms with individual hydronic HVAC systems. These systems are in accordance with ASHRAE 55-1992 requirements. The hotel also has a smoke-free stairwell exit system for use during emergencies. This system maintains air quality by pressurizing the stairwells (preventing the smoke's movement from the back to the front of the hotel), and by operating fans that blow the smoke out of the stairwells. Indoor environmental quality clearly is a priority at the Orchard Garden Hotel, and the project team members made their decisions based on budget and product availability.

Market Positioning and Consumer Response

The Orchard Garden Hotel is marketed as a "green" hotel and caters to both business and leisure customers. The hotel is a mid priced hotel with room charges in a range of $169 to $499 per night. The Orchard Garden expects to be AAA rated as a Three Diamond hotel. The general manager, Stefan Mühle, believes that a high performance hotel should not appear different from or cost more than a traditional hotel. Features such as the in-room key card system, recycling bins, and Aveda amenities invite hotel guests to participate in a green lifestyle.

Being the first LEED certified hotel in California has helped to generate significant "buzz" for the Orchard Garden. Prominent travel journalists from Condé Nast and the *New York Times* have published articles about the hotel's greening efforts. General Manager Stefan Mühle was able to open the hotel with almost no marketing budget, largely because of the low-cost publicity generated by the high performance efforts and the loyal customer base drawn from the sister Orchard Hotel.

Guests have noticed and appreciated the environmentally sustainable features at the Orchard Garden Hotel, and several who filled out comment cards mentioned recommending the hotel to friends and family who care about environmentally responsible travel. (See example responses in Table 3.)

Table 3 GUEST SURVEY RESPONSES	
Month	**Guest Responses**
December 2006	"Excellent property. I am glad that I found this and I will stay here again when we return. I will recommend this to my friends, as they, too, are Eco Greens and like to stay at these types of places to see what services are being offered."
	"My husband and I had stayed at the Orchard and have always loved it so when I saw that you had the new (green) hotel nearby, I booked it for us and two couples that we were traveling with."
	"The beds are great, the TVs are huge, and the 'green' policy is nice."
January 2007	"We enjoyed the cleanliness and the 'green' efforts of the room."
	"You do have a beautiful hotel and I fully embrace the concept of going 'green'."
	"So happy to find a 'green' hotel! The linens were wonderful and just being able to breathe was great! Thank you!"
February 2007	"I stayed at this hotel for its green status."
	"The fact that a 'green' hotel can be so comfortable and luxurious is yet another plus in your favor."
	"I am pro eco-friendly and it made me very happy to find an eco-friendly hotel. I will stay at this hotel every time I come to the city now. Thank you."

Why High Performance Construction?

The Orchard Garden developer and general manager decided to construct a new, mainstream high performance hotel because they could get a third-party certification with minimal cost being added to the construction budget (approximately $35 thousand additional cost incurred for the key card energy system, which is a 0.17% premium). The original construction documents for Orchard Garden were created before the current owner purchased the project, so limited budget changes were acceptable. The third-party certification, achieved through the USGBC LEED rating system, allows the hotel to receive low-cost publicity (marketing expenses now only approximately $5,000 a month) and to create a differentiated product. Additionally, since it was the first LEED certified hotel in San Francisco, one could speculate that the Orchard Garden received a larger amount of media coverage than it would have if it wasn't the first in the market.

There are several reasons why the high performance design and construction of the hotel and the LEED certification did not cost much more than was originally budgeted for construction:

- The 5,600-square-foot building was small enough to achieve basic energy efficiency at no to low additional cost as a result of design features including cool roof, exterior wall insulation, commissioning, and high efficiency hydronic HVAC system. Additionally, the footprint is a rectangle, which is an energy-efficient shape.
- The LEED credits pursued were mostly cost neutral.
- The significant cost items for this project were the LEED registration and certification fees, and commissioning, which were reduced because of the general contractor:
    - The general contractor internalized the LEED administration fees, costing $10 to $15 thousand, because it wanted to increase firm competency in the process, especially because it was the first online LEED submittal it had performed.
    - Commissioning is part of the general contractor's basic package and costs approximately $30 thousand.
    - The general contractor already incorporates many other LEED credits into standard construction practices, including construction waste management and indoor air quality. (The LEED credits likely to be affected include: Sustainable Sites Prerequisite 1, Materials & Resources Credit 2, and Environmental Quality Credit 3.1 and 5.)
- Code requirements and climate conditions in San Francisco allow the Orchard Garden Hotel to achieve several LEED credits at no cost. These credits include Energy and Atmosphere Credit 2 (the California Title 24 energy code is equal to this and already required), and Environmental Quality credit 7.1 (the hotel does not need humidity control in San Francisco, only temperature control). Recycled content items like concrete and tile are also available locally, which affects Material and Resources credits 4.1 and 4.2. (See the Orchard Garden's LEED scorecard in Figure 2.)

Why High Performance Operations?

One of the reasons the Orchard Garden Hotel implements practices to conserve resources is because the hotel achieves cost savings by reducing operating expenses. For example, using washable linens and curtains instead of "dry clean only" textiles introduces operating savings because conventional laundry is less costly than dry cleaning. The general manager projects these savings to be between 10–20%.

The Orchard Garden Hotel also performs high performance operations because it benefits the health and well being of hotel staff and guests. For both staff and guests, high performance operational practices tend to be more noticeable than high performance construction practices. For example, fruit-based cleaning products are much nicer for hotel staff because they are less abrasive and do not pollute the air. Recycled toilet paper, napkins, and office paper are items that guests can see and appreciate, unlike the fly ash in the concrete. For the Orchard Garden Hotel, these operational product decisions are cost neutral from a purchasing standpoint. They also garner additional, ongoing benefits over the life of the product. See Table 4 for financial highlights of high performance operations implemented.

Table 4 **FINANCIAL BENEFITS OF HIGH PERFORMANCE OPERATIONS FEATURES**

High Performance Operational Feature	Benefit
Washable linens and curtains	Dry Cleaning Cost Savings of 10–20%
Recycled paper for office printing	Cost Neutral
Recycled toilet paper napkins	Cost Neutral
Fruit acid–based cleaning products	Cost Neutral

Advantages of High Performance Construction and Operations

There are multiple advantages for the Orchard Garden Hotel in having both high performance construction and operations. First, the sustainably designed building, with its energy and water-efficient equipment, enables the owner and manager to reap the benefits of decreased utility expenses. For example, the guest room key card energy management system is expected to reduce electricity consumption in guest rooms by 20% (based on future occupancy rates and EPA data), which will lead to operational savings.

Second, the Orchard Garden Hotel obtained LEED credits for the hotel's ongoing operations. One credit was achieved for the use of environmentally friendly housekeeping products, and another for educating guests about the hotel's high performance construction features through signage and tours. Both of these items incur little cost.

A third advantage is guest comfort and awareness and employee comfort and productivity. By employing both high performance construction and operational practices, guests and employees benefit from a comfortable and healthy environment where they can identify with environmentally friendly features. This has the potential for increased employee retention and enhanced customer satisfaction. However, employee retention and customer satisfaction are difficult to quantify at the Orchard Garden Hotel because historical information does not exist yet. See Table 5 for financial highlights of high performance construction and operations practices implemented.

Table 5 **FINANCIAL BENEFITS OF HIGH PERFORMANCE CONSTRUCTION AND OPERATIONS FEATURES**

High Performance Feature	Capital Cost	Payback Period	Benefits
Guest room key card energy management system	$35,000	Two years	Estimated 20% reduction in guest room energy consumption
Low-flow bathroom fixtures	Cost neutral		Reduction in water consumption

Table 6 is a summary of high performance hotel construction and operation advantages realized by the property oversight stakeholders – the developer/owner and the management company.

Table 6 **STAKEHOLDER ADVANTAGES SUMMARY**		
Developer	**Owner**	**Management Company**
The LEED certification process, which minimally exceeded the project budget, validated the hotel's high performance claims and helped to differentiate a property that was other-wise similar to nearby hotels.	Being the first LEED-certified hotel in California attracted low-cost publicity, which reduced marketing costs.	Being the first LEED-certified hotel in California attracted low-cost publicity, which reduced marketing costs.
Attempting mostly LEED credits that had no additional cost, the project was able to achieve LEED certification while only minimally exceeding the construction budget. • The contractor absorbed LEED documentation and submittal fees because of its desire to get high performance hotel project experience, so there was no additional cost. • The LEED AP and the commissioning agent were contractor employees and their services yielded no additional costs. • San Francisco code requirements enabled the Orchard Garden Hotel to obtain certain LEED credits without additional costs.	Profit margins are projected to increase through lower operating expenses. Examples: • Guest room key card system expected to reduce electricity consumption by 20%. • There is a dry cleaning projected cost savings of 10–20%.	Profit margins are projected to increase through lower operating expenses. Examples: • Guest room key card system expected to reduce electricity consumption by 20%. • There is a dry cleaning projected cost savings of 10–20%.
	Potential employee cost savings: • Fruit acid–based cleaning products are cost neutral, healthier, and nicer for hotel staff. These have the potential for improving productivity and decreasing sick time, but these potential benefits have not been tracked.	Potential employee cost savings: • Fruit acid–based cleaning products are cost neutral, healthier, and nicer for hotel staff. These have the potential for improving productivity and decreasing sick time, but these potential benefits have not been tracked.

You really need people that understand the intentions of the USGBC to implement the project successfully.

Stefan Mühle, *General Manager,* Orchard Garden Hotel

Best Practices and Conclusions

The Orchard Garden Hotel offers an exemplary case study in effective team collaboration and high performance construction.

The following products and activities implemented at the Orchard Garden are industry best practices:

- **Energy Efficiency and Innovation – Guest Room Key Card System**
- **Environmentally Friendly Cleaning Supplies**
- **Efficient Space Planning**
- **Effective Team Collaboration**

The project team has designed and constructed a hotel that is simple, elegant, and comfortable, maximizing the use of a small building footprint. The Orchard Garden is a mainstream hotel where the incorporation of energy saving devices (such as the in-room key card for utility activation) demonstrates both the feasibility and the desirability of high performance development. At the same time, the hotel enhances the health and well being of guests and staff through high performance operational practices such as utilizing environmentally friendly cleaning supplies.

Through this project, the Orchard Garden Hotel team has discovered that, no matter how committed a company is to high performance design, sustainability cannot be accomplished without the assistance and guidance of dedicated professionals. Successful sustainable design depends on the commitment of all who are involved, including (but certainly not limited to) the property oversight team, the architect, and the contractor. Additionally, if LEED certification is identified as a goal earlier in the project timeline, it is easier to obtain a higher level of sustainability with limited budget impact.

Figure 2: Orchard Garden Hotel LEED Scorecard

LEED for New Construction v2.0/2.1

Orchard Garden Hotel
Project # 10002237
Certification Level: Certified
5/31/2007

27 | Points Achieved   Possible Points: **69**

Certified 26 to 32 points   Silver 33 to 38 points   Gold 39 to 51 points   Platinum 52 or more points

6 | Sustainable Sites   Possible Points: 14

Y

Y	Prereq 1	Erosion & Sedimentation Control	
1	Credit 1	Site Selection	1
1	Credit 2	Development Density	1
	Credit 3	Brownfield Redevelopment	1
1	Credit 4.1	Alternative Transportation, Public Transportation Access	1
1	Credit 4.2	Alternative Transportation, Bicycle Storage & Changing Rooms	1
	Credit 4.3	Alternative Transportation, Alternative Fuel Vehicles	1
1	Credit 4.4	Alternative Transportation, Parking Capacity & Carpooling	1
	Credit 5.1	Reduced Site Disturbance, Protect or Restore Open Space	1
	Credit 5.2	Reduced Site Disturbance, Development Footprint	1
	Credit 6.1	Stormwater Management, Rate & Quantity	1
	Credit 6.2	Stormwater Management, Treatment	1
	Credit 7.1	Landscape & Exterior Design to Reduce Heat Islands, Non-Roof	1
1	Credit 7.2	Landscape & Exterior Design to Reduce Heat Islands, Roof	1
	Credit 8	Light Pollution Reduction	1

2 | Water Efficiency   Possible Points: 5

Y

1	Credit 1.1	Water Efficient Landscaping, Reduce by 50%	1
1	Credit 1.2	Water Efficient Landscaping, No Potable Use or No Irrigation	1
	Credit 2	Innovative Wastewater Technologies	1
	Credit 3.1	Water Use Reduction, 20% Reduction	1
	Credit 3.2	Water Use Reduction, 30% Reduction	1

1 | Energy & Atmosphere   Possible Points: 17

Y

Y	Prereq 1	Fundamental Building Systems Commissioning	
Y	Prereq 2	Minimum Energy Performance	
Y	Prereq 3	CFC Reduction in HVAC&R Equipment	
	Credit 1.1	Optimize Energy Performance, 15% New / 5% Existing	1
	Credit 1.2	Optimize Energy Performance, 20% New / 10% Existing	1
	Credit 1.3	Optimize Energy Performance, 25% New / 15% Existing	1
	Credit 1.4	Optimize Energy Performance, 30% New / 20% Existing	1
	Credit 1.5	Optimize Energy Performance, 35% New / 25% Existing	1
	Credit 1.6	Optimize Energy Performance, 40% New / 30% Existing	1
	Credit 1.7	Optimize Energy Performance, 45% New / 35% Existing	1
	Credit 1.8	Optimize Energy Performance, 50% New / 40% Existing	1
	Credit 1.9	Optimize Energy Performance, 55% New / 45% Existing	1
	Credit 1.10	Optimize Energy Performance, 60% New / 50% Existing	1
	Credit 2.1	Renewable Energy, 5%	1
	Credit 2.2	Renewable Energy, 10%	1
	Credit 2.3	Renewable Energy, 15%	1
	Credit 3	Additional Commissioning	1
1	Credit 4	Ozone Depletion	1
	Credit 5	Measurement & Verification	1
	Credit 6	Green Power	1

7 | Materials & Resources   Possible Points: 13

Y

Y	Prereq 1	Storage & Collection of Recyclables	
	Credit 1.1	Building Reuse, Maintain 75% of Existing Shell	1
	Credit 1.2	Building Reuse, Maintain 100% of Shell	1
	Credit 1.3	Building Reuse, Maintain 100% Shell & 50% Non-Shell	1
1	Credit 2.1	Construction Waste Management, Divert 50%	1
1	Credit 2.2	Construction Waste Management, Divert 75%	1
	Credit 3.1	Resource Reuse, Specify 5%	1
	Credit 3.2	Resource Reuse, Specify 10%	1
1	Credit 4.1	Recycled Content, Specify 5%	1
1	Credit 4.2	Recycled Content, Specify 10%	1
1	Credit 5.1	Local/Regional Materials, 20% Manufactured Locally	1
1	Credit 5.2	Local/Regional Materials, of 20% Above, 50% Harvested Locally	1
	Credit 6	Rapidly Renewable Materials	1
1	Credit 7	Certified Wood	1

7 | Indoor Environmental Quality   Possible Points: 15

Y

Y	Prereq 1	Minimum IAQ Performance	
Y	Prereq 2	Environmental Tobacco Smoke (ETS) Control	
	Credit 1	Carbon Dioxide Monitoring	1
	Credit 2	Ventilation Effectiveness	1
1	Credit 3.1	Construction IAQ Management Plan, During Construction	1
	Credit 3.2	Construction IAQ Management Plan, Before Occupancy	1
1	Credit 4.1	Low-Emitting Materials, Adhesives & Sealants	1
1	Credit 4.2	Low-Emitting Materials, Paints	1
1	Credit 4.3	Low-Emitting Materials, Carpet	1
	Credit 4.4	Low-Emitting Materials, Composite Wood & Agrifiber Products	1
1	Credit 5	Indoor Chemical & Pollutant Source Control	1
	Credit 6.1	Controllability of Systems, Perimeter	1
	Credit 6.2	Controllability of Systems, Non-Perimeter	1
1	Credit 7.1	Thermal Comfort, Comply with ASHRAE 55-1992	1
	Credit 7.2	Thermal Comfort, Permanent Monitoring System	1
1	Credit 8.1	Daylight & Views, Daylight 75% of Spaces	1
	Credit 8.2	Daylight & Views, Views for 90% of Spaces	1

4 | Innovation & Design Process   Possible Points: 5

Y

1	Credit 1.1	Innovation in Design: Green Cleaning	1
1	Credit 1.2	Innovation in Design: Green Education	1
1	Credit 1.3	Innovation in Design: Environmental Management	1
	Credit 1.4	Innovation in Design	1
1	Credit 2	LEED® Accredited Professional	1

Arbutus 'Marina'

Planted by

Mayor Gavin Newsom

in honor of the Orchard Garden Hotel's opening on

October 4, 2006

WALKING TOUR
Orchard Garden Hotel

Building Exterior/Entrance

- Notice the short frontage. It is only 50 feet wide!
  What does this mean? The building footprint is only 5,600 SF and the floor plan is only 112 feet deep. As a result, the design team had to be very efficient with their planning.

- Notice the artwork on the door handles, balconies, and marquee. The Orchard Garden Hotel features the work of local artist Archie Held, from Richmond, California.

Lobby

- Notice the wood paneling. It is not wood!
  The panels are made from recycled particle board and plastic laminate, and use low VOC adhesives.

- And where there is wood (in tables, guest room desks, bed headboards, and sliding bathroom doors), it is Forest Steward Council certified from Minnesota. This means that it is harvested from forests that are responsibly managed according to FSC standards.

Roots Restaurant

- If you are at the restaurant for breakfast or lunch, notice that tablecloths are used only in the evening. This minimizes laundry operations.

- Look at the menu. The restaurant tries to use food products from local farms (within a 20-mile radius) whenever possible.

- And how can you miss the focal point in the dining room? Most of the wines featured on the wine rack are organic.

Roof

- Public access to the roof is available daily until 5:00 p.m.

Guest Rooms

- Hotel fabrics, including drapes, coverlets, and shower curtains, were developed by Luna Textiles. The drapes consist of 53% recycled polyester; the shower curtains are constructed from 86% recycled polyester; and the bed coverlets are made from 49% recycled polyester. These fabrics are machine washable and can be cleaned on site. They do not require harsh dry cleaning chemicals.

Property	The Comfort Inn & Suites Boston/Airport
	85 American Legion Highway, Revere, Massachusetts 02151
Contact Information	http://www.comfortinn.com/hotel-revere-massachusetts-MA051?amp;promo=gglocal
	(781) 485-3600
Hotel Category	Branded, Mid Rate (Select Service)
	Comfort Inn & Suites by Choice Hotels
Property Oversight	Developer: Old Bayside Partners LLC
	Owner: Saunders Hotel Group (SHG)
	Management Company: Saunders Hotel Group
Gross Square Feet (GSF)	Eight stories above grade; no basement
Number of Guest Rooms	208 rooms
Construction Type	New construction
Date Completed	September 2000
High Performance	• Site
	• Materials and Waste Management
	• Energy
	• Water
	• Indoor Environmental Quality
	• Education
	• Performance Measurement
Awards and Certifications	AH&LA Environmental Hotel of the Year
	Boston Green Tourism, Charter Member
	British Airways Tourism for Tomorrow Prize
	Choice Hotels Exceptional Environmental Awareness Award, 2002
	Ceres Company
	Climate Neutral accommodations (Cool Rooms) certified
	Co-op America, member
	Energy Star Partner of the Year
	Green Hotel Association, member
	Skal International Ecotourism Award
	NWF (National Wildlife Foundation) Corporate Excellence Award

Revere, Massachusetts

Comfort Inn & Suites Boston/Airport

Opened in September 2000, the Comfort Inn & Suites Boston/Airport is located near Boston Logan International Airport and is managed by the Saunders Hotel Group (SHG). The Saunders Hotel Group was an early pioneer of high performance operations starting from innovations implemented at the Park Plaza in 1989. SHG has been able to take the lessons learned at the Park Plaza, and later at The Lenox, and apply them to the Comfort Inn & Suites franchise in Revere, Massachusetts. SHG built the Revere property from the ground up over an abandoned municipal landfill. The hotel has deftly been able to balance high performance operational practices with Comfort Inn & Suites corporate brand standards. The Comfort Inn & Suites Boston/Airport is an excellent case study in effective team collaboration, high performance operations, performance measurement, education, and outreach.

Background

The Comfort Inn & Suites Boston/Airport is located near Boston Logan International Airport and is managed by the Saunders Hotel Group (SHG). Tedd Saunders leads EcoLogical Solutions, a sustainable consulting practice that he created as an outgrowth of environmental work with SHG. While growing up, Mr. Saunders enjoyed going on family camping trips and had developed a broad appreciation for the natural world. His mother was a holocaust survivor and raised her family with a "no waste" mentality. Mr. Saunders' father has a genuine "sense of wonder" as described by Rachel Carson in her book of the same name. This parental combination strongly influenced Mr. Saunders' commitment to corporate social responsibility.

The idea for sustainable operations took shape at the Park Plaza Hotel in Boston, which SHG managed from 1976 to 1996. At one million square feet, the Park Plaza was the largest family owned and operated hotel in the United States. The Park Plaza also had the largest private laundry in the city. Tedd Saunders evaluated their operational practices and found ways to cut their operating expenses by reducing energy and water consumption as well as the waste stream. SHG has been able to take the lessons learned at the Park Plaza property and apply them at other hotels in the company's portfolio, including The Lenox and the Comfort Inn & Suites franchise in Revere, Massachusetts. The Revere property opened in September 2000.

The lessons learned at other portfolio hotels heavily influenced SHG's approach to the construction of its eight-story Comfort Inn & Suites. An energy management system with infrared motion sensors, cooling towers, an ozone laundry system, low-flow hardware for plumbing fixtures, and efficient window glazing all were specified in the construction documents. They were cost effective, and they helped to reduce SHG's impact on the environment while lowering operational expenses. In addition, SHG built the Revere property from the ground up, constructing a steel and concrete edifice over an abandoned municipal landfill. According to the United States Green Building Council (USGBC), rehabilitating environmentally damaged sites reduces pressure on undeveloped land. This also has created a rapport between SHG and the local municipality.

Comfort Inn & Suites Boston/Airport meets both SHG's mission and Choice Hotels' branding criteria (with some operational waivers granted). It meets and exceeds guest expectations, as demonstrated by having won Choice Hotels' gold medal for excellence in every year the hotel has been in operation. At the same time, the hotel offers guests an opportunity to learn about environmentally sustainable practices, both at the hotel and in their own homes. Not only has the Comfort Inn & Suites Boston/Airport avoided sprawl by undertaking construction on previously underdeveloped land, it has also reduced energy and water consumption and takes pride in a sustainable education program that reaches out to staff, guests, the local community, and many businesses and educational groups. The hotel's Green Team, an interdisciplinary group comprising various staff, meets monthly to measure sustainability progress and identify new areas for improvement.

The Comfort Inn & Suites Boston/Airport is an excellent case study in effective team collaboration, high performance operations, performance measurement, and education and outreach.

> *Slowly but surely, energy awareness and recognition of climate change have helped green hotel activities mushroom. This is an inherently beneficial business approach – over time it will become standard. Not only is it the right thing, but it is good business – sustainable hotels reduce operating costs and build support, team spirit, and customer loyalty. I don't know of any other business strategy that can achieve all of that at the same time.*
>
> TEDD SAUNDERS, *Co-Owner*, The Lenox and Comfort Inn & Suites Boston/Airport
> *President*, EcoLogical Solutions

Organization

Project Team

The project team consists of the property oversight group – the developer, owner, and management company. In this case, the property oversight group were all from the same parent company, although they represented different subsidiaries.

Contact Information

Below is contact information for the project team.

Developer	Old Bayside Partners LLC http://www.old-bayside.com
Owner	Saunders Hotel Group http://www.saundershotelgroup.net
Management Company/ General Manager	John Mitchell Saunders Hotel Group http://www.saundershotelgroup.net JMitchell@ComfortInnBoston.com
Environmental Sustainability Consultant	Tedd Saunders EcoLogical Solutions http://www.ecological-solutions.net tsaunders@ecological-solutions.net

Developer: Old Bayside Partners LLC; Jeff Saunders, Gary Saunders, and Steve Bodi

High Performance Qualifications: Old Bayside had no specific requirements for high performance development, but did look for properties that other developers usually overlook. For example, brownfields are not typical acquisition candidates because remediation is often costly and time consuming. However, development on brownfields conserves undeveloped land and this is better for the environment.

Owner: Saunders Hotel Group; the Saunders family

High Performance Qualifications: SHG specialized in high performance hotel operations primarily because of its long relationship with EcoLogical Solutions.

Management Company/General Manager: John Mitchell, Regional Manager for the Saunders Hotel Group

High Performance Qualifications: Mr. Mitchell had no prior high performance construction or operations background.

Managerial Structure

The Comfort Inn & Suites Boston/Airport has a relatively flat organizational structure and minimal hierarchy. The Saunders family is very much involved and is on site regularly. This access to top management makes it easier to promote new ideas and implement changes. While the focus on environmental sustainability at the Comfort Inn & Suites Boston/Airport seems to be driven from the top down, the hotel's management team actually makes sure staff from all business areas serve on the Green Team. This is part of an overall approach which encourages employee involvement and appears to improve morale, increase the quality of operations, and reduce employee turnover.

Figure 1 represents the reporting structure at the Comfort Inn and Suites Boston/Airport for the administrative and managerial positions only.

Figure 1: Managerial Structure

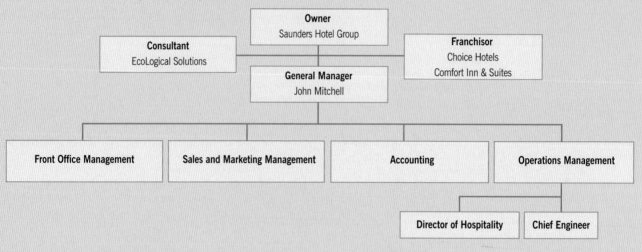

Green Team

The hotel has an active Green Team that meets monthly to discuss 15–20 items that relate to the progress of its sustainability initiatives as well as opportunities for improvement. The team has representatives from each of the hotel's key groups. Tedd Saunders from EcoLogical Solutions helps lead the meeting and brings in external knowledge as needed.

Staff Training and Compensation

The Comfort Inn & Suites Boston/Airport requires minimal sustainability training but, when it is needed, management focuses on employees in housekeeping, sales, and reservations, as well as on front desk and reception staff, so they can respond to guest questions and concerns. Management personnel at the hotel do not have to transition existing housekeeping staff to work with new products, because Green Seal–certified products have been used since the hotel opened. According to Omar Zenon, the operations manager, "The staff is not reluctant, primarily due to the fact that the hotel has been around for five years. So, it is no longer a new concept and it is not an issue. Also, it is easier, safer, and better for cleaning."

The front desk staff, receptionists, and reservationists have been trained to answer guest questions regarding the hotel's high performance program. If the front desk staff does not have the answer to the guest's concern, they take the question to the right person and then get back to the guest. The hotel also has an "eco" bulletin board in the back-of-house office space to help employees learn how to reduce their environmental footprints, both at the office and at home

At the Comfort Inn & Suites Boston/Airport, the general manager's compensation is based in part on gross operating margin and the incumbent has a significant incentive to keep costs low. Environmentally sustainable operations help to achieve this goal and have helped motivate all management staff. Guests also motivate staff through the Choice Hotels' staff recognition program. Choice Hotels offers Platinum, Gold, and Silver employee awards that are based on guest scores for service (with a rating of 60% or above).

The Comfort Inn & Suites Boston/Airport is a relatively flat organization and employees stay with the family business over the long-term. For example, there are members of the housekeeping staff who have been there since the opening of the hotel in 2000. According to one staff member,

> *Everyone is willing to go above and beyond. We are all motivated*
> *to help with the hotel because this is our second home, or maybe it is*
> *our first home – because we spend so many hours here.*

The hotel's management recognizes the needs of each staff member and assigns roles appropriately to keep individuals motivated regarding their high performance efforts. The most eco-friendly staff member receives the annual Shining Star award. Another incentive includes the monthly housekeeping award for a staff member who goes above and beyond his or her job responsibilities. The award is a day off with full compensation. The management offers this award in recognition of the fact that the staff is impacted the most by new decisions and changes, and by implementing programs and testing products. The Saunders family also offers the opportunity for a four-year scholarship at Newbury College for the children and grandchildren of Comfort Inn & Suites Boston/Airport employees.

Community Outreach and Education

The Comfort Inn & Suites Boston/Airport encourages staff members to volunteer with community greening efforts outside of work, as well as during in-house staff volunteer days. A number of managers and staff members volunteered at the Revere Beach and Franklin Park cleanup projects.

Construction and Operations

Table 1 summarizes the most prominent among the high performance features of the Comfort Inn & Suites Boston/Airport construction and operations.

Table 1 HIGH PERFORMANCE CONSTRUCTION AND OPERATIONS HIGHLIGHTS	
1. Site	• The hotel has three compressed natural gas (CNG) airport shuttle vans, and participates in a carbon offset program. • The hotel was built on a brownfield site that required environmental remediation.
2. Material and Resources, and Waste Management	• The hotel uses biodegradable hot cups for take-out coffee and tea. • Housekeeping staff use Green Seal certified cleaning supplies throughout the hotel. • Pool cleaning employs an ionization process, dramatically reducing chlorine use. • Bulk amenities and refillable dispensers are located in all guest bathrooms. • The hallway renovation used recycled content carpeting. • Food sorting for composting takes place in both the kitchen and dining area. • The Comfort Inn & Suites Boston/Airport recycles paper, rigid containers, printer toner cartridges, batteries, and cell phones.
3. Energy	• The hotel has installed Vendor Miser's motion sensors for vending machines that save 57% of the vending machine's energy use. • Motion sensors in the guest rooms control thermostat settings. • There is compact fluorescent lighting throughout the hotel. • The HVAC cooling towers, fans, LED signs, and efficient windows help to decrease the hotel's overall energy use.
4. Water	• The ozone laundry system uses cold water and environmentally friendly disinfectants. • Low-flow bathroom fixtures include toilets, showers, and faucets.
5. Indoor Environmental Quality	• Recent renovation: All hallways have been painted with low volatile organic compound (VOC) paint and Rug Institute–certified carpet and padding. • Recent renovation: All hallways have been upgraded with new carpet and wall coverings made with low VOC adhesives.

1. Site

The Comfort Inn & Suites Boston/Airport is an airport hotel built in the suburban setting of Revere, Massachusetts. The hotel is not accessible by public transportation and can only be reached by private automobile or a hotel shuttle. From an environmental standpoint, this is a limitation, because it does not promote mass transportation. However, three of the hotel shuttle vans run on compressed natural gas (CNG) and only one van runs on petroleum. Additionally, the Saunders Hotel Group is considering the purchase of carbon credits through TerraPass to offset the carbon emitted by the 30-minute shuttle service cycle between the hotel and the airport. This would cost the hotel approximately $2,800 annually to offset 300 tons of CO_2.

It is important to note that the Saunders Hotel Group preserved greenfields by building on a brownfield site that was originally zoned for industry. This is a significant sustainability feature, because building the hotel did not consume natural spaces and SHG made the land useful – land that would have been otherwise less valuable. The site was previously a municipal landfill. In order to develop the land for constructing a hotel, the site had to be capped. This ensured that previous contaminants would not harm human beings or the atmosphere.

2. Materials and Resources, and Waste Management

Comfort Inn & Suites Boston/Airport's interior design and operational practices help minimize use of new resources and materials and also reduce the waste stream from the hotel.

Interior Design

Although vinyl wall covering is used throughout the hotel, it has been installed with low volatile organic compound (VOC) adhesives. In addition, the rolled Origins carpets, manufactured by the Shaw Carpet company with recycled content, also have been installed with low VOC adhesives. The majority of the wood throughout the hotel is a laminate.

Choice Hotels recently required the Comfort Inn & Suites Boston/Airport to meet the parent company's standards by upgrading the bed sheets to a 200 thread count fabric. The hotel found that the higher thread count actually lasts longer. The hotel typically replaces the bed sheets every six months to a year and uses the retired sheets as cleaning rags before discarding them.

Operations

From a materials and resources standpoint, most of the sustainable initiatives affect the day-to-day operations of the Comfort Inn & Suites Boston/Airport. The hotel composts food scraps from the buffet breakfast, uses biodegradable hot cups instead of Choice Hotels' standard Styrofoam, and is in the process of getting a waiver from Choice Hotels to use organic fair trade coffee. The hotel intends to source this coffee from Earth Share, a company that donates the proceeds of its sales to environmental causes.

For cleaning the swimming pool, the hotel has implemented an ionization process that uses electric ions instead of chlorine to take pollutants out of the water. The hotel uses Rochester Midland cleaning supplies and Enviro-Care products for daily guest room cleaning. These cleaning products are purchased in bulk (one to five gallons) and are Green Seal certified to extend the life of fabrics and reduce health hazards for employees.

> *A dispensing system in the back of the house issues concentrated liquids that can be diluted with water on site. A room attendant typically has three days [worth] of shower gel (cleaning four showers each day) without having to refill.*
>
> OMAR ZENON, *Operations Manager*, Comfort Inn & Suites Boston/Airport

Signage in the hallways encourages guests to use the wicker recycling baskets. The hotel also recycles paper, rigid containers, printer toner cartridges, batteries, and cell phones from its back-of-house operations. In addition, to reduce waste, the hotel sought and received special permission from Choice Hotels to purchase refillable dispensers for bulk soap, shampoo, conditioner, and lotion. This has eliminated the cost of 220,000 individual amenity bottles each year.

To measure its performance, the Comfort Inn & Suites Boston/Airport solicits comments from guests specifically about environmental initiatives, using comment cards made from 100% post-consumer recycled paper. The hotel staff post their responses to guest comments, showing that they actually pay attention to guest suggestions. Every time the hotel orders a ream of paper, the paper company plants a tree.

3. Energy

At the Comfort Inn & Suites Boston/Airport, energy efficiency is primarily the result of operational equipment and technology that was installed when the hotel was built and during subsequent ongoing renovations. As mentioned earlier, in the Background section, SHG's approach to the Comfort Inn & Suites Boston/Airport construction was influenced by lessons learned at other hotels. SHG had years of operating experience with the hotels in its portfolio and was able to apply that experience because the Comfort Inn & Suites Boston/Airport was SHG's first ground-up construction project.

Operations

The Comfort Inn & Suites Boston/Airport helps guests conserve energy by using occupancy sensors installed in the guest rooms. These sensors activate or deactivate the thermostat by detecting the presence or absence of the guest. Each room is individually zoned and has its own thermostat for the guest to control within a range of 65–85°F. Almost all of the light bulbs throughout the property are compact fluorescent, which also contributes to energy savings.

SHG has installed an innovative energy-efficient feature, known as Vendor Miser, for the soda vending machines. The system controls the display lighting with motion sensors while keeping the beverages refrigerated. The decision to install this system was not difficult to make, because the payback timeframe for energy savings was only two years, with an annual 67% reduction of energy consumption over traditional machines.

Although the Comfort Inn & Suites Boston/Airport was not built according to specific high performance building standards, such as USGBC LEED (Leadership in Energy and Environmental Design) criteria, SHG incorporated features in both the building's core and shell to make the hotel highly efficient. In the building's core, the HVAC system uses roof cooling towers that inherently consume less energy than compressors do while cooling air. In the shell of the building, SHG installed rigid insulation efficient windows, compact fluorescent light bulbs, LED exit signs, and fans to reduce energy consumption. The roof is a white reflective rubber membrane that also contributes to the building's energy conservation program by reflecting the sun's heat away from the building. However, the roof requires cleaning for maximum efficiency.

4. Water

The hotel's design allowed for water-saving innovations.

Construction

SHG added low-flow water fixtures to the guest rooms and public restrooms in the initial design phase of the project to reduce water consumption. The equipment rates are: toilets at 1.6 gallons per minute, showers at 2.5 gallons per minute, and faucets at 1.5 gallons per minute.

The hotel achieves most of its water conservation through the ozone laundry equipment and the bathroom low-flow water fixtures. SGH has installed an ozone laundry system by Ozotech Inc. to conserve both energy and water. The machine is operated with cold water and the ozone acts as a disinfectant.

As a result, SHG saves heat energy (by using cold water) and conserves water (by reusing it). The hotel washes guest room linens and towels with this system. However, the hotel also provides coin-operated machines for washing personal items. Dry cleaning typically is sent off site.

5. Indoor Air Quality

At the time of the building's construction, the indoor environmental quality–enhancing features at Comfort Inn & Suites Boston/Airport were operational. Since then, additional steps have been taken to improve the indoor air quality, specifically during a recent hallway renovation project.

Operations

In order to improve the air quality in the hallways, the hotel used paints and adhesives with low VOC emissions. The adhesives included those in the carpet and in the wall covering. The renovation improved the indoor air quality and became a good marketing tool for SHG.

Business Case

Market Positioning and Consumer Response

The hotel is a Comfort Inn & Suites franchise, and the brand's parent company, Choice Hotels International, creates the standards for brand positioning and communication. Examples of the standards set by Choice Hotels include website content, guestroom layout, coffee brand, mattress quality, and online guest satisfaction surveys. Choice Hotels sets these standards to create a consistent brand image across all Comfort Inn & Suites hotels.

The Comfort Inn & Suites Boston/Airport attracts a variety of guests. A significant amount of the hotel's traffic is the result of its proximity to Boston Logan International Airport. The hotel has contracts with major airlines to house flight crews during layovers, as well as passengers from cancelled flights. The hotel offers a park-and-fly program for guests flying in and out of Logan Airport. Tour groups and leisure travelers visiting Boston on a more modest budget also tend to stay at this hotel. The hospitality business in this area is highly competitive, with a number of full-service hotels nearby (Courtyard, Hampton Inn, and Hilton). The Comfort Inn & Suites Boston/Airport must be able to maintain contracts and ensure repeat business through excellent customer service.

Few of the hotel's guests overtly seek out an environmentally sustainable hotel, but the Comfort Inn & Suites Boston/Airport is finding that Northern European and British consumers and travel agencies are more aware of environmental issues and appreciate the hotel's efforts. Upon their arrival, the majority of the guests are unaware of the hotel's commitment to sustainability. In order to keep the format and information consistent with other hotels in the chain, the Choice Hotels' website does not allow the Revere hotel to advertise its environmentally sustainable features. However, the hotel staff promotes a number of programs to educate guests once they are in the hotel. There are several environmental conservation posters and educational signs displayed throughout the hotel. For example, the men's restroom on the first floor has a sign stating that urinals consume 40% less water than is consumed by low-flow toilets. The hotel also places educational cards in guest cars that offer environmental tips on how to reduce gas usage on the road.

The "Tread Lightly" box placed at the front of the hotel lobby encourages guests to recycle old athletic shoes and offers a room discount based on the size of the shoe donated. This recycling box was designed by local art school students and helps communicate the hotel's commitment to sustainability. The sneakers are recycled by Nike into safe turf for playgrounds. There is an eco-suggestion box by the elevators that encourages guests to suggest ideas for improving the hotel's environmental performance. The bulk soap and lotion dispensers in the bathrooms are the environmentally sustainable features most noticed by guests, and they are often complimented in the remarks found on the guest comment cards.

The hotel's greening efforts do not seem to have resulted in a price premium, nor have they attracted major new business. However, the hotel has received a large amount of publicity; the hotel handles an average of three calls per week from journalists. The hotel's efforts also have resulted in awards from Energy Star, NWF, and British Airways, among others. The hotel is currently helping lead Boston Green Tourism, which is working with the Massachusetts Lodging Association, the mayor's office, the convention bureau, and others to make Boston a green destination known worldwide for its urban ecotourism leadership.

Why High Performance Construction?

LEED certification was not as popular at the time of Comfort Inn & Suites Boston/Airport's construction and the hotel was not built to any specific green construction standards. SHG did, however, install equipment that would result in energy and water savings. Since the developer, owner, and management company are all the same entity, they had a shared vision of creating a hotel that would run efficiently and be a green model.

The decision to build on a brownfield site requiring minimal clean-up helped the hotel save money on construction costs. Since it was a brownfield site, SHG was able to purchase the land for less than they would have spent on a non-brownfield site. Additionally, SHG obtained an Alternative Use License (AUL) that allowed them to build a hotel on the site as long as they capped the land. This saved time in the construction schedule, because they did not have to remove the soil and treat it, or perform an in situ remediation. We are unable to quantify the exact benefits due to confidentiality issues.

Why High Performance Operations?

The Comfort Inn & Suites Boston/Airport operations are considered high performance because they result in cost savings and because they benefit the hotel's employees and guests. Environmentally friendly operations are very important to SHG and are manifested in every aspect of the facility, including the formation of a Green Team and the educational signage throughout the hotel.

The hotel's operations incorporate both innovative operational practices as well as common industry practices. Leading innovative examples include the bulk amenity dispensers in the guest rooms (instead of single amenity containers) and the ionization pool-cleaning system instead of a chlorine system. The bulk dispensers save the hotel almost 220,000 individual amenity bottles annually. The ionizing pool-cleaning system had a two-year payback by replacing cleaning chemicals with a one-time purchase of electrodes.

Common industry practices at the hotel include the use of washable linens and curtains (washing is cheaper than dry cleaning) and the use of recycled paper for office printing.

In addition to the bulk amenity dispensers and the ionization pool cleaning system, the hotel has a few other practices with obvious benefits for hotel guests and staff. For example, environmentally sustainable cleaning products are much nicer for hotel staff because they are less abrasive and do not pollute the air. Recycled-content toilet paper and napkins are items that guests can see. These products are cost neutral.

Advantages of High Performance Construction and Operations

The Comfort Inn & Suites Boston/Airport has implemented high performance operations and has installed equipment to save money through reduced product costs and operating expenses. The Saunders family also believes it is important to run the hotel this way for the benefit of guests and employees.

The hotel's decision to install water conservation technologies in the construction phase of the project saves the hotel money during the operations phase. For example, the ozone laundry system has capital costs of $36,000 with a payback of two years. The utility costs savings include a 25% reduction in water consumption, chemicals, sewage output, and electricity. There is an 86% reduction in hot water usage.

More cost savings occur with efficient energy equipment. Vendor Miser, the vending machine lighting sensor, cuts energy costs by $189 annually and only cost $165 to install.

Less tangible but nonetheless important advantages are guest comfort and awareness, and employee comfort and productivity. By installing efficient equipment and by employing high performance operational practices, the hotel benefits guests and employees with a comfortable and healthy environment where they can identify with environmental responsibility. This has significant potential for increasing both employee retention and customer satisfaction.

Table 2 highlights the financial benefits of high performance construction and operations at the Comfort Inn & Suites Boston/Airport.

Table 2 FINANCIAL BENEFITS OF HIGH PERFORMANCE CONSTRUCTION AND OPERATIONS FEATURES			
High Performance Feature	**Capital Cost**	**Payback Period**	**Benefits**
Ozone laundry system	$36,000	Two years	A 25% reduction in water consumption, chemicals, sewage output, and electricity consumption; an 86% reduction in hot water usage.
Vendor Miser	$165	Less than 1 year	Saves electricity usage by $189 annually.

Table 3 is a summary of high performance hotel construction and operation advantages realized by the property oversight stakeholders – developer, owner, and management company.

Table 3 **STAKEHOLDER ADVANTAGES SUMMARY**

Developer	Owner	Management Company
The developers had lower project land costs because they acquired a brownfield site that was originally designated for industrial use. They built the hotel by obtaining an Alternative Use License (AUL). The site did not require major cleanup and there was no adverse impact on the construction schedule.	The owners have created an environment where staff at all levels are encouraged to contribute ideas to the high performance program. The program's success and international visibility creates higher staff retention and morale.	The management team has created an environment where staff at all levels are encouraged to contribute ideas to the high performance program. The program's success and international visibility helps create higher staff retention and morale.
	Energy Star certification and environmental awards are third-party verifications that the Comfort Inn & Suites Boston/Airport has high operating efficiency and quality environmental programs. These credentials help to promote the hotel to guests and staff.	Energy Star certification and environmental awards are third-party verifications that the Comfort Inn & Suites Boston/Airport has high operating efficiency and quality environmental programs. These credentials help to promote the hotel to guests and staff.
	Reduced operating expenses equate to higher profits. Innovations include: • Vendor Miser vending machine motion sensors reduce energy consumption by 67%. • In-room occupancy sensors cut heating and cooling costs. • Bulk toiletry dispensers for soap, shampoo, and lotion save 220,000 individual amenity bottles annually. • Low-flow bathroom fixtures that reduce water costs. • Cooling towers reduce heating, ventilating, and air conditioning (HVAC) costs. • An ozone laundry system has a payback of two years, has saved on hot water consumption and sewage bills, and has dramatically reduced usage of chemicals.	Reduced operating expenses equate to higher profits. Innovations include: • Vendor Miser vending machine motion sensors reduce energy consumption by 67%. • In-room occupancy sensors cut heating and cooling costs. • Bulk toiletry dispensers for soap, shampoo, and lotion save 220,000 individual amenity bottles annually. • Low-flow bathroom fixtures that reduce water costs. • Cooling towers reduce heating, ventilating, and air conditioning (HVAC) costs. • An ozone laundry system has a payback of two years, has saved on hot water consumption and sewage bills, and has dramatically reduced usage of chemicals.

Best Practices and Conclusions

As mentioned earlier, The Comfort Inn & Suites Boston/Airport is an excellent case study in effective team collaboration, high performance operations, performance measurement, and education and outreach.

The following best practices implemented at the Comfort Inn & Suites Boston/Airport have been identified as industry best practices for environmentally high performance construction and operations:

- **Food Composting**
- **Compressed Natural Gas Shuttle Vans**
- **Ozone Laundry System**
- **Vendor Miser**
- **Green Team**
- **Sharing Best Practices with Overall Brand**

The hotel's management team believes that sustainability cannot be accomplished without the assistance and guidance of others. Successful sustainable design depends on the commitment of all members of the team, including the guests. The hotel's Green Team continues to monitor operational practices to identify environmentally sustainable initiatives that offer a return on investment to the hotel. The Green Team continues to be a leader in the industry as well as in the community, educating guests and working closely with the Boston Chamber of Commerce to improve Boston's record of environmental responsibility.

> *It is most cost effective to accomplish initiatives using in-house resources whenever possible (if the expertise is there).*
>
> JOHN MITCHELL, *General Manager*, Comfort Inn & Suites Boston/Airport

WALKING TOUR
Comfort Inn & Suites Boston/Airport

Building Exterior/Entrance

- Notice the airport shuttle van – three out of the four vans use compressed natural gas to run the engines. In addition, the Comfort Inn & Suites Boston/Airport purchases carbon offset credits from TerraPass to offset the emissions from van travel.

Lobby

- Notice the "Tread Lightly" box placed at the front of the hotel to collect sneakers that will be recycled into flooring for playgrounds. The hotel offers a discount based on the size of the shoe donated (size 8 = $8 nightly discount). The container was designed in the shape of a running shoe by local Boston art school students. This recycling box demonstrates the depth of the company's commitment to sustainability.

- Now look up. Wow, that is a big fan! The lobby seating area ceiling reaches up to the second floor, and this area is directly across from the entrance. As a result, this design has led to loss of heat in the central lobby (heat rising and escaping) during the winter months. The large fan circulates the warm air downward and remedies this problem.

Breakfast Buffet Area

- In this area, tent cards on each table explain how to separate food wastes properly so that the Comfort Inn & Suites Boston/Airport can compost scraps appropriately.

- In addition, the hotel received special approval from its parent company, Choice Hotels, to purchase biodegradable disposable hot cups (in addition to reusable glasses and ceramic mugs) instead of the standard Styrofoam cups.

- Also, notice all the awards and recognition plaques the Comfort Inn & Suites Boston/Airport has received since its opening. These awards and plaques are displayed throughout the lobby. Additional educational materials can be found in the elevator as well as in every guest room.

- Take a look at the vending machines behind the buffet area. Are the lights on or off? Each vending machine has been equipped with a Vendor Miser to control the machine's energy use. If the motion detector senses movement, the machine turns its lights on. When no guest accesses it for several minutes, it "powers down" to conserve energy. Whether the machine's lights are on or off, it continues to keep beverages refrigerated.

Pool

- Just before you put on your swim trunks, check out the guest comment station and let the hotel know what you think about their environmental initiatives. It is worth noting that the comment cards are printed on 100% post-consumer recycled paper.

- Rest assured that when you do go swimming, the Comfort Inn & Suites Boston/Airport uses a non-toxic pool cleaning process. The ionization process employs electric ions instead of chlorine to clean the water.

Guest Rooms

- On the way to your room, check out the wicker recycling bins in the hallway. Signs just above the bins tell guests what they can and cannot recycle.

- The hotel washes linens on site, using an ozone laundry system for disinfecting. Ozone uses only cold water and has no toxic side effects. In addition, the ozone system eliminates some water consumption.

- Next, turn on your television and find the EcoChannel. The owners of the hotel produced a five-minute educational video communicating the mission, objectives, and future of green hotels. This and other entertainment videos run 24/7 for free.

- Finally, step into your bathroom. There you will notice bulk amenities for soap, shampoo, conditioner, and lotion. Using bulk containers eliminates the need to purchase and dispose of 220,000 individually packaged amenities each year. It also allows the hotel to improve the quality of the actual amenity products with the saved purchasing and disposal costs.

CONFERENCE
CENTER HOTELS

Property	Inn and Conference Center, University of Maryland University College
	3501 University Boulevard East; Adelphi, Maryland 20783
Contact Information	http://www.marriott.com/hotels/travel/wasum-the-inn-and-conference-center-university-of-maryland-university-college
	(301) 985-7300
Category	Independent, Conference Center
	Two Diamond AAA Rating
Property Oversight	Developer: University of Maryland University College
	Owner: University of Maryland University College
	Management Company: Marriott Hotels & Resorts
Gross Square Feet (GSF)	104,000 GSF
	6,850 GSF for conference space
	Five stories above grade
	One story below grade
Number of Guest Rooms	127 @ 765 GSF per room
Construction Type	New construction, Hotel expansion
Date Completed	March 2004
Project Cost	$22 million (excluding land and associated fees)
	$220/SF
	$0 for land (UMUC already owned land)
High Performance	• Site
	• Materials
	• Energy
	• Water
	• Indoor Environmental Quality
Awards and Certifications	LEED New Construction version 2.0 basic certification

Adelphi, Maryland

Inn and Conference Center,
University of Maryland University College

University of Maryland University College's (UMUC) Inn and Conference Center (ICC) addition is the first LEED (U.S. Green Building Council Leadership in Energy and Environmental Design) certified hotel in the world. UMUC pursued high performance construction and design for the expansion project in order to comply with a gubernatorial mandate at the time of the project's conception. Eventually the mandate to build in a sustainable manner was dropped, but UMUC continued with its high performance leadership position because the design had been completed and any changes would adversely affect schedule and budget. UMUC is the owner and developer of the ICC. The State of Maryland is the ultimate decision-making authority.

As a result of its pioneer position, UMUC and the entire project team experienced a large learning curve. The project team (developer/owner, contractor, and architect) was one of the first to research, test, and implement new high performance hotel products, technologies, and LEED best practices. Because of these lessons learned, UMUC is applying the best practices to its older buildings. The UMUC Inn and Conference Center is a premier case study in the influence of government regulations on high performance construction.

Background

The University of Maryland University College (UMUC) is a fully accredited institution of higher education that offers bachelors, masters, and doctoral degrees. The UMUC campus is located adjacent to the University of Maryland at College Park (UMCP) campus. The two institutions are completely separate entities, but they do leverage mutual resources when appropriate. For example, UMUC procures services such as pest control from UMCP's administration. UMCP's Department of Architecture, Engineering, and Construction (AEC) and other departments rent meeting space from UMUC.

As a Maryland state school, the University of Maryland University College is publicly funded. UMUC students are primarily soldiers located on military bases across the country and overseas, or adults who work while going to school. Due to the unique needs of the UMUC student population, the College has developed an extensive online degree program and has one of the largest online enrollments of any public university in the country. Consequently, UMUC typically leases space, as needed, from local community colleges and regional higher education facilities. The College therefore requires minimal onsite classroom space other than its conference center. The UMUC hotel and conference center accommodates a wide range of events.

The original UMUC hotel and conference facility suffered from an imbalance in the ratio between conference square footage and hotel rooms. (The conference space is 32,150 gross square feet [GSF] and the number of guest rooms is 111.) According to Marriott's calculations, UMUC's old facility had less than half the hotel rooms needed for their conference space. To correct this imbalance, UMUC decided to build the Inn and Conference Center (ICC) and pursued approval and funding for the addition.

UMUC already owned the land for the new Inn and Conference Center, but because UMUC was a state school, UMUC needed to obtain approval from both the Board of Regents and the Board of Public Works (state governor, treasurer, and controller) to finance the project. At that time, Maryland's governor, Parris N. Glendening, was a proponent of environmental issues and "led the charge" for green facilities. By executive order, Governor Glendening mandated that all buildings built by the state had to be considered environmentally sustainable, per USGBC LEED (United States Green Building Council Leadership in Energy and Environmental Design) standards. (Please see the LEED scorecard in Figure 2.) This mandate was rescinded after the governor's budget hearing because it appeared that high performance projects would cost the state a premium of 15% or more. However, by the time the mandate was rescinded, UMUC was already deeply involved in the ICC design development, so the College continued on its path in pursuit of LEED certification.

In 2001, when UMUC started designing the new conference facility, there was very little information and only a few product options in the field of high performance design and construction. In addition, UMUC was challenged with the need to balance three sets of standards during the design and construction process: (1) UMUC standards set by the University of Maryland's AEC department; (2) USGBC standards; and (3) Marriott standards. There was a huge learning curve for the project team members and they went through a great deal of trial and error. However, when the Inn and Conference Center opened in 2004 it received LEED certification for New Construction (LEED NC), making it the first hotel in the United States to receive this designation.

The UMUC Inn and Conference Center is a premier case study in the influence of government regulations on high performance construction.

> *At the time of UMUC's proposal and the governor's mandate, it cost approximately 15% more to build green, but now it is getting closer to nothing, currently 2-5%.*
>
> GEORGE TRUJILLO, *Assistant Vice President of Facilities*, Inn and Conference Center, University of Maryland University College

> *If you imagine the green design initiative like a wave, we've been building momentum over the last few years and we are now just hitting the crest. Once the wave breaks (in the next few years), green will become the standard by default.*
>
> GEORGE TRUJILLO, *Assistant Vice President of Facilities*, Inn and Conference Center, University of Maryland University College

Organization

Project Team

The project team consists of the property oversight group – the developer/owner and the management company – as well as the general contractor and architect.

Contact Information

Below is contact information for the project team.

Developer/Owner	George Trujillo University of Maryland University College http://www.umuc.edu/ gtrujillo@umuc.edu
General Manager	Mike McCarthy Marriott Hotels & Resorts http://www.marriott.com/ mmccarthy@umuc.edu
General Contractor	Bovis Lend Lease http://www.bovislendlease.com
Architect	OPX http://www.opxglobal.com

Developer/Owner: University of Maryland University College; George Trujillo, Assistant Vice President of Facilities

High Performance Qualifications: Mr. Trujillo had limited exposure to high performance construction but was supportive and interested because of the gubernatorial mandate.

Management Company: Marriott Hotels & Resorts; Mike McCarthy, General Manager

High Performance Qualifications: Mr. McCarthy had limited exposure to high performance operations.

General Contractor: Bovis Lend Lease

High Performance Qualifications: Bovis Lend Lease had limited exposure to high performance operations.

Architect/Designer: OPX

High Performance Qualifications: OPX had direct exposure with LEED and provided the LEED accredited professional (AP) for this project.

Managerial Structure

Marriott Hotels & Resorts was chosen as the management company for the ICC through a competitive bid process. Marriott was awarded a five-year contract with two additional five-year terms possible. Although it is not a Marriott franchise, the ICC must meet Marriott standards. In addition, the general manager (Marriott's Mr. McCarthy) and UMUC's Assistant Vice President of Facilities (Mr. Trujillo) both report to the UMUC Financial Operations office. The general manager has a cabinet group, and high performance operations are an item on their agenda. This group represents the Green Team and they meet on a bi-weekly basis.

The diagram below (Figure 1) represents the reporting structure for the administrative and managerial positions at the UMUC Inn and Conference Center.

Figure 1: Managerial Structure

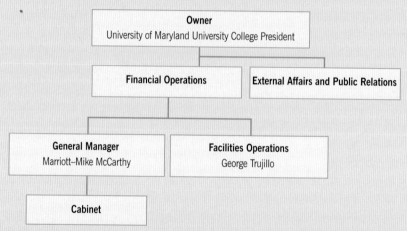

Construction and Operations

The ICC comprises mostly high performance construction elements versus operational practices.
Table 1 summarizes the most prominent among the high performance features of the Inn and Conference
Center's construction and operations.

Table 1 HIGH PERFORMANCE CONSTRUCTION AND OPERATIONS HIGHLIGHTS	
1. Site	• The hotel addition was constructed on an existing building site and shares the public parking facility and stormwater retention pond with the original Conference Center. • High-albedo exposed aggregate hardscape in the courtyard and drive-way was used to reduce the heat island effect. • 54% of the site (not including building footprint) was restored to native vegetation. • No exterior and site upward-directed lighting was installed. • An erosion and sedimentation control plan was implemented during construction.
2. Material and Resources, and Waste Management	• 53% of construction waste was recycled. • The builders purchased locally manufactured construction materials for 61% of construction materials by value; 57% of construction materials were also made from locally extracted materials. • 70% of construction materials by value were made with recycled content. • 63% of the wood, by value, used throughout the construction was Forest Stewardship Council (FSC) certified. • The Inn and Conference Center installed some paper wall covering that was adhered with water-based, environmentally friendly adhesive. • Food and beverage waste from restaurants and banquet events is recycled and/or composted, including glass, metal, plastic, paper, and cardboard. Guest room items are also recycled.
3. Energy	• The hotel addition shares energy systems with the original hotel, making both more efficient by minimizing the equipment needed and leveraging economies of scale. • The Kone elevators are 34% more efficient than standard elevators. • Energy recovery units harness energy from outgoing, exhaust air and transfers it to the incoming, outside air. Also, air handlers have carbon dioxide (CO_2) sensors that maintain constant interior CO_2 levels. The combination saves energy.
4. Water	• Landscaping does not require an irrigation system. • Bathroom fixtures include dual-flush toilets and low-flow shower heads, which result in 40% water consumption savings when compared to baseline level.
5. Indoor Environmental Quality	• Guest rooms: A combination of operable windows, thermostats, and air ventilation is used to maximize comfort. • Conference rooms: Thermostat controls are available for meeting attendees, and the air is completely exchanged four times every hour. • All wall and floor covering adhesives and wall paint have low volatile organic compound (VOC) emissions. • Air handlers have carbon dioxide (CO_2) sensors to maintain constant interior CO_2 levels.

1. Site

Although the Inn and Conference Center is located in a suburban location, there are few negative land use impacts since the ICC is an addition to an existing building site. The ICC is able to share many amenities with nearby buildings. For example, the new facility shares the parking deck with the original hotel. Also, because of close proximity to University of Maryland's College Park campus, there is access to good public transportation. A third shared element is the stormwater retention pond that was constructed next to the closest UMCP campus parking lot. This pond helps to retain and filter stormwater before it reaches the water table.

In order to reduce the heat island effect from man-made impervious surfaces, UMUC decided to install high-albedo exposed aggregate in the courtyard and driveway area. This included 17,681 square feet or 53.5% of the non-roof impervious site surfaces. Because of its light color, this pavement (with an albedo of 0.3) does not absorb as much solar energy as conventional hardscape products (such as black asphalt).

Utilizing another method to improve the site's environmental conditions, UMUC restored 54% of the site (not including building square footage) to natural vegetative conditions. This percentage amounts to 16,519 square feet. Last, in an effort to reduce night pollution, UMUC did not install any upward-directed site and exterior lighting.

Construction

The project team implemented an erosion and sedimentation control plan during ICC's construction that complies with the 1994 Maryland standards.

2. Materials and Resources, and Waste Management

In Table 2, sustainable product highlights used in the ICC are shown.

Table 2	MATERIALS AND RESOURCES
Building Core and Shell	• Brick: was acquired from a local manufacturer • Drywall: was manufactured locally and has recycled content • Roof: was made from recycled tires
Other Flooring	• Granite and marble in lobby: Daltile • Tile: Terra Green Ceramics • Traffic tile: recycled glass tile • Wood flooring stain: Ecostain • Wood flooring: Mountain Lumber Company, 3.5-inch plank flooring, heart pine
Fabrics	• Fabric wrapped panels: Carnegie Xorel Wall
Coverings	• Innovation's Innvironments: 50% wood pulp and 50% polyester fibers • Wall paint: Sherwin-Williams Harmony (low VOC paint)
Windows	• Pilkinton solar e insulating and optifloat clear, low-e double glazing

Construction

The Inn and Conference Center achieved a 53% recycling rate during construction. This was primarily the result of tracking waste throughout the project rather than waiting until the completion of the project. Bovis Lend Lease provided a few workers who were dedicated solely to waste management.

The project team purchased regionally manufactured materials for 61% of all the construction materials, by value, which included brick, aggregate, concrete, and steel. ("Regionally" is defined as within 500 miles of the project site.) Purchasing materials from within the region reduced energy consumption and emissions from fossil fuel–based transportation. In addition, of those regionally manufactured materials, 57% by total materials value were manufactured with raw materials that were harvested and extracted within the region. All of the brick used in the expansion was from the state of Maryland.

Seventy percent of total construction materials, by total materials value, were made with recycled content. These materials included steel, drywall, wallpaper, roof shingles, concrete, and window treatments.

Interior Design

The University of Maryland University College chose to use earth tone color palettes for furniture and interior spaces in the new conference facility, made with a range of environmentally sensitive materials. UMUC used paper-based as well as vinyl wall covering. The project used vinyl wall covering (which is not environmentally friendly) in high traffic areas such as corridors, and paper wall covering in areas where less durability was acceptable, such as conference meeting rooms. For the vinyl wall paper, UMUC used an environmentally friendly water-based adhesive. In addition, 63% of the facility's wood, by total wood value, was Forest Stewardship Council (FSC) certified. This included veneers as well as solid woods. For example, the panels in the lobby are veneers, but they are also FSC certified.

UMUC experimented with bamboo floors but ultimately chose not to use that product for that purpose because of durability concerns. Instead, the hotel used the sample bamboo to line the interior of the elevators.

Operations

Currently, Marriott recycles back-of-house paper, corrugated cardboard, and rigid containers, and there are recycling options available in the guest rooms. Food and beverage waste from restaurants and banquet events is recycled – including glass, metal, plastic, paper, and cardboard. Food is also composted – up to 1,000 pounds per day! Diverting this food waste from the trash dumpster is saving money, as the per-ton charge to remove composting material is half of what it costs to remove solid waste.

In addition, the hotel uses only china and silverware (not paper and plastic) in the conference areas, and retired terry cloth towels become cleaning rags. Concentrated green cleaning supplies come from EcoLab and are purchased in bulk to minimize waste from individual bottles, but these supplies are not Green Seal–certified. Marriott is currently consulting with UMUC's maintenance provider to obtain information regarding the Green Seal–certified cleaning solution used at other UMUC facilities.

The hotel donates unused guest room amenities such as shampoo and conditioner to a local women's shelter, and follows the Green Meeting Industry Council's (GMIC) guidelines for Green Meetings. Finally, in an effort to minimize paper usage, all guests can request electronic receipts at checkout and meeting planners can receive all planning materials electronically.

3. Energy

Energy-efficient features that are incorporated into the core of the ICC building include Kone elevators, fluorescent lighting, indirect lighting, energy recovery units, CO_2 sensors on the air handlers, and an insulated building shell. The efficiency features represent a 19% reduction in energy consumption as compared to the ASHRAE 90.1-1999 standards. (This calculation does not include energy consumed in lamp lighting, which is a large part of ICC's lighting, because ICC is evaluated with LEED version 2.0.) The Kone elevators are 34% more energy efficient than standard elevators because of the overhead cable pulley system that they use. Fluorescent lighting is used for all overhead lighting, and daylighting provides some indirect light.

The combination of energy recovery units with CO_2 sensors on the air handlers is the most energy-efficient technology in the ICC addition. The energy recovery units create an energy saving system that captures energy from outgoing exhaust air and transfers it to the incoming outside air. This narrows the range that the outside air needs to be heated or cooled. As a result, the air handlers heat or cool tempered air and the CO_2 sensors reduce the amount of outside air that is introduced to the building. The combination of these systems creates a much more energy-efficient system that provides a healthier indoor environment.

The ICC building shell is also efficient through its low-e windows and roof construction. The windows are low-e glass windows that allow daylight to enter. Since the windows are operable, however, the amount of energy efficiency realized is more difficult to control. The roof is constructed entirely of recycled rubber material. On the flat section, a white reflective roof has been installed that absorbs less solar energy than the steeper section of the roof that is a dark red color (that was chosen to match the design of the original hotel).

The Inn and Conference Center's HVAC&R systems are also efficient, since they are shared with the original hotel, so together the two buildings are more efficient than if they were isolated buildings. The original building's systems previously were oversized – that is, there was too much machinery for its energy needs. Now, however, there is adequate capacity to serve both buildings. This is an example of economies of scale. From a LEED perspective, the Inn and Conference Center building is more efficient because it requires minimal additional building equipment. Commissioning the building's energy systems to an advanced level also improved efficiency.

4. Water

At the Inn and Conference Center, there are no formal irrigation systems installed for the landscaping. This is because the plantings are native (indigenous to the locale) and drought tolerant. Beyond natural rain water, the only watering that occurs is the hose watering of the flowering annuals.

The most innovative water conservation feature of the hotel addition is the installation of dual-flush toilets in the guest bathrooms. Currently, a standard water conservation practice is the use of low-flow toilets with a rate of 1.3 gallons per flush. However, the Caroma brand dual-flush toilet uses .7 gallons and .9 gallons per flush, respectively, depending on whether the half or the full button is pressed. In addition to the dual-flush toilets, the guest bathrooms have low-flow showerheads that conserve water at a rate of two gallons per minute. This Body Spa brand showerhead had the lowest water flow and the best "feel" out of the four tested by UMUC staff.

Through the building's water-efficient features, ICC is able to conserve 40% of water consumption compared to a baseline level (as determined in LEED calculations).

If it's a new product, go home and test it!

GEORGE TRUJILLO, *Assistant Vice President of Facilities*, Inn and Conference Center, University of Maryland University College

5. Indoor Environmental Quality

ICC maintains a quality indoor environment for its guests and employees through its selected adhesives, paints, energy systems, no smoking policy, operable windows, and mechanical ventilation. All wall coverings employed water-based adhesives with low VOC emissions. There are also painted walls throughout the facility with low VOC content. Additionally, the hotel used only water-based stains for floors and wall panels.

Since ICC couples its HVAC&R system with the existing UMUC hotel and convention center, no CFC's or ozone-depleting substances are used in the expansion's on-site energy systems. ICC's no smoking policy and post-construction indoor air quality testing also ensures a healthy indoor environment.

The Inn and Conference Center's operable windows allow guests to naturally control their thermal comfort and ventilation. Additionally, there are thermostats in the guestrooms and throughout the common areas and conference rooms to ensure that guests are comfortable. Although this is a nice amenity, it can conflict with energy conservation efforts, depending on how often and on what scale temperature changes occur.

The ICC provides additional ventilation mechanically in the conference rooms and guest rooms. The air is exchanged four times each hour through the mechanical systems in the conference rooms. This is more than the office standard of three times per hour. Also, those same systems can dehumidify and humidify the air, as needed, which is not typical of office or hotel buildings. The constant CO_2 levels achieved by the CO_2 sensors on the air handlers can have a positive affect on the energy level of guests and employees. The guest rooms are also ventilated directly outside through the energy recovery units, which is not typical of hotel design.

Business Case

Market Positioning and Consumer Response

UMUC's marketing and advertising budget is relatively small relative to the size of the Two Diamond AAA rated hotel, so the public relations initiatives usually come from the Marriott Corporation. There are no educational materials about the hotel's high performance features for guests to peruse on site. UMUC does not market the high performance attributes, nor does the College differentiate between the new addition and the original hotel. However, Marriott.com features the Inn and Conference Center on the greenhouse gas and climate change website, and Marriott promotes the hotel with marketing materials and sales kits at trade events. Marriott also reaches out to Marriott reward program members.

In change since the UMUC interview, Marriott now highlights UMUC's LEED certification on its website. The management company can now benefit by receiving free publicity for UMUC's actions, since "green" is a trendy topic. In addition, the property launched a website for green operation reference information (www.umucmarriottgreen. com) and produced other marketing materials such as fact sheets and entrance banners.

In the past, legislators have asked about ICC's high performance features and have communicated the information back to their constituents and meeting planners. Government agencies such as NASA (National Aeronautics and Space Administration), as well as the state of Maryland and the Chesapeake Bay Foundation, have asked for building information when booking reservations. Contracting with high performance hotels is not a mandate for any of these entities, but environmentally sustainable features enter into the decision-making process.

Why High Performance Construction?

As mentioned above, the University of Maryland University College constructed a high performance building because that was the government mandate when construction began. When high performance construction was no longer a mandate, it would have been too expensive not to construct the building the way it had been designed. All decisions for the high performance construction features were based on first cost, not on payback or internal rate of return. UMUC's goals were to stay within budget, pursue environmentally sustainable leadership, and meet Marriott's standards. In order to pursue LEED certification there was an approximate 15% premium, but that was mainly a result of high performance products offered in the marketplace not yet being up to par.

Why High Performance Operations?

Marriott, since the hotel interview, has been working on high performance standards that will be implemented in the near future. Additionally, since the Inn and Conference Center is the only high performance building UMUC owns, it is also working on changing operating procedures.

Advantages of High Performance Construction and Operations

Since constructing ICC as a high performance building, UMUC and the management company have realized operational cost savings. For example, the energy usage has stayed relatively flat after the addition was added. Utility savings breakdowns by technology or operational practice implemented, however, are not currently tracked by UMUC.

Table 3 is a summary of high performance hotel construction and operation advantages realized by the property oversight stakeholders – the developer/owner and the management company.

Table 3 STAKEHOLDER ADVANTAGES SUMMARY		
Developer	**Owner**	**Management Company**
UMUC owned the land prior to construction.	Energy usage has remained relatively flat after addition was added and is a result of energy efficient equipment installed. Examples: • Energy recovery units in combination with CO_2 sensors • Kone efficient elevators • Dual-flush toilets	Energy usage has remained relatively flat after addition was added and is a result of energy efficient equipment installed. Examples: • Energy recovery units in combination with CO_2 sensors • Kone efficient elevators • Dual-flush toilets
• The need for land is reduced by sharing existing parking facilities and the stormwater detention pond. • Energy system capital expenditures are reduced because ICC shares systems with existing hotel.	The owner gains free public relations now for being the first LEED hotel in the United States. LEED certification has become trendy, and this results in marketing cost savings.	The management company gains free public relations now for being the first LEED hotel in the United States. LEED certification has become trendy, and this results in marketing cost savings.

Best Practices and Conclusions

The UMUC Inn and Conference Center is a premier case study in the influence of government regulations on high performance construction.

The following products and activities implemented at the Inn and Conference Center at UMUC are industry best practices and innovations:

- **Energy Recovery Units Combined with CO_2 Sensors**
- **Kone Efficient Elevators**
- **Dual-Flush Toilets**
- **Sharing Best Practices**

In 2001, the Maryland state government regulated the University of Maryland University College to pursue the construction of a high performance building. Some of the high performance innovations that UMUC installed include energy recovery units with CO_2 sensors, Kone efficient elevators, and dual-flush toilets, which all result in resource efficiency.

Because UMUC was among the high performance construction pioneers, UMUC paid a 15% premium in order to build sustainably, which was much higher than current premiums. The entire project team experienced a tremendous learning curve as it moved through high performance product and technology testing and learned about LEED best practices. As a result of this early sustainable construction work, the project team has learned some extremely valuable lessons that UMUC now implements in its older buildings and Marriott is considering implementing across its brand.

> *It may have cost more up front to bring on the general contractor earlier on in the process, but it saved money in the end.*
>
> GEORGE TRUJILLO, *Assistant Vice President of Facilities*, Inn and Conference Center, University of Maryland University College

Figure 2: UMUC Inn and Conference Center LEED Scorecard

LEED-NC

Inn & Conference Center Addition, LEED® Project # 0249
LEED Version 2 Certification Level: CERTIFIED
June 9, 2005

31 Points Achieved — Possible Points: **69**

Certified 26 to 32 points   Silver 33 to 38 points   Gold 39 to 51 points   Platinum 52 or more points

7 Sustainable Sites — Possible Points: 14

Y			
Y	Prereq 1	Erosion & Sedimentation Control	
1	Credit 1	Site Selection	1
	Credit 2	Urban Redevelopment	1
	Credit 3	Brownfield Redevelopment	1
1	Credit 4.1	Alternative Transportation, Public Transportation Access	1
1	Credit 4.2	Alternative Transportation, Bicycle Storage & Changing Rooms	1
	Credit 4.3	Alternative Transportation, Alternative Fuel Refueling Stations	1
1	Credit 4.4	Alternative Transportation, Parking Capacity	1
1	Credit 5.1	Reduced Site Disturbance, Protect or Restore Open Space	1
	Credit 5.2	Reduced Site Disturbance, Development Footprint	1
	Credit 6.1	Stormwater Management, Rate and Quantity	1
	Credit 6.2	Stormwater Management, Treatment	1
1	Credit 7.1	Landscape & Exterior Design to Reduce Heat Islands, Non-Roof	1
	Credit 7.2	Landscape & Exterior Design to Reduce Heat Islands, Roof	1
1	Credit 8	Light Pollution Reduction	1

4 Water Efficiency — Possible Points: 5

Y			
1	Credit 1.1	Water Efficient Landscaping, Reduce by 50%	1
1	Credit 1.2	Water Efficient Landscaping, No Potable Use or No Irrigation	1
	Credit 2	Innovative Wastewater Technologies	1
1	Credit 3.1	Water Use Reduction, 20% Reduction	1
1	Credit 3.2	Water Use Reduction, 30% Reduction	1

4 Energy & Atmosphere — Possible Points: 17

Y			
Y	Prereq 1	Fundamental Building Systems Commissioning	
Y	Prereq 2	Minimum Energy Performance	
Y	Prereq 3	CFC Reduction in HVAC&R Equipment	
2	Credit 1.1	Optimize Energy Performance, 20% New / 10% Existing	2
	Credit 1.2	Optimize Energy Performance, 30% New / 20% Existing	2
	Credit 1.3	Optimize Energy Performance, 40% New / 30% Existing	2
	Credit 1.4	Optimize Energy Performance, 50% New / 40% Existing	2
	Credit 1.5	Optimize Energy Performance, 60% New / 50% Existing	2
	Credit 2.1	Renewable Energy, 5%	1
	Credit 2.2	Renewable Energy, 10%	1
	Credit 2.3	Renewable Energy, 20%	1
1	Credit 3	Additional Commissioning	1
1	Credit 4	Ozone Depletion	1
	Credit 5	Measurement & Verification	1
	Credit 6	Green Power	1

6 Materials & Resources — Possible Points: 13

Y			
Y	Prereq 1	Storage & Collection of Recyclables	
	Credit 1.1	Building Reuse, Maintain 75% of Existing Shell	1
	Credit 1.2	Building Reuse, Maintain 100% of Existing Shell	1
	Credit 1.3	Building Reuse, Maintain 100% Shell & 50% Non-Shell	1
1	Credit 2.1	Construction Waste Management, Divert 50%	1
	Credit 2.2	Construction Waste Management, Divert 75%	1
	Credit 3.1	Resource Reuse, Specify 5%	1
	Credit 3.2	Resource Reuse, Specify 10%	1
1	Credit 4.1	Recycled Content	1
1	Credit 4.2	Recycled Content	1
1	Credit 5.1	Local/Regional Materials, 20% Manufactured Locally	1
1	Credit 5.2	Local/Regional Materials, of 20% Above, 50% Harvested Locally	1
	Credit 6	Rapidly Renewable Materials	1
1	Credit 7	Certified Wood	1

8 Indoor Environmental Quality — Possible Points: 15

Y			
Y	Prereq 1	Minimum IAQ Performance	
Y	Prereq 2	Environmental Tobacco Smoke (ETS) Control	
1	Credit 1	Carbon Dioxide (CO_2) Monitoring	1
	Credit 2	Increase Ventilation Effectiveness	1
1	Credit 3.1	Construction IAQ Management Plan, During Construction	1
1	Credit 3.2	Construction IAQ Management Plan, Before Occupancy	1
1	Credit 4.1	Low-Emitting Materials, Adhesives & Sealants	1
1	Credit 4.2	Low-Emitting Materials, Paints	1
	Credit 4.3	Low-Emitting Materials, Carpet	1
	Credit 4.4	Low-Emitting Materials, Composite Wood	1
1	Credit 5	Indoor Chemical & Pollutant Source Control	1
1	Credit 6.1	Controllability of Systems, Perimeter	1
1	Credit 6.2	Controllability of Systems, Non-Perimeter	1
1	Credit 7.1	Thermal Comfort, Comply with ASHRAE 55-1992	1
	Credit 7.2	Thermal Comfort, Permanent Monitoring System	1
	Credit 8.1	Daylight & Views, Daylight 75% of Spaces	1
	Credit 8.2	Daylight & Views, Views for 90% of Spaces	1

2 Innovation & Design Process — Possible Points: 5

Y			
1	Credit 1.1	Innovation in Design: Exemplary Performance WEc3	1
	Credit 1.2	Innovation in Design:	1
	Credit 1.3	Innovation in Design:	1
	Credit 1.4	Innovation in Design:	1
1	Credit 2	LEED® Accredited Professional	1

WALKING TOUR

Inn and Conference Center,
University of Maryland University College

Building Exterior/Entrance

- Before entering the hotel, stand in the middle of the courtyard and face the new Inn and Conference Center by Marriott. Notice that all outdoor lighting is directed downwards to reduce light pollution concerns. The exposed aggregate on the driveway is light in color to reflect heat (not absorb it) and reduce the heat island effect. The driveway aggregate was also purchased locally. If you turn around, you will notice bike racks that encourage visitors and employees to bike instead of drive. Showers are provided on site to freshen up after a long bike ride.

- You should be able to see that the facilities are near main roads and a bus route. This promotes commuting by public transportation and reduces vehicle emissions.

- Now look up at the roof of both buildings, old and new. The pitched roof on the new facility is covered with a material made from recycled rubber tires and shaped to look like slate shingles that match the rest of the UMUC campus, while also maintaining the aesthetics of the original building. It is a darker color (reddish) and, for UMUC, it is a great option because it comes with a 50-year warranty. The flat roof, which is not visible from the ground, is covered with a white (reflective) material and therefore reduces the heat island effect (similar to the benefit of the light-colored aggregate on the driveway).

- You may have noticed already that the guest rooms are equipped with operable windows that take advantage of natural ventilation and fresh air.

- And finally, watering is not required for the facility's landscaping because it has only drought toler-ant, indigenous grasses and plants (with the exception of the annuals in the center of the courtyard that require minimal watering).

Lobby

- The first thing you will probably notice in the lobby is the gold LEED medallion hanging on one of the front columns. This certifies that the construction of the Inn and Conference Center meets the United States Green Building Council's criteria for sustainable buildings.

- You will also notice extensive use of wood in the main lobby. The wood throughout the facility is FSC-certified, which means that it is harvested from forests that are responsibly managed according to FSC Standards.

- Another feature of the lobby is the abundance of natural light, as well as the possibility for guests to control the temperature by using one of the centrally located thermostats. Creating local controls for air temperature ensures that the hotel is not over-heating or over-cooling the site.

Guest Rooms

- In the guest rooms, you will find that all light bulbs are fluorescent, not incandescent. In the conference rooms, these lights are dimmable.

- Now, look at the fixtures in the bathroom. Two-button toilets made in Australia (Caroma brand) are manufactured with two cartridges for flushing 0.7 gallons per minute and 0.9 gallons per minute. A standard low-flow toilet usually flushes 1.3 gallons of water per minute. To avoid toilet back-ups, which are common with other low-flow toilets, the Caroma technology pushes the contents out of the bowl instead of requiring a vacuum or pressure-assisted system.

- In addition, low-flow showerheads have been installed in each guest room. UMUC tested a number of products prior to selecting the Simply Central by Body Spa, which uses two gallons per minute. This product was installed in the homes of the hotel's senior management to make sure the pressure was acceptable.

Property	Airlie Center 6809 Airlie Road, Warrenton, Virginia 20187
Contact Information	http://www.airlie.com
	(540) 347-1300
Category	Independent, Conference Center
	Equivalent to Four Diamond AAA Rating
Property Oversight	Developer: Airlie Foundation
	Owner: Airlie Foundation
	Management Company: Airlie Foundation
Gross Square Feet (GSF)	100,000 GSF
	Seven sleeping lodges with a range of 4 to 34 rooms
	Eight conference buildings with 17 flexible meeting rooms accommodating 5 to 550 people
	Land covering 2,800 acres, of which 1,800 are developed
Number of Guest Rooms	150 @ 667 GSF per room, distributed throughout the sleeping lodges
Construction Type	Renovations and retrofits
Date Completed	Ongoing
Project Cost	Not applicable (N/A)
High Performance	• Site
	• Energy
	• Water
	• Materials and Waste Management
	• Indoor Environmental Quality
	• Education
	• Performance Measurement
Awards and Certifications	Best of Best Practices by International Association of Conference Centers (IACC) in 2005
	E2 Awarded 2003
	E3 Awarded 2004
	Environmental Excellence Program
	Green Seal Awarded 2004
	Virginia Department of Environmental Quality (VA DEQ)*

Warrenton, Virginia

Airlie Center

The Airlie Center is located in Virginia's rural Piedmont foothills on 2,800 acres and is home and protector to one of the largest population of swans in the world. The conference center opened in 1960 to provide a unique environment for the creative exchange of ideas, later referred to by *Life* magazine as "an island of thought." The Center can accommodate up to 550 people for any given event.

The Airlie Center's commitment to sustainable practices is led by staff who voluntarily seek out operational improvements and perform top notch audits on a quarterly basis.

By empowering employees and implementing a cost-saving high performance operations program, the Airlie Center is a case study in doing the right thing for the environment while balancing guest expectations and fiduciary responsibilities.

* The Virginia Environmental Excellence Program is a program of the Virginia DEQ's Office of Pollution Prevention (P2). The E2 level of participation is for those organizations that are interested in beginning or are in the early stages of implementing an environmental management system (EMS). The E3 level of participation is for those organizations with a fully-implemented EMS, pollution prevention program, and demonstrated environmental performance.

Background

In 1956, Dr. Murdock Head and his wife purchased a large farm in the state of Virginia. Their plan was to create a place where individuals and organizations could meet without distraction in a natural setting to discuss and exchange ideas. Converting old farm buildings into lodging and conference meeting room space, Dr. Head created a relaxed yet up-to-date atmosphere for the guests. In 1959, Dr. Head established the Airlie Foundation. The Airlie Foundation and its conference center operate in tandem to develop and sponsor educational, environmental, and cultural programs. Together they host over 600 non-profit, government, and private sector groups annually. The Center does not accommodate transient guests, but it does host approximately 20 weddings each year.

The Airlie Center's mission is "to study, promote, encourage and foster knowledge, understanding and appreciation of the interrelationships which exist in the physical and social sciences." The Center is situated as a secluded retreat in the heart of Virginia's Piedmont foothills, an area noted for its rich history and diverse habitat. Airlie's employees pay careful attention to the delicate balance between the natural environment and the Center's operations. They consider themselves to be stewards of the 2,800 acres forming the Center's central campus and surrounding wetlands, meadows, and woodlands.

The Airlie Center must meet Green Seal standards on an ongoing basis in order to maintain Green Seal certification (e.g., there are no mercury thermostats on site). In addition, the Center must adhere to the meeting practice standards of the International Association of Conference Centers (IACC) (e.g., providing dimmable lights, ergonomic seating, and tackable wall surfaces), as well as comply with the requirements of the state of Virginia's Department of Environmental Quality (DEQ) Environmental Excellence Program. As a result, the Center has created a Green Team to monitor and balance these standards while pursuing the mission of the Airlie Center's founder.

Airlie's environmental stewardship predated the national advent of the green movement (even Earth Day was conceptualized on site). Environmentally sound practices and land stewardship had always been a part of Dr. Head's mission and part of Airlie's culture. The mission of the Airlie Green Team is to ensure the longevity of Dr. Head's philosophy by primarily focusing on the Center's day-to-day operations.

Airlie implemented recycling officially in 2001 as part of a comprehensive property-wide Environmental Management Program (EMP). The Green Team, led by employees, meets two times per month to monitor progress, introduce staff recommendations for approval, conduct internal audits, and stay informed about new environmentally friendly technologies, increase employee awareness, and maintain the EMP records. The Airlie Foundation and Conference Center considers itself a steward of the land because it is the "right thing to do."

At the Airlie Center, environmental impact is the first consideration when considering any new product or service. The results are weighed against organizational costs. Life cycle assessments, multiple option comparisons, payback evaluations, and net present value (NPV) analyses are common for large investments. Cost is therefore a critical variable in the decision-making process, but it is always weighed against the efficacy of sustainability measures. If the Center spends irresponsibly, then other programs will be sacrificed. As a result, cost can be a prohibiting factor when considering the implementation of a more sustainable technology.

That said, the Airlie Center pursues green certification because it promotes stewardship and aligns with the Center's culture. However, green certification does not necessarily improve the Center's ability to attract guests. The Center always strives to exceed the requirements of certification programs. However, the Center only began to tell guests about its sustainability efforts in 2003, 36 years after many of the programs were initiated. In the hospitality industry, the Airlie Center provides a case study in doing the right thing for the environment while balancing guest expectations and fiduciary responsibilities.

Organization

Project Team

The project team consists of the Airlie Foundation property oversight group.

Contact Information

Below is contact information for the project team.

Developer/Owner/ Management Company	Airlie Foundation
General Manager	Kevin Carter
	Airlie Center
	http://www.airlie.com
	kcarter@airlie.com
Director of Rooms and Engineering	Jean LaChance
	Airlie Center
	http://www.airlie.com
	jlachance@airlie.com

Managerial Structure

There were approximately 170 employees on the Airlie Center payroll. Figure 1 below represents only the Senior Management of the Center's Management Team. Reporting to these managers are the department heads, including (among others) the Executive Chef and Head of Security.

Figure 1: Managerial Structure

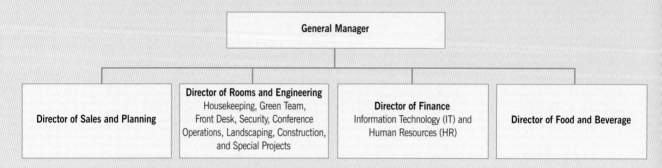

Green Team

High Performance Qualifications: The majority of members have no formal education in environmental sustainability. Personal interests drive the progress of the Green Team, and everyone is very inquisitive.

Staff Training and Compensation

> There is a high level of commitment and communication between all employees and management. The Center's employees provide a tremendous amount of input. All suggestions, no matter who they come from, are encouraged, welcomed, and considered as solutions or improvements to our green initiatives.
>
> GINA CLATTERBUCK,
> *Special Projects Aide,*
> Airlie Center

The Airlie Center appointed a Culture and Training Manager to maintain the strength of the Center's "soul" while business operations continue to grow. Management does not want the Center to lose its sense of culture and history, or to become "too commercial and cold." An emphasis on culture is part of every employee's training. The Airlie Center's management believes the Center's culture is one of the reasons for low employee turnover. The range of housekeeping and engineering staff tenures is five to 30 years. This does not include one staff member who lived at Airlie when he was seven and still works there. The highest turnover appears to be among the wait staff.

In addition to culture training, every staff member receives an award-winning manual describing the Airlie Center's environmental policy. There are currently more than 150 of these manuals in circulation. A tour of the property is included in each new employee's orientation, with a focus on the environmental features. Guests also have the opportunity to learn about the Center's environmental practices by reading posters and flyers that are placed around the buildings, and by attending the many lectures hosted by the Center.

In Fauquier County, Virginia, it is often difficult to find new employees because the unemployment rate is 1%. As a result, the Center makes a serious effort to create a pleasant work environment, encourage employee loyalty, and reduce employee turnover. As an incentive, the Airlie Center provides educational and professional development assistance through a tuition reimbursement program for all employees. The Center also provides all employees with lunch and dinner. The Airlie Center is the third-largest employer in Fauquier County. The hospital and the local schools are the first and second largest employers, respectively.

In general, there are no financial incentives encouraging Airlie employees to be more environmentally sensitive. However, there is both spoken and written recognition of employee environmental efforts. As an employee benefit, and to generate enthusiasm about sustainable efforts on site, the Airlie Center sponsors several activities during Earth Week – activities in which the employees can have fun and learn about sustainable practices. Employees can gather honey with the beekeeper, participate in swan research, work in the local garden, and make and hang bluebird feeding boxes. Earth Week typically ends with a lunch and ice cream social, and a raffle that includes environmentally themed prizes such as carbon credits.

Community Outreach and Education

The Local Food Project at Airlie creates a bridge to the community. An organic culinary garden was created on campus to supply fresh herbs, vegetables, and flowers to Airlie Center's kitchen. This program is now nearly ten years old. It originated as a partnership between the Humane Society of the United States (HSUS) and the Airlie Foundation, and it represents the Center's most extensive public outreach.

The Center invites guests and local residents to attend free seminars about sustainable agriculture. The program attracts more than 150 people per year and is especially popular with those who grow (or want to grow) vegetables in their own backyards. Airlie Foundation and HSUS use the Local Food Project as a way to demonstrate the benefits of sustainable agriculture and local food systems. The groups sponsor seminars, tours, and conferences to promote sustainable food production using natural methods designed to protect air and water quality while improving soil fertility with organic compost, mulching, and green cover crops.

Educational materials and sessions are offered to conferees and the general public to promote the advantages of local food systems for the well-being of communities. The Airlie Center believes that when consumers know where their food comes from, they can choose products that meet their expectations for health, quality, taste, environmental sensitivity, and the treatment of farm animals.

The Airlie Center's management also supports and provides a venue for environmental conferences. Center directors frequently speak on panels and/or give presentations to conference attendees. The Center's management worked on the Ceres Green Hotel Initiative for event planners, and the United States Green Building Council (USGBC) holds board meetings on site. In addition, the Center hosts a reception in the garden every Wednesday for all in-house guests.

Finally, the Airlie Center leases some of its land to local farmers to produce hay for their cattle.

Construction and Operations

Table 1 summarizes the most prominent among the high performance features of the Airlie Center's construction retrofits and operations.

Table 1	HIGH PERFORMANCE CONSTRUCTION AND OPERATIONS HIGHLIGHTS
1. Site	• The Airlie Center is an environmental steward of its 2,800-acre site through natural preservation, environmental programs, and operational practices. • Alternative transportation, such as walking and biking, is encouraged by the close proximity of sleeping rooms to the meeting space and the availability of complimentary bicycles. • On-campus buildings incorporate reflective material for flat roofs, and 50-year asphalt shingle tiles contain recycled content.
2. Material and Resources, and Waste Management	• An on-site sustainable garden supplies the Airlie Center kitchen with 4,500 pounds of food annually. • Biodegradable hot-and-cold cups are manufactured from sugarcane. • The Center provides water in pitchers for conferences; bottled water is available only upon request. • The facility composts 20 tons of food scraps annually. • Housekeeping staff use non-toxic, biodegradable cleaning products. • The Center recycles more than 38 tons of waste each year. • There are two on-site hybrid vehicles for shuttling guests. • In a recent renovation, all the materials had recycled content and the furniture was purchased locally.
3. Energy	• The Airlie Center planned to reduce energy consumption by 25% between 2004 and 2009 with HVAC and lighting upgrades. By 2006, the Center was 11.7% more energy efficient. • The Center uses packaged thermal air conditioning (PTAC) HVAC units in most of the buildings. These units naturally ventilate space with outside air if the temperature is appropriate. • There is an average Seasonal Energy Efficiency Ratio (SEER) of 15 across all Airlie Center HVAC units. • The Center uses Honeywell 8000 programmable thermostats in the meeting rooms. • Water extractors have been installed on the three on-site commercial laundry machines to pull water out of the material. Reduced drying time saves energy.
4. Water	• There is no outside irrigation system installed on the grounds. • The Center has replaced most plumbing fixtures with water-saving equipment such as low-flow water closets, showerheads, and faucets that adhere to Green Seal standards as part of its retrofits and renovations projects. • The dishwasher recycles the rinse water.
5. Indoor Environmental Quality	• The Airlie Center's PTAC HVAC units require no ozone-depleting substances (chlorofluorocarbons [CFCs], hydrochlorofluorocarbons [HCFCs], or halons) to operate. • Housekeeping staff use environmentally friendly cleaning products. • Throughout the campus, all paints and adhesives have low volatile organic compound (VOC) emissions. • Guest rooms provide individual heating and cooling systems to maximize guest comfort.

1. Site

Construction

The Airlie Center's conference attendee accommodations are conveniently located in close proximity to Airlie House, the Center's main building. This encourages alternatives to driving. Guests can easily walk from any of the seven lodging buildings to any other place on campus. The Center owns and maintains complimentary bicycles for guest use during their stay.

Other features of the Airlie Center site help to preserve the local habitat. Buffer zones surround the lakes and ponds, protecting both wildlife and habitat. The gas fuel tanks located on site are double insulated and Environmental Protection Agency (EPA) grade to ensure that the liquid propane or oil does not leak and contaminate surrounding areas. The Airlie Center also has installed industry standard light-colored roofing on the flat roofs of the buildings, which helps to reduce the heat island effect by reflecting solar heat gain. On the shingled steeper roofs, the Center is planning to install rubber-content shingles that have a less negative environmental impact than traditional asphalt shingles.

Operations

The Airlie Center's 2,800-acre site previously was a complete natural habitat (i.e., a greenfield site). Currently, 1,800 acres are developed. The Center has been an excellent environmental steward of the land, and continues that stewardship through its environmental education programs as well as through natural preservation and operational practices.

The Airlie Center encourages responsible land stewardship most directly through habitat preservation – maintaining trails and gardens and protecting unspoiled natural areas for wildlife. The Center boasts that it is home to one of the largest swan populations in the world, and the grounds are certified as National Wildlife Habitat. The Center's environmental study programs conduct research on the swans and other native fauna and flora. The Peterson Butterfly Garden provides a pesticide-free, carefully structured habitat of native woodland, meadow, and wetland species of nectar and host plants that encourage a myriad of caterpillars, butterflies, and moths. Other environmental programs include hosting a honey bee keeper and supporting a sustainable garden operation. Also, land that is not used for conference guests is leased to a local farmer to grow hay for his cattle.

2. Materials and Resources, and Waste Management

In an effort to identify the most sustainable products on the market, the Airlie Center initiated a challenge to existing vendors and business partners to help find new and improved products, even if those products were items that the vendors currently did not supply. As a result of the good working relationship with "friends," it was very easy for the Center to work with its business partners to identify appropriate resources. And, when the vendors could not carry the new product, they would refer the Center to other companies in order to maintain the friendly relationship.

Interior Design

The Airlie Center is installing ceiling tiles with recycled content in the renovation of the Federal Room. The ceiling tile manufacturer also will take back the existing tiles (as well as the newly installed product at the end of its useful life) to recycle back into new ceiling tiles for the future.

The Airlie Center tested a variety of no/low volatile organic compound (VOC) latex paints and found that these paints peeled frequently. As a fix, the Center used a primer, and that seemed to solve the problem.

The drapes in newly renovated rooms are either made from linen (a natural fiber) or, in the case of the solar shades in the Federal Room, contain recycled content.

At Silo House, almost all materials, including the furniture, contain recycled content. The Center purchased most material locally within a 500-mile radius of the Center. On the exterior, and in order to preserve the look of the original structures, the Center maintains the existing stucco and also applies stucco to newly renovated buildings to match the original farm house and campus buildings. The interior log cabin structure will remain in buildings with this kind of interior.

Operations

The Kitchen – As mentioned, the Center's organic culinary garden is a sustainable agricultural project initiated by the Airlie Foundation in partnership with the Humane Society of the United States. The garden, known as the Local Food Project at Airlie, employs an organic farmer who collaborates with Airlie chefs and supplies a wide variety of vegetables, herbs, and edible flowers for the Center. The food alone amounts to 4,500 pounds annually. In addition, the Food and Beverage department has initiated a safe seafood program that bans Chilean sea bass, swordfish, and Mako shark. The department has added organic wines to the wine selection. For dining, the Center uses no disposable serving products, individual bottles of water, or individual condiments (except sugar). When a disposable hot-and-cold cup is needed, the Airlie Center uses a product it has sourced from the Co-op America website – a product that is manufactured from sugarcane and is completely biodegradable. The Center serves water in pitchers with glasses, and condiments in larger packages for use by the entire table. The Center collects 20 tons of food scraps annually for the local garden compost, including egg shells, fruits, vegetables, tea, and coffee. Cooking oil is taken away by a third-party company to be used as a raw ingredient for shampoo.

Housekeeping – The Airlie Center uses non-toxic, biodegradable cleaning products for general all-purpose cleaning. Although the products themselves are not Green Seal certified, the product line is accepted for Green Seal lodging certification. The Airlie Center also buys concentrated products in bulk to reduce the waste associated with individual bottles.

In additional efforts to minimize waste, all Airlie Center printers default to duplex mode, and new paper binders come from the Sustainable Group, a vendor that sells Rebinder. This product contains recyclable (and replaceable) corrugated cardboard and reusable metal binder rings. The facility uses recycled content paper products throughout, including toilet paper. In fact, toilet paper was one of the Center's most scrutinized decisions, with guests, employees, and vendors all seeming to weigh in. Ultimately, the Center decided on a Green Seal certified product.

The Airlie Center has made on-site recycling convenient for both the staff and the guests. Containers at the side of the Center are clearly labeled and color coded to differentiate landfill waste from recyclable material. Gray bins are for dirty trash, white buckets are for compost, and blue bins are for recyclables.

For guests, there are no in-room recycling bins, only a waste bin, but there are recycling centers for the sleeping room buildings in each lobby. There are also custom-made wooden mixed-use bins in all meeting areas throughout the campus, to collect plastic, glass, and paper. The housekeeping staff is trained to collect wire hangers from closets, and to sort the contents of guest room waste bins. The recycling vendor, Waste Management, sorts the remaining waste off site at its own facilities. There are durable outdoor bins as well, for collecting recyclables. The Airlie Center previously made a decision to purchase the outdoor bins even though the purchase involved a significant premium. The managers made this decision to reiterate their commitment to doing the right thing.

The Airlie Center recycles more than 38 tons of waste each year, including, but not limited to, glass, office paper, newsprint, cardboard, aluminum, steel, plastic, wood pallets, motor oil, kitchen grease, and Freon. The Center donates textiles such as blankets to the local SPCA (Society for the Prevention of Cruelty to Animals), and old towels are used as rags. Light bulbs, batteries, and ballasts are recycled by a third-party recycler in Ashland, Virginia.

The Guest Rooms – At the Airlie Center, toiletries such as soap and shampoo are made from natural ingredients and packaged in recycled-content paper and bottles which can be recycled further at the end of their use. The unused shampoo in the opened bottles is collected by housekeeping staff and consolidated in larger bottles. These are used by Airlie employees or donated to homeless shelters. Housekeeping staff also consolidate the unused pieces of bar soap and used them for spot cleaning.

Miscellaneous – The Airlie Center has procured two hybrid vehicles for transporting guests on site and for running errands. A third vehicle has been ordered for security operations. The Center does not allow lead in the ammunition and saucers used for skeet shooting, nor does it permit lead sinkers for fishing.

3. Energy

The Airlie Center began tracking metrics for energy consumption in 2004. The Center's goal was to reduce energy consumption by 25% by 2009 through lighting and HVAC retrofits. In 2004, the Center was using 2.06 million kilowatt hours (kwh) of energy. By 2006, the Center was using 1.82 million kwh, an 11.7% reduction.

By 2007, the Center had replaced 75% of its conventional lighting with compact fluorescent and standard fluorescent lighting. This project involved the updating of all lighting across campus to meet Green Seal certification standards. The Center switched over the lighting in high-occupancy areas first to reduce the largest amount of energy consumption and obtain the greatest impact. Management decided to replace the exit signs with light emitting diode (LED) technology before changing the guest room lights. The Center estimated a five-year payback period on the investment in energy-efficient lighting.

The HVAC retrofits to the Airlie Center were the "greenest" technology that met the financial and project objectives. The management employed energy consultants to provide energy modeling and to help determine what HVAC systems to purchase. Through this process, the Airlie Center's management learned the benefits of long-term financial analysis. Since the Airlie Center is the developer, owner, and manager of the campus, it has additional motivation to consider long-term investments. Most of the HVAC systems have been upgraded to packaged thermal air conditioner (PTAC) units. The most energy-efficient aspect of PTAC HVAC systems is that they automatically use outside air to heat and cool a building if the air temperature is at a level that can be utilized. For example, if a building needs to be cooled, and the outside air temperature is cooler than the indoor temperature, the outside air will be vented to the inside before the HVAC cools additional air. An additional feature of the PTAC units is that they do not use CFCs, HCFCs, or halons (all ozone-depleting substances) as refrigerants.

For all of the HVAC units used on the Airlie Center campus, the average efficiency rating is 15 SEER. The government-mandated minimum requirement is 13 SEER. The Airlie Center always tries to stay a couple of steps ahead of the government regulation.

In addition to the lighting and HVAC upgrades, the Airlie Center incorporates other energy-efficient features. The meeting rooms are all equipped with adjustable thermostats that result in large energy savings. An added bonus of these thermostats is that they are mercury free, which is a Green Seal certification requirement. When the Center's office equipment and dishwashers have to be replaced, they are upgraded to Energy Star–compliant models.

The Center also participates in an off site energy conservation program that offers carbon offsets for meeting planners who book conferences on site.

The Airlie Center also planned to install thermal solar shades with recycled content in place of heavy drapes across the campus. These perforated shades allow daylight to filter in while shading enough of the building's space to maintain energy efficiency. The Center was also considering on-site energy production (e.g., geothermal) once it became cost-effective.

Sometimes the result has a smaller impact, but [is] nonetheless positive with regard to sustainability. The cost is also less.

KEVIN CARTER, *Airlie Center General Manager,* Airlie Center

4. Water

Construction

The Airlie Center has installed multiple pieces of water conservation equipment. All of the sleeping lodges have been retrofitted to be compliant with Green Seal standards for low-flow bathroom water fixtures. The water fixtures include water closets that have a maximum water flow rate of 1.6 gallons per flush, showerheads with a rate of 2.5 gallons per minute, and faucets with a rate of 2.2 gallons per minute. The Center's dishwasher conserves water by recycling rinse water to be used in the washing cycle. Water extraction systems have been installed on the three laundry machines that are used to wash guest room linens and towels. By reducing the amount of water in those materials, the Center saves energy in the drying cycle.

Operations

As part of its environmental stewardship program, the Airlie Center is diligent about conserving water. Both the Warrenton reservoir and a man-made pond are on the Center's campus. The only potable water comes from a well. The Center does not have any irrigation systems installed on the property, and has minimal hose bibs. When new trees are planted, they are kept moist during their infancy by using Gator bags filled with lake water. Rainwater collected in a cistern is used to irrigate the gardens.

5. Indoor Air Quality

Construction

The Airlie Center has enhanced the indoor environmental quality of its buildings by installing appropriate HVAC systems and using materials with low VOC emissions. The PTAC units, which are the primary HVAC systems across the campus, operate without ozone-depleting substances such as CFCs, HCFCs, or halons. Additionally, each PTAC unit in the sleeping lodges provides individual heating and cooling controls so that guests can manage their own comfort directly. The Airlie Center uses low VOC-emitting paints on the walls throughout the campus, and adhesives are specified as low VOC in all construction projects, including drywall and projects that require adhesive.

Operations

Within the last five years, the Airlie Center mandated that its buildings would be smoke-free. This helped to improve the overall indoor environmental quality of the buildings.

As mentioned, the Center uses EcoLab cleaning products that Green Seal's program allows for certification, even though the products themselves are not Green Seal certified.

Business Case

Market Positioning and Consumer Response

The Airlie Center's marketing efforts are limited and the Center attracts most of its business via word of mouth.

Among the Center's guests, 50% are domestic travelers and 50% are foreign. Eighty-five percent of the Center's guests travel for work (40% from government, 40% from non-profit organizations, 5% from corporate entities, and 15% for other reasons). Repeat customers represent 60% of the Airlie Center's business. September through November and the spring months are the Center's busiest times. During these months the Center has an average occupancy rate of 80%. The Airlie Center runs at an occupancy rate of 45% to 50% during the remainder of the year (summer and winter), although summer traffic is both steady and predictable. All 150 of the Center's guest rooms are booked several times each year. In the down season, the Airlie Center does not shut down any of its lodges. However, if the Center grows to approximately 200 rooms, management would be able to close some of the lodges during the slow period.

Recently, corporate clients have begun to inquire about the Airlie Center's environmentally sustainable meeting practices. Although the Center attracts some conference attendees as a result of its high performance initiatives, the bulk of the Center's guests are attracted by the surroundings – the natural beauty of 2,800 reclusive acres. Social responsibility and environmental sustainability are now appearing as criteria in corporate requests for information. In addition, people who desire to have environmentally sustainable weddings often select the Airlie Center as their venue.

The Airlie Center does not publish typical advertisements. Management finds ways to get the word out, primarily through educating clients, enhancing the Center's website, participating in the DEQ website, and gaining mention in green lodging news, press releases, Earth Week celebrations, emails, interviews, and editorials.

The Airlie Center's management does not believe that corporate clients are willing to spend more for environmentally sustainable accommodations. Corporate clients typically have more resources when compared to government and nonprofit clients, but corporations are more astute negotiators. Even so, the Airlie Center's managers believe they can charge a premium for local sundries and other amenities, such as organic food.

The Airlie Center tracks consumer preferences by distributing comment cards that the guests submit through the Front Desk. There are four different comment cards on-site, and these are distributed at random. The Center develops the cards (content and design) and a third-party vendor compiles the data. Management tracks the results against a star segment in the same category. That is, they benchmark the Airlie Center against similar competing hotels. The third-party vendor also compiles open-ended responses for the Airlie Center. The questions focus primarily on services and products. Currently, there are no environmentally sustainable feedback questions on any card. However, guests communicate their comments about the Center's green attributes in their answers to the open-ended questions.

Why High Performance Construction?

The Airlie Center has buildings on its campus that date from the 1890s. The Center is retrofitting old buildings with equipment upgrades that make them more energy and water efficient. Management is doing this purely to achieve operational savings.

Why High Performance Operations?

The Airlie Center promotes high performance operating practices because management believes it is the right thing to do to maintain the Center's culture and enhance the guest experience. Environmental stewardship is a big piece of the Airlie Center's culture, as seen through its land stewardship, environmental programs including green team and organic garden, and the environmentally sustainable educational resources provided to staff and guests.

Many of the Center's high performance operational practices are either cost neutral or less costly. New practices, such as disposable biodegradable cups, are implemented primarily for the benefit of guests and staff. The Airlie Center also has an extensive recycling program and composts a large amount of waste on-site. Additionally, water pitchers are available for conference goers on-site and bottled water is only offered upon request. The Center owns two shuttles which are hybrid vehicles.

Advantages of High Performance Construction and Operations

The Airlie Center has implemented high performance operations, and has retrofitted equipment and facilities, to save money. The Center achieves savings through reduced product costs and operating expenses but, until recently, the high performance initiatives have been more for the benefit of guests and staff. Currently, the Center's management evaluates equipment upgrades in terms of the largest cost savings. As long-term owners, they have shifted their mindset to an evaluation of new products and equipment based on full life cycles, and this has resulted in significant cost savings.

After product evaluations, the next largest cost savings comes from energy-conserving equipment and, to a much lesser extent, from water-conserving equipment. The Center achieves most of its savings by upgrading HVAC units to more efficient PTAC units, by retrofitting lighting to compact and standard fluorescents, and by installing programmable thermostats in the meeting spaces. The Center reduces water consumption through low-flow bathroom fixtures and dishwashers that recycle rinse water. The Center's reduced water consumption does not result in as much cost savings as that produced by the energy conservation improvements. However, reduced water consumption could help save more money in the future as potable water prices increase. Currently, the Airlie Center does save money by not installing or operating an irrigation system.

Table 2 is a summary of high performance hotel construction and operation advantages realized by the property oversight stakeholders – the developer/owner/management company.

Table 2 **STAKEHOLDER ADVANTAGES SUMMARY**		
Developer	**Owner**	**Management Company**
In the Airlie Center case, the advantages for the developer are the same as for the owner and the management company because they are all the same entity. Existing buildings are retrofitted with high performance construction practices so there are currently no new construc-tion tax incentives or other tax benefits.	The Airlie Center is Green Seal–certified and has a beauti-ful property site, both of which help to increase the number of its green conference customers.	The Airlie Center is Green Seal–certified and has a beauti-ful property site, both of which help to increase the number of its green conference customers.
The developer gained an ad-vantage by constructing Airlie Center at its current rural Virginia site with beautiful surroundings. Consumers are drawn to the site primarily because of the natural setting.	Profit margins have increased by lowering operating expenses achieved from energy and water conservation equipment upgrades. Examples: • Management projected a 25% decrease in energy consump-tion between 2004 and 2009 through heating, ventilating, and air conditioning (HVAC) and lighting upgrades. • Low-flow bathroom systems and water-efficient dishwashers reduce water consumption.	Profit margins have increased by lowering operating expenses achieved from energy and water conservation equipment upgrades. Examples: • Management projected a 25% decrease in energy consump-tion between 2004 and 2009 through heating, ventilating, and air conditioning (HVAC) and lighting upgrades. • Low-flow bathroom systems and water-efficient dishwashers reduce water consumption.
	Potential employee cost savings: • The Green Team and other on-site environmental pro-grams encourage a quality culture and a positive work environment, thus reducing employee turnover. • Green cleaning products are cost neutral and healthier for Airlie Center staff, potentially increasing productivity and/ or reducing sick-time days.	Potential employee cost savings: • The Green Team and other on-site environmental pro-grams encourage a quality culture and a positive work environment, thus reducing employee turnover. • Green cleaning products are cost neutral and healthier for Airlie Center staff, potentially increasing productivity and/ or reducing sick-time days.

Best Practices and Conclusions

As mentioned above in the Case Overview, the Airlie Center provides a case study in doing the right thing for the environment while balancing guest expectations and fiduciary responsibilities by empowering employees and implementing a cost-saving high performance operations program.

The following programs implemented at the Airlie Center have been identified as industry best practices toward creating high performance hospitality operations:

- **Green Team and Staff Motivation**
- **Organic Farm and Food Composting Onsite**
- **Extensive Recycling Program**
- **No Bottled Water Onsite**
- **Two Hybrid Shuttles**
- **Endangered Species Protection**

> *Energy projects result in the largest savings over the life of the project.*
>
> JEAN LaCHANCE, *Director of Rooms and Engineering*, Airlie Center

The Airlie Center team is driven toward improving the Center's operations because they see it as an opportunity to align with the original mission of Airlie's founder to "green" the land. The improvements occur as retrofits and renovations since the facilities have been in operation since the 1960s. That said, the Airlie Center has been able to achieve significant reductions and savings in energy and water conservation.

> *Periodically audit supply chain and business partner practices.*
>
> JEAN LaCHANCE, *Director of Rooms and Engineering*, Airlie Center

By implementing these programs and learning from past experiences, the Airlie Center team understands the importance of measuring progress. Quarterly audits are performed to make sure programs stay on track and hit target goals. These progress updates are communicated to Airlie staff and it has been found to motivate team members to participate in developing new high performance programs. The team also found that participating in third-party certification programs such as Green Seal and IACC standards provides an incentive to prioritize audit efforts. External validation and certification deadlines create an impetus to remain on a regular audit cycle.

A final key learning from the Airlie Center is the importance of balancing cost with environmental impact. As mentioned, the Airlie Center must stay within budget when implementing environmentally sustainable strategies. If the Center spends irresponsibly, then other deserving programs will be sacrificed. The Airlie Center performs due diligence prior to approving any project by evaluating lifecycle assessments, multiple-option comparisons, payback evaluations, and net present value (NPV) analyses in order to make the best, most comprehensive and relevant decision for the property.

WALKING TOUR
Airlie Center

Site

- Upon entering the Airlie Center grounds, you will notice that the expanse of the property is 2,800 acres and that there is no sprinkler or irrigation infrastructure on site. In an effort to conserve water, there are very few hose bibs. Gator bags are used to water newly planted trees.

- You may notice also the swans with the black "necklaces." The Swan Research Program is a private research program that began in 1969. It is the nation's only organization dedicated to the study of the family cygnus. The Airlie Center's research swan collection is one of the largest in the world.

- In addition to walking the Center's miles of paths and trails, guests can use bikes to explore the campus or ride in one of two hybrid SUVs to get around. For those interested in skeet shooting or fishing, please note that lead is not permitted in the skeet ammunition and saucers or in the sinkers used for fishing.

- If you have some free time between meetings, definitely head toward The Local Food Project, where you will find a huge compost pile breaking down the Center's kitchen scraps into nourishment for the soil. You will see the fertile land that grows 4,500 pounds of food annually for Airlie Center guests, and interact with the on-site sustainable gardener, Pablo Elliot. Be aware that The Local Food Project is always looking for volunteers who are willing to lend a helping hand.

Building Exterior/Entrance

- In order to preserve the original structure, the Airlie Center applied stucco to the outside of the Lake Cottage so that it matched the rest of the campus. The inside of the log cabin was preserved. You can explore some of the smaller lodges to see if you can find the original log cabins that were built in the early 1960s.

- As you walk among the buildings, do not be surprised if you happen upon large murals that were painted by the same artist who created posters for the Ringling Bros. and Barnum & Bailey circus.

Dining Room

- Notice that only china is used (no disposable products) and there are no individual condiments (with the exception of sugar). Also, the food that is grown in the local garden has a little yellow sticker on the placard that indicates the dish's contents.

Meeting Rooms

- Upon entering the Federal Room, you will notice that it is brightly lit through the large panoramic windows. Instead of using heavy drapes, the Airlie Center chose solar shades to allow natural light to enter the room while still permitting the guest to see the natural landscape outside. In addition, in every meeting room you will notice that you are only a few steps away from a door that leads to the outside. If you need a breath of fresh air, you do not have to go too far!

- All lights in the Federal Room are energy-efficient compact fluorescent and the ceiling tile is an Armstrong product that contains recycled content. In addition, the carpet is made from wool, a natural fiber that can be steam-cleaned with water.

- At the Airlie Center, you will not find any bottled water on site. Instead, the Center serves water in pitchers and glasses to minimize the waste generated from disposable plastic bottles.

- Got meetings? If so, have you considered offsetting the carbon emissions associated with your conference? The Airlie Center will help you to determine how many offsets you need to purchase and they will procure the credits on your behalf.

Guest Rooms

- You have control over the temperature in your room. Is it just right outside? If so, try not to utilize the PTAC unit in your room!

- Also, when entering the bathroom, notice that the toiletries are made with natural ingredients, and that the wrapping and containers not only contain recycled content but can be recycled as well. Look for the recycling bins located in all common areas. And, if you have dead batteries or an inoperable cell phone, bring them to the front desk and the Center will recycle these on your behalf.

- Finally, please try to conserve water and energy by hanging up your towels in the bathroom after you use them. Housekeeping will then not take them away for laundering after every use. Do not forget to fill out the guest comment card and applaud the Airlie Center's sustainable efforts in your answers to the open-ended questions.

Property	Hilton Vancouver Washington and Vancouver Convention Center 301 West 6th Street, Vancouver, WA 98660
	Branded, Conference Center
Contact Information	http://www1.hilton.com/en_US/hi/hotel/PDXVAHH-Hilton-Vancouver-Washington-Washington/index.do
	(360)993-4500
Category	Three Diamond AAA rating
Property Oversight	Developer: FaulknerUSA
	Owner: City of Vancouver (owns hotel and convention center)
	Management Company: Hilton Hotels Corporation
Gross Square Feet (GSF)	225,000 GSF
	30,000 GSF for conference space
	7 stories above grade
	1 stories below grade
Number of Guest Rooms	226 @ 863 GSF per room
Construction Type	New construction
Date Completed	June, 2005
Project Cost	$62 million
	$276/SF (excluding land and associated fees)
High Performance	• Site
	• Materials and Waste Management
	• Energy
	• Water
	• Indoor Environmental Quality
	• Education
	• Green Team
Awards and Certifications	2006 Global Vision Award from *Travel + Leisure* magazine
	Environmental Management Award from Washington State Hotel & Lodging Association
	Green Seal certification (audit completed, certification pending)
	LEED New Construction version 2.1 basic certification

Vancouver, Washington

Hilton Vancouver Washington and Vancouver Convention Center

The Hilton Vancouver Washington and its addition, the Vancouver Convention Center, together represent the second LEED (Leadership in Energy and Environmental Design) certified hotel in the United States. And, Hilton was able to achieve LEED Certification with only a 0.29% premium to construction costs. This project helped to lead the way in the sustainable construction and operations movement, and soon will be the first hotel in the world to have both LEED and Green Seal certification. As a result of having both certifications, the Hilton Vancouver is able to achieve market differentiation.

In addition to focusing on high performance construction and operations, the Vancouver hotel and convention center project is rooted in the local community as part of a city revitalization effort. This effort emphasizes maximizing the return on Vancouver's investment in downtown redevelopment and promoting sustainability through commerce with local suppliers and manufacturers. A hotel Green Energy Management Team (GEM) collaborates with local companies to benchmark best practices that can be incorporated into the Hilton Vancouver's sustainable operations.

The Hilton Vancouver Washington and Vancouver Convention Center complex is a premier case study of city revitalization and of how a high performance building pioneer keeps pushing the boundaries to maintain a competitive advantage.

Background

Vancouver, Washington, a small city bordering Portland, Oregon, is not well known and often is confused with Vancouver, British Columbia. By the year 2000, downtown Vancouver was in need of major revitalization. The city was surrounded by rural areas and the downtown needed private investment and an identity rebirth to attract people and dollars into the area.

Through public/private partnerships, the city of Vancouver began the downtown rejuvenation process with the rehabilitation of Esther Short Park. The city's main partner was Burgerville, a local fast-food chain run on 100% alternative energy that had a large customer base. In addition to the park, the city developed residential units and small retail stores in the area. In 2000, the City of Vancouver contemplated building a hotel, but there was no funding – not even for a feasibility study. A group of local business leaders, calling themselves "Identity Clark County," funded a market feasibility study through the consulting firm HVS. The group saw this as a way to improve economic conditions in the area – an improvement that would benefit them in the future. The Hilton Vancouver Washington and Vancouver Convention Center were the joint result of this optimistic study.

The city learned that state funds could be utilized to build a convention center because that effort would spur economic development. Also, the city could use lodging sales taxes for the same purpose. The hotel portion of the project had to be created as a separate entity, and the city funded that project through revenues from the operations of the hotel and convention center.

Fletcher Farr Ayotte was selected as the architectural firm for the project. The firm focused on orientation and site characteristics, incorporating the renovated park across from the site as a strategic asset for the development. Gerry Link, with the Hilton Hotels Corporation, joined the project team in 2004. The idea to pursue LEED (U.S. Green Building Council Leadership in Energy and Environmental Design) building certification originated with the architects and involved slight changes in the development's original design. (Please see the LEED scorecard in Figure 2.) Even though the city supported this initiative, their main objective for the hotel and convention center was for the complex to be an economic beacon and create job growth. It was more important to the city that the hotel and convention center utilize local suppliers and materials in its construction and operations.

While the Hilton Vancouver was to be the second LEED certified hotel in the world, its focus on achieving both LEED and Green Seal (a third-party verification of high performance operations) certification was revolutionary. Hilton's association with Vancouver's high performance hotel and convention center was a turning point for the sustainable design and construction movement. With corporate brand support, what was once considered a "hippy, tree hugger" movement became an idea with credibility.

The Hilton Vancouver Washington and Vancouver Convention Center complex is a premier case study of city revitalization and of how a high performance building pioneer keeps pushing the boundaries to maintain a competitive advantage.

> *"The hotel provided an economic stimulus to the growing re-development of the downtown area."*
>
> GERRY LINK, *General Manager*, Hilton Vancouver Washington and Vancouver Convention Center

Organization

Project Team

The project team consists of the property oversight group – the developer, owner, and management company – as well as the architect.

Contact Information

Below is contact information for the project team.

Developer	FaulknerUSA www.faulknerusa.com
Owner	City of Vancouver, Washington www.cityofvancouver.us
General Manager	Gerry Link Hilton Hotels Corporation www.hiltonmanagementservices.com Gerry_Link@hilton.com
Architect	Phil Rude, Eric Wilcox, and Mike Shea Fletcher Farr Ayotte www.ffadesign.com

Owner: City of Vancouver, Washington

High Performance Qualifications: The city originally had no previous experience with high performance buildings, but now city and state buildings in Washington must be LEED certified.

Developer/General Contractor: FaulknerUSA

High Performance Qualifications: The firm had no previous high performance building experience, but it had worked on other municipally owned hotel buildings in Omaha and Texas.

General Manager: Gerry Link

High Performance Qualifications: Mr. Link was attracted to this project because of its community revitalization focus, and, although he did not have explicit experience with high performance building, he saw it as a way to maximize the property's positive effects on the area.

Architect/Designer: Fletcher Farr Ayotte (Phil Rude, Eric Wilcox, and Mike Shea, a LEED Accredited Professional (AP)

High Performance Qualifications: The firm's partners had limited high performance building experience at project conception, and they wanted to use this project to gain competence.

Managerial Structure

The following diagram (Figure 1) depicts the reporting structure for the Hilton Vancouver Washington and Vancouver Convention Center. Gerry Link reports to the City of Vancouver on all matters except those regarding financial assets. The City of Vancouver hired Warnick & Company as a third-party asset manager. Mr. Link supplies information to the asset manager, who develops a summary for the city. This ensures that Hilton's proprietary data, such as occupancy statistics and room rates, is retained as confidential business information.

Figure 1: Managerial Structure

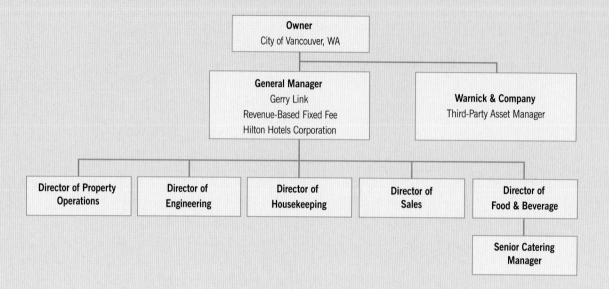

Green Team

In March 2006, employees from each department of the hotel and convention center organized themselves into a Green Energy Management Team known as GEM. This group was formed because of the employees' passion for sustainability. The team currently researches and implements sustainable operations initiatives. No one on the GEM team has formal environmental training. The team exists because of the members' desire to implement, at work, the environmentally sustainable values they live by. The group is led by the Director of Engineering and the Senior Catering Manager. At the time of our interview, the team was focused on completing the Green Seal certification audit.

The GEM team's ideas for the future include a chef's garden on the third floor (using kitchen compost as fertilizer) and partnering with other organizations (such as Burgerville) that operate sustainably to share best practices. The GEM team submits waiver exemption forms to the Hilton Corporation for operational changes the team wants to make. There is no fee and the forms are accepted at any time. Hilton Hotels Corporation encourages the use of sustainable practices within its properties, and has been receptive to the GEM team's changes as long as they don't compromise Hilton's brand standards.

> *"We are learning from others who have paved the way and finding many of our own innovations as a result."*
>
> MELINDA HINKLEY, *Senior Catering Manager*,
> Hilton Vancouver Washington and Vancouver Convention Center

Staff Training and Compensation

The project architects performed the initial staff training on sustainable construction, bringing the sales team, and especially Gerry Link, up to speed. The architects still contact him with new sustainability-related information.

The GEM team is responsible for educating hotel and convention center staff on environmental operations initiatives.

As is typical in the hospitality industry, Mr. Link as general manager is paid a revenue-based fixed fee from the hotel owner. This contract between the city of Vancouver and the Hilton Corporation undergoes an annual review. Since the fee is revenue-based, Mr. Link does not currently have any financial incentive to reduce expenses (e.g., through lower energy use). This may change, however, after the hotel's fourth year in operation.

Community Outreach and Education

Gerry Link shares sustainability knowledge through speaking engagements and tries to create mutually beneficial partnerships. He has spoken to several groups, including the Washington State Recyclers Association, the Clark County Sustainability Conference, and local utility companies.

The Vancouver Convention Center hosts at least twenty events each year, at cost (30–35% below retail), for local 501(c)(3) organizations. Many of these events feature the environmentally sustainable meeting space as a benefit. The hotel sponsors movie nights in the park and other community events, including the display of local artwork throughout the facility.

In addition to local outreach efforts, the Hilton Vancouver tells hotel guests about its sustainable initiatives through documentation at the front desk and online at Hilton's website. The convention center also educates its guests on the benefits of high performance construction and operations, such as the use of carbon dioxide sensors in meeting rooms to help maintain a healthy environment.

Construction and Operations

The Hilton Vancouver Washington and Vancouver Convention Center have a fairly even balance of high performance construction elements versus high performance operational practices. Table 1 provides an overview of these high performance features.

Table 1	HIGH PERFORMANCE CONSTRUCTION AND OPERATIONS HIGHLIGHTS
1. Site	• The project is an example of urban infill development, designed to maximize the benefit of public open space. • All parking is underground, which helps reduce heat island effect. • 100% of stormwater that reaches the development is infiltrated on site. • Erosion and sedimentation control best practices were implemented during the construction.
2. Material and Resources, and Waste Management	• 80.5% of construction waste was recycled. • Steel, drywall, ceiling tiles, and light fixtures were specified with recycled content. • 25.6% of the construction and interior design materials used were extracted locally, and 26% of the materials used were manufactured locally. • Every guest room provides in-room recycling and Hilton now composts and offers biodegradable disposable hot cups. • The project used carpet backing with recycled content from Bentley Prince Street.
3. Energy	• Demand controlled ventilation using carbon dioxide sensors (CO_2) narrows the indoor air temperature range to minimize energy used for heating and cooling. • A highly reflective roof covering decreases the heat island effect and saves energy. • The hotel and convention center utilize multiple sensor technologies, such as motion controls and occupancy sensors, to increase energy conservation. • The building's central hydronic heating and cooling system is more efficient than a fan coil system. • The practice of commissioning improved energy efficiency by ensuring that equipment performance met design specifications. • Heat, as a byproduct of the pool pack equipment, heats the pool.
4. Water	• Local off-site bulk washing uses environmentally friendly techniques. • Outdoor landscaping is native and drought tolerant. Watering is performed with off-peak controlled irrigation.
5. Indoor Environmental Quality	• CO_2 sensors in meeting rooms maintain constant fresh air levels. • The building's HVAC system requires no ozone depleting substances (CFCs, HCFCs, or halons). • Housekeeping staff use environmentally friendly cleaning products from Johnson Diversity and Ecolab. • Adhesives, paints, carpet systems, and composite wood have low volatile organic compound (VOC) emissions. • Thermal control is handled through operable windows and thermostats in the guest rooms, as well as thermostats in meeting spaces.

1. Site

The Hilton Vancouver Washington and Vancouver Convention Center are located in the heart of the City of Vancouver and help to stimulate economic development at the city's center. The development was constructed in an urban infill location, previously a run-down bus depot, across from Esther Short Park. This public park, recently renovated by the city, augments the aesthetics of the hotel and convention center. The architects sited the hotel and convention center to maximize views of this scenic amenity. Most rooms either look out over the park or the nearby Columbia River. The hotel and convention center span 225,000 gross square feet, including 30,000 square feet of convention space. The complex resides within a pre-existing surrounding urban fabric of approximately 86,081 square feet per acre (according to LEED calculations).

Vancouver considered sound environmental practices not only in its high performance building project, but also in its transportation plan. The hotel and convention center are near two bus lines, and all of the single occupancy vehicle parking (158 spaces) is underground. This underground parking space has an alternative use as an exhibition hall for large conventions. By constructing underground parking, the amount of hardscape exposed to sun energy is minimized, reducing the heat island effect. Additionally, locating impervious pavement underneath the building, instead of at street level, maximizes the potential for stormwater infiltration.

One section of the roof is composed of gravel and stones artistically laid out on top of reflective roofing. This public art display mimics the Columbia River that is within view.

Taking the surrounding environment into consideration, the project team ensured that 100% of the stormwater runoff from the site was infiltrated on site by pumping it into tanks underneath the building. This hydrology feature controls the rate and quantity of stormwater that flows to the municipality's sewer systems and cleans the stormwater through filtration before it reaches the water table.

Construction

During construction, the project team implemented best practices to limit erosion and control sedimentation in nearby waterways. These practices included a silt fence, storm drain inlet protection, and sediment traps.

2. Materials and Resources, and Waste Management

Materials used in the hotel and convention center construction and interior design came from local and regional suppliers, and many of these materials were manufactured with recycled content. Of the overall construction materials, 25.6% were sourced locally and 32% were manufactured locally (within 500 miles of the project site), based on cost. Table 2 describes some of the materials and their sources.

Table 2 MATERIALS AND RESOURCES	
Building Core and Shell	• Steel frame: Dietrich Metal Framing; Reinforcement: Farwest Steel • Steel doors with recycled content: Curries • Foam board insulation • Pre-cast concrete: Morse Brothers; Concrete: Glacier Northwest • Brick: Mutual Materials
Interior Walls and Ceilings	• Ceilings: USG, Celotex • Ceiling tiles with recycled content: Armstrong Ceiling Systems • Drywall with recycled content: Georgia-Pacific • Low VOC paint: Pittsburgh Paints
Carpeting	• Carpet: Brintons USA, Atlas, Mannington Mills, Couristan Inc., Bentley Prince Street, and Mohawk Industries
Wood	• Zero formaldehyde casework: Sierra Pine, Panolam • Wood doors: Algoma Hardwoods Inc. • Guest room case goods: Northland Manufacturing
Chandelier Light Fixtures	• Recycled aluminum light fixtures: Eleek Inc.
Other	• Compostable disposable guest cups • Environmentally friendly cleaning products: Johnson Diversity and Ecolab

Construction

The underlying structure of the Hilton Vancouver Washington and Vancouver Convention Center is a steel frame with pre-cast concrete, and the interior is insulated with foam board. The project recycled 80.5% of the construction waste.

Interior Design

The hotel and convention center are luxury designed spaces with high performance building components that have local and recycled content.

Flat-screen monitors are used outside the conference rooms to help convention guests navigate. While these screens use energy, they save the cost of the material and labor needed to create hard-copy signs.

Some of the carpet used in the hotel and convention center has recycled-content backing. The supplier is Bentley Prince Street. The casework installed in the lobby and dining room of the hotel and convention center has no extra formaldehyde added. Also in the lobby, the chandelier light fixtures are made by Eleek Inc. and consist of recycled aluminum. The lobby drapes are standard sheer fabrics that require dry cleaning because of their size.

With the exception of the board room, all of the meeting rooms use flexible furniture that is stored on site. The exercise equipment in the fitness room is made by Nautilus, a local manufacturer.

In the hotel guest rooms, the amenities are individually packaged containers from Crabtree & Evelyn. Unused products are donated to local charities because health codes do not permit consolidation and reuse. The Crabtree & Evelyn products are not available in bulk, but the packaging is made with recycled content. Guest room case goods, such as night stands and dressers, are made by Northland Manufacturing in Bend, Oregon.

Operations

Hilton Vancouver's RFPs (requests for proposals) do not stipulate environmental requirements. However, the GEM team is working to change that. One idea the team recently implemented was changing disposable cups from conventional to compostable. This change was part of the Hilton Vancouver's Green Seal certification effort and was cost neutral. In the meeting rooms, Hilton serves bottled water only if requested by the customer. Ninety percent of the customers drink tap water presented in pitchers. Hilton's housekeeping staff currently use environmentally friendly cleaning products from Johnson Diversity and Ecolab.

The Hilton Vancouver has now broadened its recycling operation to include composting. Again, this is part of the hotel's Green Seal certification goal. Currently, guest rooms have one recycling container, and housekeeping staff sort the waste. The loading dock is too small to accommodate recycling, but the Hilton Vancouver is considering the installation of a lift to help remove containers from the area.

While Hilton's management is working toward the use of new and more sustainable products, the marketplace does not always have high performance products that meet hotel durability standards. For example, the bathroom tissue does not have 100% recycled content because testing determined that 100% recycled-content tissue did not meet hotel quality requirements.

In Grays At the Park, Hilton Vancouver's bistro, the chef uses locally grown and organic ingredients whenever possible. He frequently sources food from the Vancouver Farmers Market, located in the Esther Short Park across from the hotel and convention center.

The Hilton Vancouver uses the vendor Shady Grove for composting services. Even though waste goes first to Portland, Oregon, and then comes back to Washington State (there is insufficient demand for local composting services), the cost is less than sending the waste to landfills. The Hilton Vancouver is trying to reduce the amount of landfill waste by 50%. Goals can be tracked through the Green Seal certification process. Waste Connections, the waste hauler, assists in this effort by providing free waste reports.

3. Energy

Considerable energy efficiency improvements are achieved from the use of various sustainable components in the core and shell of the hotel and convention center. These components include efficient electric lighting; improved insulation; occupancy sensors; hydronic heating, ventilating, and air conditioning (HVAC); and demand-controlled ventilation. These elements combine to create energy savings of 22.6%, comparing the design case to the base case based on ASHRAE (American Society of Heating, Refrigerating and Air-Conditioning Engineers) 90.1-1999 (from LEED calculations).

Tall windows used throughout the hotel and convention center are a quality design feature. Daylighting from these large windows, combined with a 90% use of compact fluorescent bulbs, reduces lighting demand and results in lower energy use. Also, the meeting spaces utilize a dimming system from Electronic Theater Controls.

Focusing on the shell of the building, improved insulation helps reduce energy consumption. All windows are double-paned and low-e from Kawneer North America. Most of the roof area consists of a common rolled reflective roof covering from Johns Manville (Denver, Colorado). The light color of the roofing material helps to reduce the heat island effect and moderate building temperatures. The building's Trane HVAC system is hydronic, and is more efficient than a fan coil unit. With the hydronic system, air-cooled chillers and compressors supply chilled water to fan coil units in the guest rooms. Heat is transferred from hot water boilers across coils in variable air volume (VAV) units and into the different rooms. The chillers are from McQuay International and the air handlers are from AAON Heating and Cooling Products, McQuay, and Desert Aire. The pool pack system, which controls humidity and temperature in the pool area, is another water-based heating system. This equipment generates heat that is reused to heat the pool.

Motion and occupancy sensors, as energy saving features, were easy to implement. Motion sensors were installed in low-use areas, such as hallways. Occupancy sensors that are set for a pre-determined amount of time turn off the lights and return the heating or cooling to pre-set conditions and are utilized in areas such as the conference rooms and bathrooms.

The most significant energy saving feature in the hotel and convention center is demand-controlled ventilation using CO_2 sensors. The widely variable occupancy of the rooms makes this ventilation system especially useful. The system uses outside air except during July and August. Energy recovery units are not needed in the temperate Washington climate. With two chillers and air handlers using variable speed drives, all building air systems are run on demand.

The project team took the quality assurance step of commissioning the building systems to verify and document that the energy systems met performance requirements. Commissioning can reduce energy costs, limit change orders during construction, and help ensure a building will operate efficiently. Commissioning is a prerequisite for LEED certification. Additionally, Hilton employs energy management computer software that collects energy metrics for easy monitoring and controls equipment, including the HVAC system, lighting, and ventilation equipment, so that adjustments can be made (even off-site).

The Hilton Vancouver also uses some energy-efficient appliances and office equipment. For example, public appliances, some office equipment, and guest room television sets are all Energy Star products.

4. Water

Water efficiency is maintained outside the hotel and convention center. The use of native, drought-tolerant plants and timing-controlled irrigation reduces by 50% the amount of potable water needed for landscaping.

The hotel team also implemented some water-conserving laundry practices inside the building. The linen program allows guests to choose to reuse their towels, which reduces the frequency that towels are washed, thus conserving energy and water. There is no on-site laundry equipment (except for one small staff machine). Both regular laundry and dry cleaning is sent off-site to a local cleaner in Portland, Oregon, that is reputed to use environ-mentally friendly techniques.

5. Indoor Environmental Quality

The project team also focused on a healthy indoor environment, an important element in a convention center where guests spend a considerable amount of time in one place. The indoor environment is maintained by controlling the ventilation to maximize fresh air indoors, enforcing the state ban on cigarette smoking, limiting materials that emit VOC gases, and providing indoor environmental quality control.

To maintain the most beneficial mix of fresh air, the Hilton Vancouver installed carbon dioxide (CO_2) monitoring equipment in all non–guest room spaces where carbon dioxide levels are not regulated by the number of people in the space. These CO_2 sensors were set with a differential of 530 ppm (parts-per-million) above ambient levels. The normal ventilation baseline for unoccupied space is 420 ppm. The hotel and convention center also made sure the building met ASHRAE 62-1999 standards for a building's ventilation rate. There are operable windows in the guest rooms, as well as vents to bring in fresh air at tempered levels separate from the variable air volume (VAV) unit.

Initially, the hotel and convention center were built with smoking rooms exhausted to the outside. In June 2007 a state mandate made the hotel and convention center smoke-free.

The materials specified to be no or low VOC included adhesives, sealants, paints, carpet, and composite wood. The complex used plant-based adhesives to adhere the vinyl wall covering and the carpet. Additionally, it used paint that qualified for low VOC compliance for Green Seal certification, and the carpet complied with the Carpet and Rug Institute (CRI) Green Label Program. The composite wood met the low VOC requirement, since it did not contain added urea formaldehyde resins.

Additional methods of minimizing indoor pollutants included the installation of walk-off mats at major entryways to the building, and exhausts in janitor closets. And, the HVAC system was free of polluting CFCs, HCFCs (chloro and hydro chloro fluoro compounds), and halons.

The Hilton Vancouver also provided for indoor thermal comfort and control. For example, it constructed building systems that would maintain humidity and temperature levels to meet the Addenda 1995 standards of ASHRAE 55-1992. Also, guest rooms have operable windows and a thermostat, and meeting rooms and other public spaces have individual thermostats.

Construction

To ensure pollutants did not contaminate the building during construction, the project team followed an Indoor Air Quality (IAQ) plan. The IAQ plan was developed in accordance with SMACNA (Sheet Metal and Air Conditioning Contractors' National Association) IAQ guidelines for occupied buildings under construction. When construction was finished, the project team installed air filters with a minimum efficiency reporting value (MERV) of 13.

Operations

In addition to implementing healthy indoor environment technology during building construction and operations, Hilton's management continues to instruct housekeeping staff to clean with environmentally friendly products. The environmentally friendly cleaning products that Hilton uses are from Johnson Diversity and Ecolab.

Business Case

Market Positioning and Consumer Response

The Hilton Vancouver caught the media's attention as early as opening weekend. The complex was featured in the *New York Times* travel section for targeting LEED certification. The project team had not anticipated the repercussions of media interest. After the opening, Hilton's entire executive management team became "quick studies" and champions of applying LEED concepts, where possible, throughout the Hilton brand. The press touted the project team members as experts who were "leading the [sustainable construction] field." Such accolades appeared in publications ranging from *Lodging* to *Travel + Leisure*, the latter naming the Hilton Vancouver "Eco-hotel of the Year" in 2005.

Gerry Link's current marketing strategy is to leverage off the extensive publicity and key differentiation from other local hotels in order to increase traffic and influence guests' brand loyalty. The hotel and convention center received an estimated $2.98 million of free publicity during the first nineteen months of operation. At first, the publicity did not translate into higher occupancy rates. One limiting factor was thought to be the Vancouver location. The Hilton Vancouver's customer base is regional and is composed of convention guests (56%), business travelers (31%), and leisure travelers (13%). As of July 2007, Mr. Link had started focusing on marketing to regional event and meeting planners, especially targeting green meeting planners. These efforts have been successful, because Mr. Link has been able to directly connect the marketing and public relations effort to increased revenues. Mr. Link estimates that the approximately $2 million in revenues are attributable to customers that value Hilton Vancouver's high performance features.

> "*Based on that response, [the project team] knew it had something big.*"
>
> GERRY LINK, *General Manager*, Hilton Vancouver Washington and Vancouver Convention Center

The hotel and convention center communicates its environmental position via Hilton's website, magazine articles, and outreach events attended by the general manager. Hotel rooms are in the $125–$200 per night range and the convention hotel has a Three Diamond AAA rating. The hotel and convention center are luxury spaces that have environmental features the guests would not know about without reading the educational materials.

Why High Performance Construction?

Both the architectural firm and the developer were interested in high performance construction for the Hilton Vancouver Washington and Vancouver Convention Center. These players wanted to gain experience in the newly developing area of sustainable design and construction, and the additional construction costs were minimal – estimated at no more than $187,000 (0.29% premium). The total construction budget was $64 million (not including land), and the payback was projected at six years. With the construction documents already completed, the only design change required was improving HVAC equipment with items like air handlers. The city of Vancouver thought it would be the "right thing" for them to do. The local Clark County Court House already was a LEED building, the result of a legislative mandate that government buildings achieve at least a LEED Silver ratings. As the hotel management company, Hilton Hotels Corporation was not an active participant in the decision making process, however it was attracted to the idea of including a high performance hotel in its portfolio.

Initially, the project team did not realize how much public attention they would attract. At the time of our interview, the Hilton Vancouver had received the equivalent of approximately $3 million in free publicity and video, and they had spent only $25,000. This was a significant savings in the marketing budget and changed the payback from LEED certification from 6 years to 1 year. The media attention and targeted marketing approach is directly related to increased consumer traffic. Mr. Link attributes $2 million in increased revenue to guests who value Hilton Vancouver's high performance features.

Why High Performance Operations?

The Hilton Vancouver property practices sustainable operations for several reasons. Firstly, the hotel staff felt it was counterintuitive to work in a high performance building, but not operate in a high performance manner. The passion of the GEM team and the initiatives they have implemented thus far show their dedication to sustainability. Secondly, the management was aware of the cost savings through lower utility bills.

By maintaining high performance operations, Hilton Vancouver aims to achieve a Green Seal certification, a third-party verification of high performance operations. The cost of LEED certification was paid from the construction budget, while Green Seal certification costs will be covered by the operating budget. The city supports the expense because dual certification will enhance the high performance image of the hotel and will most likely lead to market differentiation.

Operational changes resulting from the Green Seal audit included replacing disposable cups with compostable ones and installing a cardboard baler. This allowed the Hilton Vancouver's recycling operation to expand and include composting. The cups were cost neutral and the baler had a payback of one year.

Advantages of High Performance Construction and Operations

Ultimately, the main advantage of high performance construction and operations for the Hilton Vancouver Washington and Vancouver Convention Center is to differentiate themselves from their main competitors in the regional marketplace. This property will be the first among its competitors to have achieved both LEED and Green Seal certification. Being first with dual certification will be an enormous asset for increased and free-of-cost promotion and public relations. Additionally, third-party verification in both construction and operations makes the high performance claims credible. In the American Northwest, environmentally friendly practices are considered mainstream. The nearby Portland Doubletree and Portland Hilton already operate in an environmentally sustainable manner and are Green Seal certified. Not only will the Hilton Vancouver be the first in the region with this dynamic combination – both LEED and Green Seal certification – it will be the first hotel in the world to have this competitive advantage.

Table 3 is a summary of high performance hotel construction and operation advantages realized by the property oversight stakeholders – developer, owner, and management company.

Table 3 **STAKEHOLDER ADVANTAGES SUMMARY**		
Developer	**Owner**	**Management Company**
FaulknerUSA developed and constructed the project and benefited by gaining experience in high performance building.	The city of Vancouver realizes resource savings from high performance construction practices. Examples include: • Demand controlled ventilation with CO_2 sensors • Occupancy controls • Efficient irrigation	Hilton Vancouver realizes resource savings from high performance construction practices. Examples include: • Demand controlled ventilation with CO_2 sensors • Occupancy controls • Efficient irrigation
The developer was able to achieve LEED certification with only a 0.29% premium.	The city gained free public relations from having a LEED certified hotel and will gain more when it becomes the first hotel in the world to have both LEED and Green Seal certification. The publicity results in marketing cost savings.	The hotel gained free public relations from being LEED certified and will gain more when it becomes the first hotel in the world to have both LEED and Green Seal certification. The publicity results in marketing cost savings.
	The city leveraged state funds to revitalize a blighted downtown area.	The hotel chain gained experience in high performance-building management and sustainable operations. These best practices can be shared throughout the hotel chain.
	Local commerce and tax revenues have increased through an emphasis on local suppliers and additional hotel and conference guest spending.	

Best Practices and Conclusions

The Hilton Vancouver Washington and Vancouver Convention Center complex is a premier case study of city revitalization and of how a high performance building pioneer keeps pushing the boundaries to maintain a competitive advantage.

The following products and activities implemented at the Hilton Vancouver Washington are industry best practices:

- **Sharing Best Practices with Brand**
- **Local Products and Suppliers**
- **Environmentally Friendly Cleaning Supplies**
- **Green Team**
- **Food Composting**

The Hilton Vancouver Washington and Vancouver Convention Center continue to be showpieces for sustainability. The hotel team has implemented innovative high performance operational practices, including utilizing environmentally friendly cleaning products, composting, and forming a Green Team. The construction project team members were pioneers in this field. Everyone on the project team and hotel management team has learned a lot, and Hilton Vancouver can now share its high performance construction and operations best practices across the Hilton brand.

Gerry Link realizes the importance of staying true to the core hotel business while progressing along the frontier of sustainability. The Hilton Vancouver's competitive advantage comes from being on that frontier and from achieving both LEED and Green Seal certification. At the same time, Hilton Vancouver has implemented the City of Vancouver's desires of sourcing local products and materials and ultimately boosting economic development in the area.

> *Find ALL local partners from the beginning to share successes and enable you to continue to use the property as a showpiece.*
>
> GERRY LINK, *General Manager*, Hilton Vancouver Washington and Vancouver Convention Center

Figure 2: The Hilton Vancouver Washington and Vancouver Conference Center LEED Scorecard

LEED for New Construction v2.0/2.1

Vancouver Conference Center & Hotel
Project # 2136
Certification Level:Certified
10/9/2006

26 Points Achieved		**Possible Points: 69**

Certified 26 to 32 points   Silver 33 to 38 points   Gold 39 to 51 points   Platinum 52 or more points

8 Sustainable Sites		Possible Points: 14
Y		
Y	Prereq 1	Erosion & Sedimentation Control
1	Credit 1	Site Selection	1
1	Credit 2	Development Density	1
	Credit 3	Brownfield Redevelopment	1
1	Credit 4.1	Alternative Transportation, Public Transportation Access	1
1	Credit 4.2	Alternative Transportation, Bicycle Storage & Changing Rooms	1
	Credit 4.3	Alternative Transportation, Alternative Fuel Vehicles	1
1	Credit 4.4	Alternative Transportation, Parking Capacity & Carpooling	1
	Credit 5.1	Reduced Site Disturbance, Protect or Restore Open Space	1
	Credit 5.2	Reduced Site Disturbance, Development Footprint	1
1	Credit 6.1	Stormwater Management, Rate & Quantity	1
1	Credit 6.2	Stormwater Management, Treatment	1
1	Credit 7.1	Landscape & Exterior Design to Reduce Heat Islands, Non-Roof	1
	Credit 7.2	Landscape & Exterior Design to Reduce Heat Islands, Roof	1
	Credit 8	Light Pollution Reduction	1

1 Water Efficiency		Possible Points: 5
Y		
1	Credit 1.1	Water Efficient Landscaping, Reduce by 50%	1
	Credit 1.2	Water Efficient Landscaping, No Potable Use or No Irrigation	1
	Credit 2	Innovative Wastewater Technologies	1
	Credit 3.1	Water Use Reduction, 20% Reduction	1
	Credit 3.2	Water Use Reduction, 30% Reduction	1

3 Energy & Atmosphere		Possible Points: 17
Y		
Y	Prereq 1	Fundamental Building Systems Commissioning
Y	Prereq 2	Minimum Energy Performance
Y	Prereq 3	CFC Reduction in HVAC&R Equipment
2	Credit 1.1	Optimize Energy Performance, 15% New / 5% Existing	1
	Credit 1.2	Optimize Energy Performance, 20% New / 10% Existing	1
	Credit 1.3	Optimize Energy Performance, 25% New / 15% Existing	1
	Credit 1.4	Optimize Energy Performance, 30% New / 20% Existing	1
	Credit 1.5	Optimize Energy Performance, 35% New / 25% Existing	1
	Credit 1.6	Optimize Energy Performance, 40% New / 30% Existing	1
	Credit 1.7	Optimize Energy Performance, 45% New / 35% Existing	1
	Credit 1.8	Optimize Energy Performance, 50% New / 40% Existing	1
	Credit 1.9	Optimize Energy Performance, 55% New / 45% Existing	1
	Credit 1.10	Optimize Energy Performance, 60% New / 50% Existing	1
	Credit 2.1	Renewable Energy, 5%	1
	Credit 2.2	Renewable Energy, 10%	1
	Credit 2.3	Renewable Energy, 15%	1
	Credit 3	Additional Commissioning	1
1	Credit 4	Ozone Depletion	1
	Credit 5	Measurement & Verification	1
	Credit 6	Green Power	1

4 Materials & Resources		Possible Points: 13
Y		
Y	Prereq 1	Storage & Collection of Recyclables
	Credit 1.1	Building Reuse, Maintain 75% of Existing Shell	1
	Credit 1.2	Building Reuse, Maintain 100% of Shell	1
	Credit 1.3	Building Reuse, Maintain 100% Shell & 50% Non-Shell	1
1	Credit 2.1	Construction Waste Management, Divert 50%	1
1	Credit 2.2	Construction Waste Management, Divert 75%	1
	Credit 3.1	Resource Reuse, Specify 5%	1
	Credit 3.2	Resource Reuse, Specify 10%	1
	Credit 4.1	Recycled Content, Specify 10%	1
	Credit 4.2	Recycled Content, Specify 20%	1
1	Credit 5.1	Local/Regional Materials, 20% Manufactured Locally	1
1	Credit 5.2	Local/Regional Materials, of 20% Above, 50% Harvested Locally	1
	Credit 6	Rapidly Renewable Materials	1
	Credit 7	Certified Wood	1

8 Indoor Environmental Quality		Possible Points: 15
Y		
Y	Prereq 1	Minimum IAQ Performance
Y	Prereq 2	Environmental Tobacco Smoke (ETS) Control
1	Credit 1	Carbon Dioxide Monitoring	1
	Credit 2	Ventilation Effectiveness	1
1	Credit 3.1	Construction IAQ Management Plan, During Construction	1
	Credit 3.2	Construction IAQ Management Plan, Before Occupancy	1
1	Credit 4.1	Low-Emitting Materials, Adhesives & Sealants	1
1	Credit 4.2	Low-Emitting Materials, Paints	1
1	Credit 4.3	Low-Emitting Materials, Carpet	1
1	Credit 4.4	Low-Emitting Materials, Composite Wood & Agrifiber Products	1
1	Credit 5	Indoor Chemical & Pollutant Source Control	1
	Credit 6.1	Controllability of Systems, Perimeter	1
	Credit 6.2	Controllability of Systems, Non-Perimeter	1
1	Credit 7.1	Thermal Comfort, Comply with ASHRAE 55-1992	1
	Credit 7.2	Thermal Comfort, Permanent Monitoring System	1
	Credit 8.1	Daylight & Views, Daylight 75% of Spaces	1
	Credit 8.2	Daylight & Views, Views for 90% of Spaces	1

2 Innovation & Design Process		Possible Points: 5
Y		
1	Credit 1.1	Innovation in Design	1
	Credit 1.2	Innovation in Design	1
	Credit 1.3	Innovation in Design	1
	Credit 1.4	Innovation in Design	1
1	Credit 2	LEED® Accredited Professional	1

WALKING TOUR
Hilton Vancouver Washington

Building Entrance

- If you're like most visitors to this area, you probably arrived at the Portland, Oregon, airport, crossed over a bridge (which is also the borderline between the state of Washington and Oregon), and landed at the entrance to the USGBC LEED certified Hilton Vancouver Washington (NOT Vancouver, British Columbia)!

- Before entering the hotel, take a look around you and notice the surroundings. First of all, there is a newly rejuvenated park directly opposite the hotel entrance. Secondly, *the Columbian* newspaper (serving Clark County) opened its Gold LEED certified headquarters office next door using geothermal heating by tapping into the water table. Finally, you might notice a number of cranes dotting the skyline of the city. These are all important signs of Vancouver's renaissance and revitalization, partly due to the Hilton Vancouver Washington hotel's commitment to bringing business back to downtown Vancouver.

- Upon entering the lobby, you might be thinking, "This isn't your father's Hilton!" That is because the designer of this lobby incorporated lightness and brightness into the space through lots of windows as a contrast to the Pacific Northwest's gray and dreary winters. If you look up, you will see a chandelier made from recycled (and recyclable!) aluminum, and all of the wood in the lobby and dining room comes from sustainably managed forests.

- As a side note, during the construction of this hotel, the construction crew recycled 80.5% of the construction waste and only 19.5% was sent to a landfill. Also impressive, the design team was able to source 25.6% of the raw materials to be extracted locally and 26% of the materials to be manufactured locally.

Dining Room

- The Hilton Vancouver Washington hotel is not only LEED certified, it is also trying to be a good local Citizen. In order to do this, the management had to forego some Hilton standards. For example, Pepsi products are stocked instead of Coca-Cola products, because there is a Pepsi bottler in Vancouver. The dining staff buys locally baked goods, and coffee is locally roasted by Boyd Coffee Company, which is owned by a third-generation Vancouver family.

- The hotel also partners with a group that supplies organic foods primarily to Northwest clients. All food scraps are taken offsite and composted. You probably didn't notice that the coffee cups are compostable as well!

Parking Lot and Roof

- I know what you're thinking now. "Why should I go to the underground parking lot?!" Well, first of all, it's underground, so it does not require additional land. Secondly, this space is actually used for conventions when the need arises. And thirdly, check out the electric vehicle plug-in stations. The garage can accommodate seven vehicles of this nature.

- We won't make you head to the roof, but you should know that it is a light color that is extremely reflective so that it decreases the heat island effect (this effect creates warmer environments in cities, since heat is absorbed by surfaces such as concrete and asphalt) and saves energy because the hotel does not have to cool the interior as much as it would if the roof absorbed heat.

Meeting Rooms

- First, take a look at the LCD flat screens outside each of the meeting rooms. These monitors use Microsoft PowerPoint slides to indicate room reservations and, as a result, save paper, sign materials, and labor.

- You may also notice the bright colors used throughout the conference space. This is intended to create another diversion from the typically downcast Pacific Northwest weather. That said, the conference rooms still maximize natural daylighting opportunities, and there are only two rooms without windows.

- CO_2 sensors in meeting rooms maintain constant fresh air levels. There are also thermostat controls to adjust the temperature as needed.

- Also, you will find that most events are catered with water in pitchers and glasses to minimize the waste generated from disposable plastic bottles.

Guest Rooms

- If the temperature isn't comfortable for you, go ahead and adjust the thermostat. Otherwise, you can open your windows (which are also energy efficient) if the temperature outside is ideal.

- Also, when entering the bathroom, take a look at the Crabtree & Evelyn amenities. The bottles are made from recycled content. If you leave partially used products, the hotel will donate the remaining shampoos and lotions to local charities.

- Did you notice the lighting? Energy-efficient compact fluorescent light bulbs can be found throughout your room.

- One thing you probably won't notice is that your room was cleaned using environmentally friendly cleaning supplies purchased from JohnsonDiversey and EcoLab. These eliminate the need for toxic chemicals, improve the air quality, and does not dry out the skin of housekeeping staff. These products are also purchased in bulk and in concentrate to minimize packaging waste.

- Along these same lines, the hotel used plant-based adhesives for the wall covering to reduce the amount of volatile organic compound emissions.

- Do not forget to read the LEED information brochure in your room and, if you have a minute, fill out the guest comment card to share some environmentally sustainable improvement ideas of your own!

LUXURY HOTELS

Property	Mauna Lani Resort
	68-1400 Mauna Lani Drive; Kohala Coast, Hawaii 96743-9796
Contact Information	http://www.maunalani.com
	(808) 885-6622
Category	Independent, luxury resort
	Four Diamond AAA rating
Property Oversight	Developer: Tokyu Corporation of Japan
	Owner: Tokyu Corporation of Japan
	Management Company: Tokyu Corporation of Japan
Gross Square Feet (GSF)	210,000 GSF
	18,600 GSF for conference space
	6 stories above grade
	0 stories below grade
Number of Guest Rooms	343 @ 475 GSF
Construction Type	Renovation
Date Completed	Ongoing
Project Cost	$10.7 million for 2005 renovation and new construction (conference)
High Performance	• Site
	• Materials and Waste Management
	• Energy
	• Water
	• Indoor Environmental Quality
	• Education
	• Green Team
Awards and Certifications	• 2003 Green Business Award from the Chamber of Commerce of Hawaii and Department of Health
	• 2007 Top 100 Golf Resorts in North America and the Caribbean from *Condé Nast Traveler*
	• 2007 World's Best Service from *Travel + Leisure*
	• 2007 *Meetings & Conventions* Gold Tee Award
	• 2007 World's Best Values from *Travel + Leisure*
	• 2008 World's Top Earth Friendly Getaways by *Condé Nast Traveler*
	• September 2004 Green Power "Leadership Award for Onsite Generation" from the United States Department of Energy and the Environmental Protection Agency

Kohala Coast, Hawaii

Mauna Lani Resort

The Mauna Lani Resort includes a 343-room luxury hotel, award-winning spa, and 36 holes of golf on 3,200 acres of pristine coastline. In addition to protecting the endangered green sea turtle, treating sewage and waste water on site, and managing a compost pile for its on-site sod and plant farms, the Mauna Lani Resort boasts the first commercial photovoltaic (PV) solar panel installation to be used by a resort in the United States. By collaborating with the hotel's parent company (Tokyu Corporation), leveraging a long-standing banking relationship, and exploiting local utility and federal tax incentives, the Mauna Lani management team has been able to pursue leading-edge technology that produces long-term benefits without adversely affecting the luxury guest experience.

This case study is an example of how innovation and leading-edge initiatives can be mutually beneficial for both the environment and hotel operations.

Background

The land can be said to contribute to the life of the spirit. You must protect your land's natural beauty and spirit of place to retain and sustain your own spirit.

KENNETH BROWN, *Chairman of Mauna Lani Resort*

Visitors travel to Hawaii to enjoy its remote location and pristine condition. Without the natural beauty beckoning at the Mauna Lani Resort's doorstep, it is unlikely that the guests would travel to the Kohala Coast. Consequently, the Mauna Lani Resort is sensitive to protecting its investments, both as a luxury tourist destination and as a culturally and environmentally friendly development.

Tokyu Corporation of Japan owns the Mauna Lani Resort, a Four Diamond AAA hotel, located on 3,200 acres of Hawaiian coastal property that was the ancestral home of Hawaiian royalty. The resort includes the Mauna Lani Bay Hotel and Bungalows, Mauna Lani Spa, 36-hole Mauna Lani Golf Course, a fitness club, a sewage treatment facility, and sod and plant farms. The land sits amid four mountains: Mauna Kea, Mauna Loa, Hualalai, and Kohala. Fifteen acres of ancient, spring-fed Hawaiian fishponds and historic petroglyph preserves also are located on the property.

The Mauna Lani Resort opened its doors on February 14, 1983. The management company is a Tokyu Corporation subsidiary, Mauna Lani Resort Operations Inc. In 1979, the president of Tokyu Corporation envisioned an environmentally sensitive mission for the Mauna Lani site, which meshed with the parent company's eco-initiative. As a result, the Mauna Lani Resort recycles 90% of its green waste and mixes it with the effluent (discharge) from the sewage treatment plant to create composted fertilizer used at the on-site sod farm and nursery, which includes a commercial tree farm. In addition, the hotel markets itself as an environmentally designed facility with naturally ventilated corridors and an atrium designed with waterfalls, fish and sea life ponds stocked with endangered Hawaiian green sea turtles, abundant trees, and native flora. The hotel's design allows 90% of the rooms to have ocean views and 10% of the rooms to have views of Mauna Kea. The Mauna Lani Resort also employs a spiritual guide to oversee the resort's continuing effort to spread the wisdom of Hawaiian culture, particularly the rich heritage of the Kalahuipua'a Fishponds.

The hallmark project at the Mauna Lani Resort is the photovoltaic (PV) solar panel system. This PV system has grown to more than 600 kWp (kilowatt peak) since its original installation in 1998. The solar panels generate enough power to meet the air conditioning and lighting needs of all the guest rooms on site. The management team began to investigate solar possibilities in 1997 with PowerLight (now SunPower Corporation). Instead of avoiding a new technology, the Mauna Lani Resort forged a path for others to follow by completing a detailed analysis, taking advantage of the local geography and climate conditions, and leveraging a long-standing banking relationship. While completing the analysis, the team also identified several utility-based rebates and federal tax incentives that made the project financially feasible. The Mauna Lani Resort solar panel system installation was the first commercial resort installation of its kind. The hotel has been able to experience significant energy savings without affecting the luxury guest experience. Consequently, this case study is an example of how innovation and leading-edge initiatives can be mutually beneficial for both the environment and hotel operations.

Organization

Project Team

The project team consists of the property oversight group – the developer, owner, and management company. In this case, the developer, owner, and operator is Tokyu Corporation of Japan. In addition, the project team also consisted of a solar power consultant.

Contact Information

Below is contact information for the project team.

Developer/Owner	Tokyu Corporation of Japan
General Manager	Brian Butterworth Mauna Lani Resort www.maunalani.com/ bbutterworth@maunalani.com
Project Manager/ Photovoltaic Solar Power Consultant	Riley Saito SunPower Corporation, Systems www.sunpowercorp.com rsaito@sunpowercorp.com

Developer/Owner: Tokyu Corporation, Japan

High Performance Qualifications: Tokyu Corporation had an environmentally sustainable mission and some experience implementing high performance programs at hotels in Japan.

Management Company: Mauna Lani Resort Operations Inc. (subsidiary of Tokyu Corporation)

Brian Butterworth, General Manager

PV Contractor: PowerLight Corporation

Thomas Dinwoodie, CEO, PowerLight Subsidiary

High Performance Qualifications: The Company was a leading global provider of large-scale solar power systems.

Managerial Structure

The Mauna Lani employs approximately 400 people per day at the hotel and 300 people working elsewhere on the property. Of those 700 staff members, 480 are full-time employees. Figure 1 below depicts the ownership and management structure.

Figure 1: Managerial Structure

Staff Training and Compensation

At Mauna Lani, leadership at the top drives environmental stewardship. The president of Tokyu Corporation, which is also the owner and manager of the resort, believes in sustainability. Management communicates these values to employees during training and ongoing educational programs. The management team tries to inculcate the staff with the corporation's view of environmental sustainability, as well as point out environmental applications specific to each employee's job.

Tours of the entire resort are part of employee orientation and include the composting and wastewater treatment facilities and farms on site. The management team describes the history of the land, the resort, and the company. This communication between the management team and employees helps align employees' thinking with Tokyu Corporation's environmental objectives.

Tokyu Corporation owns and manages the resort. This management structure promotes long-term investment thinking and supports sustainability goals. While the management team endorses sustainability goals, they provide no incentives for the employees to identify new environmental opportunities. Neither performance evaluation forms nor the balanced scorecard for the resort mentions sustainable project suggestions. The hotel measures success primarily based on financial return, which explains the hotel's focus on energy-related innovations where the return on investment is higher.

Community Outreach and Education

The Mauna Lani Resort has a strong community outreach program. The hotel actively engages in preserving Hawaii's cultural traditions and environment. The hotel shares information about the PV project with the local community. Eva Parker Woods, the great-granddaughter of John Palmer Parker, who built the Parker Ranch, lived on the property about 80 years ago, and the hotel has preserved her cottage. The hotel hosts a free monthly event at the cottage on the Saturday of the full-moon week for hotel guests and the local community. Local healers and artists perform and interact with the community. On average, 300 people attend this event and stay connected to the traditions of Hawaii.

The resort's spa was inspired by the traditional Hawaiian belief that the lava tubes represent the womb of the land (aina). The resort spa recreated a lava tube to simulate a healing or rebirthing water experience in the aina. The hotel hired at-risk youths from the community to help with the construction work. Because of this training, some of those people now work in the rock construction business.

The hotel also participates in a charity walk in conjunction with the Hawaii Hotel Association and raises money for on-island charities. In 2008, Mauna Lani raised $65,000 and was the island's largest fundraiser.

The Mauna Lani works with National Marine Fisheries to protect endangered green turtles. The hotel helps to care for and raise the green turtles until they are ready for release back into the sea. The green turtles graduate to different environments as they age. The caretakers release the mature turtles into the wild on July 4, which is a large celebration with educational booths – affectionately called Turtle Independence Day.

Mauna Lani also shares information about the PV project with the United States Department of Energy and Environmental Protection Agency, and with environmental groups from other countries, including the Philippines and Taiwan.

Construction and Operations

Table 1 below highlights the sustainable features of the Mauna Lani Resort's construction and operations. The hotel focused its efforts on respecting the local culture and preserving the natural environment, while managing budgets and minimizing the impact on the guest experience. This translated into environmentally sensitive features in both construction and operations with a strong focus on conserving energy and water resources.

Table 1	HIGH PERFORMANCE CONSTRUCTION AND OPERATIONS HIGHLIGHTS
1. Site	• The site takes advantage of the ocean and mountain views. • The site takes advantage of the natural sea breeze. • There is on-site wildlife protection of the endangered Hawaiian green sea turtle. • There is preservation of 3,200 coastal acres.
2. Material and Resources, and Waste Management	• The hotel works with local farmers to supply the Mauna Lani Resort food and beverage operations. • Food composting goes off site to local pig farmers. • The hotel processes green waste composting on site. • There is a diverse recycling program in the back-of-house area. • Materials are locally extracted. • Public restrooms use cloth towels instead of paper products.
3. Energy	• Photovoltaic solar panels distributed throughout the property generate more than half a megawatt of energy. • Thermostats are equipped with occupancy sensors and programmed with appropriate setback temperatures to conserve energy in vacant rooms and other areas of the hotel. • The hotel provides Energy Star equipment, such as liquid crystal display (LCD) television sets, in guest rooms. • Energy-efficient compact fluorescent lighting is used in guest rooms. • Indirect lighting in meeting rooms diffuses the light and requires less energy. • There is a solar thermal heater for heating the pool. • There is a computerized energy management system. • There are variable speed drives for the cooling tower. • There are installed chiller upgrades.
4. Water	• Endemic, indigenous, and introduced plants surrounding ancient fishponds are drought tolerant and act as natural pesticides. • There is on-site sewage and waste water treatment. • The hotel uses reclaimed graywater. • The hotel uses treated water for on-site composting activities. • The hotel installed Paspallum grass throughout the landscaped areas to take advantage of the local brackish water. • There are showerheads, faucets, and toilets equipped with low-flow hardware and aerators. • The off-site dry-cleaning process is perchlorethylene (PERC) free. • There is a towel and linen reuse program.
5. Indoor Environmental Quality	• There is natural ventilation in common areas and corridors. • There is thermal control with guest room operable windows, lanai doors, and individual thermostats.

1. Site

The architects paid special attention to the building orientation and layout to maximize the natural surroundings; 90% of the guest rooms in the hotel overlook the ocean and the other rooms have views of the Mauna Kea.

The Mauna Lani Resort shares the land with protected, ancient, spring-fed Hawaiian fishponds and historic petroglyph preserves. The resort must comply with coastal zone regulations mandating state ownership of the land 20 feet from the high water mark. These regulations preclude development on these strips of land and require the resort to preserve the integrity of these spaces.

The resort has also created a haven for the endangered Hawaiian green sea turtle inside the atrium and in the surrounding ponds. Since 1989, this wildlife preservation project has nurtured and released more than 125 juvenile green sea turtles into the wild.

Operations

The Mauna Lani Resort landscaped the surrounding grounds with drought-, wind-, and salt-tolerant plants. The photovoltaic solar panel system provides power for the well to pump three million gallons per day of brackish water for landscape and irrigation purposes. The water is not filtered, so salt-tolerant plants thrive and weed growth declines.

The resort spent $20 million to convert the 36-hole golf course from Bermuda grass to salt-tolerant Paspallum grass. One benefit of this reseeding was that Paspallum grass does not require fertilization, so fewer chemicals and less labor are required. Eliminating fertilizer protects the reefs, which are a major source of tourism revenue. When the resort experienced high tides and waves crashing onto the grounds, the Paspallum lawn thrived.

2. Materials and Resources, and Waste Management

Construction

The Mauna Lani Resort opened the golf course in 1981 and the hotel in 1983 as a concrete, post-tension steel building. In 1997, the hotel renovated all guest room bathrooms by installing Italian marble. In 2005, they updated all guest room soft goods, cabinets, and carpeting.

The lava rocks used throughout the spa facility were from the resort. The natural lava sauna is at a lower elevation, and the sauna designers created a lava rock berm to control erosion and sedimentation by reducing the rate of surface runoff. The lava and dry mud radiate heat up to 145 degrees, creating a natural, outdoor, dry sauna. Flat and smooth river stones are also used. Eight underprivileged youths, 15 to 20 years old, who had no previous rock project experience helped with the project. Currently, several of these people are working for the rock wall building company because of their experience at the Mauna Lani Resort.

Operations

When Hawaii introduced a recycling law in 2006, the Mauna Lani Resort had been recycling waste for more than ten years. Most of the recyclable material originates in the back-of-house operations. Hotel staff separate aluminum cans, glass, and plastic for daily removal. Hawaii implemented a bottle-recycling bill in 2005 that offers incentives for consumers to return "HI-5" bottles for a $0.05 rebate. As a result, the island recycles 85% of sold HI-5 bottles, without curbside pickup.

The Mauna Lani Resort recycles cooking oil, wet waste, food scraps, and green waste. The resort hired a local company to haul away used cooking oil that is resold as biodiesel fuel. A local pig farmer recycles food scraps. The resort composts green waste on site. The compost and effluent become soil amendments three miles from the resort and are used instead of chemical fertilizers. To date, there have not been any odors or guest complaints about the compost site, which sits at a distance from the hotel. Composting is part of a cycle. New plants take up nutrients from the compost, grow in the landscaping, and eventually become green waste to be composted again. The green waste compost procedures are: (1) mound up the green waste; (2) moisten the pile with reclaimed graywater; (3) allow the temperature to rise; (4) turn over the pile to add oxygen; and (5) allow the mixture to decompose into humus.

The Mauna Lani Resort works with local farmers to supply the hotel's food and beverage operations. The resort supports diversified agriculture. According to the General Manager, Brian Butterworth, "By working closely with local farmers, we honor those who came before us and those who take care of the land today."

The Mauna Lani Resort used to bale cardboard and prepare it for recycling but, unfortunately, there is no demand for cardboard on the island because there are no local paper mills. The resort is recycling other paper products.

3. Energy

Operations

The Mauna Lani Resort was able to take advantage of the breezy, tropical, Hawaiian climate, where the average daily temperature is in the low 70s. The resort built an open air (not air conditioned) atrium and corridor, dramatically reducing energy demand.

The resort uses other unobtrusive energy-efficient practices throughout the facility, including compact fluorescent lighting (100% usage in guest rooms), indirect lighting in meeting rooms, guest room programmable thermostats with occupancy sensors, Energy Star Sony Bravia television sets, and the first commercial installation of photovoltaic solar panels. Occupancy sensors are easy-to-implement energy-saving devices. Occupancy sensors reduce heating or cooling if they detect no motion in the room over a specified period. These sensors are part of the InnCom programmable thermostats in each guest room. Housekeeping staff regularly monitor the units, especially when it is humid, to avoid mildew and musty odors. Housekeepers may override the system and turn on the air conditioning, even if the room is unoccupied, depending on outside temperature conditions. When the resort is at high occupancy, the turnover rate (time between guests checking out and checking in) is fast and the high humidity is not a problem.

The Mauna Lani Resort also installed a computerized energy management system that requires no technical expertise to make it successful. Although the system is not linked to the room reservation system, it controls meeting room temperatures, specifically the variable speed drives, air handlers, and lighting controls for the banquet rooms, and the solar thermal heater for the pool water. The solar pool heater eliminated the need for a $55,000 heat pump by directing 100 gallons per minute of 110 degree water into the pool.

The climatic conditions of Hawaii allow the Mauna Lani Resort to utilize several photovoltaic energy systems to capture and convert solar energy. The 250 kWp–rated photovoltaic PowerTracker™ system, manufactured and installed by PowerLight Corporation of Berkeley, California, is a proprietary sun-tracking solar electric system that gave Mauna Lani the distinction of having more solar electric generating capacity (half a megawatt) than any resort in the world.

The original photovoltaic installation was an 80 kWp–rated array and produced 3% of the resort's total needs. Dedicated in May 1998, the installation consisted of ASE panels by PowerLight that have a 25-year warranty. The guest rooms are located below the PV system. The panels, acting as roof insulation, behave like an air chiller and lower the building temperature, which means it takes less energy to cool the guest rooms.

Installed in 2003, the PV system over the ballroom is a 110 kWp–rated array manufactured by Mitsubishi-Sanyo. The PV system over the hotel is rated 190 kWp. Installed in 2000, this PowerTracker system is a 250 kWp single-access tracking system. It tracks the sun's east to west movement throughout the day. It is not an East-West-North-South tracking system, but the tracker does maximize panel energy production. The power generated by the tracker first goes to the wells to pump water used for landscaping and irrigation, and then any excess power goes to the sewage treatment plant.

The Mauna Lani Resort is not constrained for space. Although photovoltaic systems are large, especially the tracking system, the Mauna Lani had adequate land for the installation. The resort has recouped its investment. The PowerTracker's ability to follow the sun makes it more efficient and generates 25–35% more electricity.

Installed in December 1998, a 110 kWp–rated PV system sits on the golf course maintenance warehouse, provid-ing power for the clubhouse restaurant and recharging the electric golf carts.

The Mauna Lani Resort does not store any generated power, as there are no batteries on site. The site consumes all the generated power; they do not return power to the utility grid. According to the resort's analysis, the monetary charges for overproducing are more than the net metering cap credits, so the hotel decided to avoid this cost.

In total, there is enough energy generated on site to provide power to all the guest rooms during the day. According-ing to the Mauna Lani Resort, the PV system has not required maintenance or cleaning since it was installed.

4. Water

Operations

The property manager expects the number of residential homes located on the Mauna Lani property to increase from 600 to 1,000 in the next few years. The resort depends on the county water system for potable water and is required to observe the county's consumption restrictions, which protect the limited resource. As a result, the Mauna Lani developments have a water consumption cap. If they surpass the cap, the county will not allow the development company to sell the homes. Therefore, the Mauna Lani Resort is committed to reducing its potable water demand to ensure the marketability of the residences on site. The hotel has implemented a number of water conservation projects, including the planting of drought-tolerant indigenous trees and plants such as sugar cane, palm trees, hibiscus, and bougainvillea.

The Mauna Lani Resort also developed an on-site wastewater treatment facility to filter sewage for reuse in irrigation and composting. The resort uses brackish water for landscape irrigation. They installed Paspallum grass to replace the Bermuda grass because Paspallum has a high tolerance for brackish water.

All water features on site use recirculated, potable water. The ponds hold salt water, which also minimizes potable water consumption.

Inside the hotel, guest rooms feature showerheads, faucets, and toilets equipped with low-flow hardware and aerators. Housekeeping staff manage the towel reuse program to minimize wasteful washing of clean, unused towels. The hotel does not wash guest room linens every day unless the guest requests it. The Mauna Lani Resort hired an outside laundry company with modern equipment that recycles water, is water efficient, and has high-technology dryers. Minimal laundry is completed on site. Three local companies handle dry cleaning off site. Two of the three dry cleaners use perchlorethylene (PERC) in their cleaning process and the third is a new laundry supplier with better, more modern equipment.

5. Indoor Environmental Quality

The Mauna Lani Resort maximizes fresh air indoors and provides guests with indoor environmental quality control in their rooms. The open-air atrium and corridors take advantage of the natural sea breezes and eliminate the need to provide conditioned air.

Business Case

Market Positioning and Consumer Response

Mauna Lani is an independent, AAA Four Diamond hotel and markets itself as a luxury destination resort. It caters primarily to leisure travelers and hosts some meetings and business conventions.

Mauna Lani's sustainability efforts, however, are paying off by attracting environmentally responsible organizations. Organizations such as Toyota Motor Corporation and IEEE (formerly Institute of Electrical and Electronics Engineers, Inc.) selected Mauna Lani for key meetings because they perceived the hotel as a truly environmentally sustainable resort. Lexus, a division of Toyota Motor Corporation, introduced the RX 400h SUV at the Mauna Lani. The event filled half the guest rooms at the hotel for five weeks. The resort's marketing brochures highlight the resort's high performance efforts. The resort hopes that these efforts will help attract more conference groups and corporate guests who are looking for hotels with environmentally sustainable programs.

Why High Performance Construction?

The resort was developed, is owned, and is managed by the same entity. This structure helps the developer benefit from investments in high performance design elements such as naturally ventilated corridors and open areas. These eliminate the need for air conditioning and result in energy savings during the use phase of the building.

Why High Performance Operations?

Mauna Lani's high performance efforts focus primarily on back-of-house opportunities for energy and water conservation, and for waste management. The goal of most of these activities is to reduce costs without compromising the guest experience.

Mauna Lani's hallmark innovation was installing PVs in 1997. It would have been cost-prohibitive to use solar panels for power generation without federal and state tax credits. At the time of the installation, Mauna Lani was experiencing negative earnings and could not leverage tax credits available to install solar panels. However, the resort was interested in reducing energy costs and was able to test the technological innovation through a creative deal with First Hawaiian Bank. The bank bought the panels and leased them back to Mauna Lani on a seven-year lease.

The bank received a federal tax credit of 10% and an additional state credit of 35% on the cost of the panels. The state mandates ownership of the panels for five years, or it assesses penalties. The bank depreciated the panels over a five-year period. The leasing arrangement was profitable for the bank and the bank later made more money by selling the panels at fair market value to Mauna Lani at the end of the seven-year lease. Table 2 below summarizes the financials from the bank's perspective.

Table 2 FIRST HAWAIIAN BANK – PV PANEL FINANCIALS	
	Cash Flows
Cost of PV panels	$(1,000,000)
10% federal tax credit	$100,000
35% state tax credit	$350,000
Mauna Lani lease payments over seven years	$600,000

Mauna Lani experienced mixed energy costs with this lease arrangement. For the first five years of the lease, the lease payment amount exceeded the cost of equivalent energy consumption purchased through the utility. During the last two years of the lease, the payment amount was lower and the cost of generated power was less than the cost of purchased power. The details of the lease structure are not available.

Mauna Lani was very satisfied with the first PV installation and decided to add five more PV projects using the same lease structure. The hotel developed their initial projections for the PV project based on a 2% annual increase in energy prices beginning in 1997. They have, instead, seen energy costs increase more than 100%. The hotel now estimates a payback of 2.5 years with the tax incentives. The federal tax rebate is now 30%, making PV installations even more economically feasible. Table 3 below summarizes the financial benefits to Mauna Lani from the PV project.

Table 3 MAUNA LANI – ENERGY SAVINGS FROM PV PROJECT	
	Cash Flows
Energy generated by six PV installations	7% of total energy used by hotel
Utility charge for energy	$0.28/kwh Cost
of energy through PV	$0.12/kwh
Savings	**$0.16/kwh**

The average temperature on the roof of the resort is 145 degrees Fahrenheit while the temperature under the PV panels is 90 degrees. The resort believes that this lower temperature helps protect the roof membrane and will reduce the need for repairs on that portion of the building. However, these benefits have not been quantified.

The resort's PV system also has helped to generate significant publicity. The resort believes that the PV installation in the spa alone generated about $3 million in free media coverage and helped promote the resort's redesigned spa.

The resort also is testing solar thermal technology to heat the pool water. The resort believes that the solar thermal water heater helped to reduce the need for a $55,000 heat pump. The local utility, Hawaiian Electric Company, provided a $5,000 incentive for the heat pump. The resort also has received rebates from the utility company for lighting upgrades, such as the conversion from incandescent to compact fluorescent light bulbs in the guest rooms.

Additionally, the resort is taking major steps to conserve water. They decided to convert the landscaping and golf course grass from Bermuda to Paspallum because the latter can survive on brackish water and does not need fertilizer. A detailed cost benefit analysis was unavailable.

The resort has on-site composting and a sewage treatment facility. They pay for recycling and garbage collection by weight, so composting reduces the waste management fees. The composting and sewage facilities also allow the resort to further develop the property without adding significant burden to the county's landfills and sewage systems, thus making it easier to obtain expansion permits. However, we do not have data to quantify this business rationale.

Advantages of High Performance Construction and Operations

With a focus on lower operating costs, the Mauna Lani Resort is a leader in energy savings, water conservation, and waste management. Because their bank packaged energy tax credits with a buy-and-lease-back arrangement, the resort has benefited from energy efficiency.

Table 4 is a summary of high performance hotel construction and operation advantages realized by the property oversight stakeholders – developer, owner, and management company.

Table 4 STAKEHOLDER ADVANTAGES SUMMARY		
Developer	**Owner**	**Management Company**
The developer also is the owner and manager of the site. All investments in high performance design (e.g., open-air common areas requiring no air conditioning) in the construction phase of the hotel have benefited the development company. The benefits include reduced expenses and higher profit margins in the operational phase of the building.	The open-air site design lowers operational expense since no air conditioning is needed in common areas.	The open-air site design lowers operational expense since no air conditioning is needed in common areas.
	The energy and water conservation programs (e.g., photovoltaic systems and Paspallum grass) reduce operational expenses and increase profit margins.	The energy and water conservation programs (e.g., photovoltaic systems and Paspallum grass) reduce operational expenses and increase profit margins.
	On-site composting and the sewage treatment plant allow the owner to develop the remaining land without adding burden to the county's municipal systems.	Protecting endangered turtles onsite adds a tourist attraction and could help increase occupancy rates and improve relations with environmental groups, perhaps averting resistance to further development.
	Protecting endangered turtles on site adds a tourist attraction and could help increase occupancy rates and improve relations with environmental groups, and perhaps avert resistance to further development.	

Best Practices and Conclusions

This case study is an example of how innovation and leading-edge initiatives can be mutually beneficial for both the environment and for hotel operations.

The following programs implemented at the Mauna Lani are industry best practices leading to high performance hospitality operations:

• Energy Efficiency and Innovation – PV Installation
• Minimal Guest Impact
• Onsite Composting and Graywater Recycling
• Endangered Species Protection

As evidenced by their commitment to photovoltaic solar panels, the Mauna Lani management team members are open to researching new products and services. Change management does not discourage them, and they have selected and implemented a technology that has improved the hotel's operations.

The photovoltaic installation typifies the open-minded, innovative culture of the Mauna Lani team. They assessed their geographical surroundings and realized the potential benefits of solar power. They researched available products that could meet their needs. For change management, the team worked with the diverse perspectives of multiple entities, including third-party consultants, hotel owners, and a lending institution. The team successfully managed the discussion and approval process and was able to implement a pilot installation. Following the success of the first phase, the hotel rolled out four more phases, quantifying the success of each phase as supporting data to obtain approval for future phases.

Guests of the Mauna Lani Resort are aware that some of the power used by the hotel is generated by solar panels on the roof. They want visible programs clearly aligned with the overall "Hawaiian" experience. Protecting the endangered Hawaiian green sea turtle differentiates the hotel, is good for the environment, and adds a cultural aspect to the guest's experience. In contrast, the hotel's composting pile and sewage treatment plant are consistent with the hotel's environmental stewardship but are not openly communicated to the guests. Mauna Lani's management team members are diligent about balancing the needs of the environment with the expectations of the guests, and they have found a successful way to address both.

WALKING TOUR
Mauna Lani Resort

Site

- Step into the open-air atrium that takes advantage of natural sea breezes and eliminates the need to provide conditioned air.

- Walk farther and notice the cascading waterfall adjacent to the atrium steps. This water feature recirculates water to minimize potable water consumption.

- After admiring the pleasant sound of trickling water, step deeper into the atrium and look at the saltwater pond. Very soon, you will spot your first endangered Hawaiian green sea turtle. Find out when the feedings are and get all your questions answered by the resident in-house turtle expert.

Photovoltaic Solar Panels

- The staff at the Mauna Lani Resort is quite accommodating. If you express interest in seeing some of the photovoltaic solar panels, you might get a tour of the roof, the on-site spa, or the East/West PowerTracker solar system.

Landscaping

- Take a walk outside. While admiring the views, the saltwater ponds teeming with fish, and the reef sharks, do not forget to notice the Paspallum grass throughout the property. This wind-resistant, salt-tolerant plant thrives on brackish water and does not require fertilizer.

Guest Rooms

- You have control over the temperature in your room. Is it just right outside? If so, turn the power off by using the thermostat and relax on your balcony with the doors open.

- Also, do not forget to hang your towels so that housekeeping does not replace them with new towels. If you want your sheets cleaned more frequently, you can always use the smooth stone provided in your room to indicate your desire to the housekeeping staff. Two items you can replicate in your own home are the Energy Star LCD television set and energy-efficient compact fluorescent bulbs.

Mauna Lani Spa

- There is one more stop you have to make. Head toward the spa and check out the open-air dry sauna made from locally extracted lava rock.

Property	The Fairmont Banff Springs
	405 Spray Avenue, Banff, Alberta CANADA T1L1J4
	Branded, luxury resort
Contact Information	http://www.fairmont.com/banffsprings
	(403) 762-2211
Category	Four Star Mobil rating, Four Diamond AAA Rating
Property Oversight	Developer: Canadian Pacific Railway
	Owner: Ontario Municipal Employees Retirement System (OMERS)
	Management Company: Fairmont Hotels & Resorts
Number of Guest Rooms	768
Construction Type	Renovation
Date Completed	Ongoing; most recent project completed June 2008
Project Cost	$25 million conference center addition (1991)
	$12 million spa addition (1995)
	$4.5 million golf course restoration (1997)
	$75 million restoration (1999)
High Performance	• Site
	• Waste Management
	• Indoor Environmental Quality
	• Education
	• Green Team
Awards and Certifications	• 2001, 2002, 2003 Gold Key Award, *Meetings & Conventions*
	• 2001-2002 Pinnacle Award, *Successful Meetings*
	• 2002 "500 Best Hotels in the World," *Travel + Leisure* (inaugural list)
	• 2002-2003 Readers' Choice Award, *Meetings & Incentive Travel*
	• 2002 Greens of Distinction Award, *Corporate & Incentive Travel* award recognizing "outstanding golf facilities and service for corporate meeting and incentive travel programs"
	• 2004 "Best Spa in Canada" Readers' Choice, *Luxury SpaFinder*
	• 2006 Global Tourism Business Award
	• Certified Audubon Cooperative Sanctuary for the golf course
	• Member of the Audubon Green Leaf Eco Rating Program for hotels
	• Top 20 Non-US Resorts in the World, *Condé Nast Traveler*

Banff, Alberta; Canada

The Fairmont Banff Springs

The Fairmont Banff Springs is the largest of three Fairmont hotels in the Banff/ Jasper area of Alberta, Canada. All three properties are located within Canadian national parks, and the hotels must adhere to strict guidelines that ensure proper care of the surrounding natural environment. Visitors travel to the area for the views and setting. The Fairmont Banff Springs, built by the Canadian Pacific Railway in 1888 as part of the Grand Hotel Series, is a Canadian icon. Fairmont Hotels & Resorts has managed this 120-year-old historic hotel since 1999, and has brought a profound corporate commitment to environmentally sustainable hotel operations and preserving the surrounding national parks.

This case underscores the benefits of a public/private partnership that pursues land conservation and historic landmark preservation, and highlights Fairmont's corporate leadership in sustainable operations.

Background

In 1885, the ten square miles (26 square kilometers) around the northern slopes of Sulphur Mountain, an area known as Banff, became Canada's first national park. On June 1, 1888, the area celebrated the opening of the Banff Springs, designed in the style of a Scottish baronial castle and in a manner that complements the ever-green trees found in the surrounding landscape. The Canadian Pacific Railway built the 778-room Banff Springs as part of the Grand Hotel Series. The hotel is now a Canadian icon, and was designated a national historic site in 1992. The Banff National Park has grown to encompass 6,641 square kilometers (2,564 square miles).

Today, Banff National Park and the 8,700 residents of the town of Banff annually welcome more than five million visitors who come to enjoy the wildlife and spectacular scenery. Tour buses and shuttles from the nearby airport arrive throughout the day. In the fall of 1999, Fairmont Hotels & Resorts acquired the Banff Springs property and brought a corporate commitment to operating an environmentally sustainable hotel, as well as to preserving the surrounding national park. The Fairmont Banff Springs is the largest hotel in the area. The hotel is surrounded by a Stanley Thompson–designed 27-hole golf course. Other hotel amenities include a health club and spa with indoor and outdoor pools, nine restaurants, four lounges, a business center, gift shop, laundry services, horseback riding and hiking trails, movie theater, and bowling alley.

Fairmont manages three hotel properties in the Banff/Jasper area of Alberta. All three properties are located within Canadian national parks. The hotels must adhere to strict guidelines that ensure proper care of the surrounding natural environment. Canada has a strong affinity for its national parks and a tradition of enabling people to experience and enjoy the landscapes and natural surroundings.

While Fairmont is an acknowledged environmental leader in the surrounding area, its actions are still subject to the scrutiny of public hearings and environmental assessments. The Fairmont Banff Springs interacts with many groups: hotel owners, guests, Canadian citizens, and the Parks Canada Agency, a government agency that manages the national parks. These groups have diverse, and sometimes conflicting, interests. There is also a strong Canadian sense of pride in ownership, and Fairmont must deal with Canada's perception of the national and historical significance of the Grand Hotels. The Fairmont Banff Springs team attempts to meet the expectations of all these interests. Because it operates in a national park, Fairmont must complete environmental impact studies for all relevant proposals. All vested groups consider Fairmont an environmental steward, and since it is the largest business in the area, they expect Fairmont to be a leader and to share its research with the community and other local businesses.

Fairmont's corporate reputation for sound environmental operations and practices allows it to maintain a close relationship with the Parks Canada Agency and the local community. Fairmont's obvious concern for the local ecology helps them with the approval process for renovation and restoration projects.

This case underscores the benefits of a public/private partnership that pursues land conservation and historic landmark preservation, and highlights Fairmont's corporate leadership in sustainable operations.

Organization

Project Team

The project team consists of members from the property oversight group – in this case, the developer, the owner, and the management company led the high performance efforts.

Contact Information

Below is contact information for the project team.

Owner	Ontario Municipal Employees Retirement System (OMERS) http://www.omers.com
Developer/General Contractor	Canadian Pacific Railway www.cpr.ca
Regional Director of Public Relations Alberta	Lori Grant Fairmont Hotels & Resorts www.fairmont.com lori.grant@fairmont.com
Chief Engineer	Marty Schenk Fairmont Hotels & Resorts www.fairmont.com marty.schennk@fairmont.com

Developer: Canadian Pacific Railway

High Performance Qualifications: The hotel was originally built in 1888 when green construction, operations, and conservation were not formalized.

Owner: Banff National Park (Parks Canada)

High Performance Qualifications: Parks Canada is the government agency responsible for national parks and has a long history of promoting conservation.

Land Lessee; Property Owner: OMERS

Management Company: Fairmont Hotels & Resorts

High Performance Qualifications: The company is a recognized industry leader in green operations.

Managerial Structure

The hotel complex employs 1,100 staff members during the peak season and 600 to 700 staff members the rest of the year. The Willow Stream Spa in the hotel has an additional 200 employees. The hotel uses a combination of permanent staff and temporary workers during the peak season. Figure 1 below highlights the hotel's management structure.

Figure 1: Managerial Structure

Environmental Committee

The Fairmont Banff Springs considers itself an integral part of the Banff National Park vacation. The hotel is committed to responsible management of the locale. The hotel has a Green Team charged with identifying innovative green operations and sharing new information with the community and Fairmont corporate headquarters. The Green Team co-chair is the Director of Public Relations and Engineering and team members are volunteers from the following groups within the hotel:

1. Rooms (housekeeping, front office, and guest services – including bell staff)
2. Food and Beverage (kitchen, restaurants, in-room dining, stewarding, and recycling)
3. Sales
4. Human Resources
5. Accounting
6. Spa
7. Grounds/Turf Care
8. Reservations
9. Royal Service
10. Engineering

The team meets once a month for one hour, and staff members from all shifts attend the meetings. The Green Team serves as a liaison to all departments and is responsible for identifying new ideas and suggestions. The Green Team forwards meeting minutes to a corporate brand team that works to share ideas with other hotels within the brand. According to Lori Grant, the Regional Director of Public Relations,

> *Members of the Green Team are people who want to make a difference, and who abide by the Girl Scout philosophy of leaving something better than the way they found it.*

The Green Team currently is working to generate innovative ideas to improve environmental performance at the hotel using the Natural Step Framework, an internationally accepted approach to achieve consensus on issues of sustainability. Mr. Roberts, then General Manager and Regional Vice President, believes the company has been successful with environmental initiatives and will benefit from following Natural Step to re-energize the staff and make green ideas a priority.

Staff Training and Compensation

Fairmont brand's standard operating procedures specify that housekeeping staff complete a 14-day training that encompasses green procedures and that is reinforced with a buddy/job shadow system. The training covers the hotel's recycling and cleaning procedures. A bulletin board outside the staff cafeteria highlights a housekeeping tip of the week. The Green Team is trying to roll out this concept to all internal departments.

Fairmont hotels sponsor the Fairmont Environmental Eco-hotel of the Year competition across all their hotels. These programs spark innovation and help the staff realize what it means to be a sustainable hotel. For example, the groundskeeper led the effort to have the hotel golf course certified by the Audubon Society.

There are no bonuses for green practices but all hotel employees work toward improving green performance. The management team believes that green practices increase staff enthusiasm. The staff understands that greener cleaning products, for example, enhance their quality of life and that they are giving back to the community.

Community Outreach and Education

As the area's largest business, the hotel believes it is its responsibility to care for the natural heritage of Banff and to give back to the community. All of the hotel's common spaces are open to the public, and the hotel encourages people from the community to utilize these spaces. The hotel also is working with the Town of Banff on a pilot composting program. They sponsor a clean-up day two times a year where hotel employees help clean the local highway. The hotel is sponsoring a UNESCO (United Nations Educational, Scientific and Cultural Organization) training program that will certify local residents as World Heritage Program Guides. Guides with permits take guests around the park and explain the culture, environment, and history of the area.

Operating in a national park increases scrutiny of the hotel's operating practices. The hotel recently sponsored a golf match for five generations of popular golfers at the Banff Springs Golf Course. There were 4,500 tickets sold. The hotel sought Park approval and worked with environmentalists on the project. The hotel set up parking lots and coordinated with the Town of Banff to develop a transportation plan to bring the extra influx of people to the golf course.

The hotel educates guests by placing information about their green efforts in guest folios. The restaurant menus highlight organic, sustainable food and local purveyors when possible. The Green Team and the public relations department also invite environmental leaders to speak to hotel guests and the local community. For example, the company recently hosted Dr. David Suzuki, a noted author, geneticist, and host of Canadian Broadcasting Corporation's television series *The Nature of Things* to talk about local foodstuffs.

The hotel works with its supply chain to enforce green practices. Suppliers understand the hotel's environmental standards and know they will lose the contract if they do not meet the hotel's standards. Fairmont obligates supplier compliance to green practices at all levels of the corporation. The Fairmont Banff Springs knows other hotels are cooperating to leverage their buying power to promote the green movement.

The Fairmont Banff Springs is not just the castle across the bridge, it's more than that.

LORI GRANT, *Regional Director of Public Relations*

Construction and Operations

Table 1 highlights the environmentally sustainable features of the Fairmont Banff Springs construction and operations. As seen below, the hotel implements high performance features mostly in the operation phase.

Table 1 HIGH PERFORMANCE CONSTRUCTION AND OPERATIONS HIGHLIGHTS	
1. Site	• The project is an example of historic preservation of a landmark building. • There is on-site wildlife protection. • The Fairmont Banff Springs is an environmental steward of its site through natural preservation and environmental programs. • Grounds vehicles run on biodiesel fuel.
2. Material and Resources, and Waste Management	• The hotel uses locally extracted stone material. • The hotel uses Environmentally Preferred Products (EPP). • There is an extensive recycling program for guest room and back-of-house waste. • There is food composting.
3. Energy	• The hotel utilizes occupancy sensors in guest rooms. • An energy-efficient lighting program includes compact fluorescent light (CFL) bulbs.
4. Water	• Faucets are equipped with aerators. • Toilets are equipped with low-flow hardware. • There is a towel and linen reuse program. • The hotel uses graywater for plant and landscaping irrigation.
5. Indoor Environmental Quality	• Housekeeping staff use non-toxic, green cleaning products from Ecolab. • Adhesives and paints have low or no volatile organic compound (VOC) emissions.

1. Site

The Fairmont Banff Springs is located within Banff National Park. As a result, the hotel must adhere to strict guidelines that ensure protection of the surrounding natural environment. The Fairmont Banff Springs' management knows that visitors travel to the area for the views, the setting, and the opportunity to explore the mountains. Fairmont has an incentive not to damage their source of income. In addition, The Fairmont Banff Springs is a Canadian icon that warrants preservation. This status creates additional challenges for the hotel. For example, regulations for managing a historic landmark prohibit new external construction on the site or expanding the footprint of the existing buildings. Retrofitting a building from the late 1800s offers its own challenges as well.

The hotel is located at the convergence of the Bow and Spray rivers in the midst of animal migratory paths. Cougars, coyotes, and human beings all traverse the land surrounding the Fairmont property. Elk like the area because the tall grass pokes through the snow making it easier to find nourishment during the cold winter months. The hotel once offered a cross-country skiing program, but the trail crossed animal migratory paths, so the Fairmont, in conjunction with Parks Canada, decided to eliminate the program. There are no animal fences (which might deter elk) and animals always have the right of way, even on the golf course.

According to the Audubon International organization, "Fairmont Hotels & Resorts is a good example of a company that has adopted sound environmental management practices. Its golf courses are enrolled in the Audubon Cooperative Sanctuary Program (ACSP)." The hotel also is a member of the Hotel Association of Canada's Green Key Eco-Rating program. The introductory level of commitment of this program educates hotels on environmental and eco-efficiency issues. The second level provides hotels with a rating, a report that details how to get to the next level of performance, and an audit that verifies each property's eco-efficiency functioning. The Fairmont Banff Springs is a four-key-rated hotel.

The ACSP is an award-winning education and certification program that helps golf courses protect the environment and preserve the heritage of the game of golf. The ACSP serves as a vital resource, helping to enhance valuable natural areas and wildlife habitats, improve efficiency, and minimize the potentially harmful impacts of golf operations.

Fairmont achieves its operational goals by ensuring a positive guest experience but also by paying attention to the area and its surroundings.

LORI GRANT, *Regional Director of Public Relations*

2. Materials and Resources, and Waste Management

Construction

Originally, the hotel was a wooden structure, but in 1926 a fire devastated the building. Work on the restored hotel began in 1928 and continued for the next 28 years. The hotel is now a steel and brick structure with a Rundle Stone exterior face.

Operations

Canada has a longer recycling history than does the United States. The Fairmont Banff Springs has leveraged this experience and has developed an extensive on-site reuse and recycling program.

The kitchen team constantly identifies opportunities for improving the sustainability of its operations. For example, local suppliers in Alberta provide food in large Styrofoam containers. The kitchen staff reuse these containers to pack lunches for the large tour groups that go in and out of the hotel daily. In addition, the team works with the Town of Banff on a local composting project. The hotel takes all food scraps off site for processing by the town.

In the dining room, table settings use china when possible, instead of paper products. These standards are consistent with the hotel's Four Star/Diamond ratings. The hotel has ordered organically grown flowers for weddings and other events. The Fairmont Banff Springs proximity to British Columbia (with greenhouses producing food throughout the year) and Alberta (a local source of meat) make purchasing local food easier.

The Fairmont Banff Springs offers bottled water only if requested by guests and collects empty plastic bottles for recycling. The spa provides water jugs along with disposable cups instead of individual water bottles. Reusable mugs, as opposed to disposable cups, do not meet sanitary regulations of the health codes.

The hotel purchases green cleaning supplies from Ecolab, and the contract specifies products in concentrated form and bulk packaging. The toilet paper in guest rooms contains recycled content, as do some other paper products used on site.

Blue boxes in every guest room encourage guests to separate recyclables. There is dedicated space in the back-of-house operations for collecting, sorting, and consolidating all recyclables. These large recycle bins are in a central location to facilitate pick-ups. The staff separates recyclables, and housekeeping carts have three bags for sorting paper, glass, bottles, and cans.

Fairmont's corporate-wide bathroom amenity standard is to provide individual Miller Harris shampoo and lotion bottles that are recyclable. In addition, staff consolidate used products for reuse at the on-site staff accommodations, which are subsidized condominiums across the street from the hotel. If there is toilet paper remaining on the roll, staff also will reuse these in their accommodations. Due to the seasonal nature of the hospitality and tourism industry, The Fairmont Banff Springs staff typically is a transient population; people come and go at the beginning and end of each season. The hotel collects abandoned items at the end of each season and distributes them to needy individuals.

The hotel's Green Team started a cell phone recycling program. Also, a collection bin in the back-of-house encourages donating old sneakers to the homeless. Finally, used furniture is reupholstered and reused on site.

Additionally, the hotel uses organic fertilizer on the entire golf course, since the wildlife feed on the grass.

3. Energy

Operations

The Fairmont Banff Springs collaborated with a third party to complete an energy audit. The performance contract limited payment to the vendor until the hotel actually realized the promised savings. Following the study, the hotel implemented a lighting retrofit and increased the HVAC controls.

A Canadian mandate states that all light bulbs must be compact fluorescent bulbs by the year 2010. The Fairmont Banff Springs already has met 95% of this goal and is continuing to make progress in this area.

In addition, The Fairmont Banff Springs has installed a Honeywell building system and each guest room is equipped with Inncom thermostats that have occupancy sensors to determine if a room is vacant or not. The building system is tied to the room reservation system so if the room is unregistered or vacant, the HVAC system will use a predetermined temperature that varies according to time of day. When the guest checks in, the thermostat will respond appropriately. Housekeepers know to keep doors closed while cleaning. There are no occupancy sensors in common areas but the system is programmable so the HVAC is not used unless there is an event.

Finally, the management team recently approved a proposal for indirect free cooling from outside air to remove heat from the chilling medium. This technology emits less greenhouse gas and requires less power.

4. Water

Operations

Inside the hotel guest rooms, there is information and a place card in each bathroom describing the linen and towel reuse program. Housekeeping staff manage the towel and linen reuse program to minimize wasteful washing of clean, unused towels, and linens are not washed every day. Each guest room is equipped with low-flow toilets and faucets with aerators to reduce potable water consumption. In addition, The Fairmont Banff Springs reuses graywater from the golf course, and irrigates the landscaped areas with well water.

Together with the Fairmont hotel in Lake Louise, the Banff Springs property sends all laundry and dry cleaning off site to the same facility, taking advantage of bulk processes.

5. Indoor Environmental Quality

Operations

The healthy indoor environment at The Fairmont Banff Springs results from a variety of activities, including the use of environmentally friendly products manufactured by Ecolab for cleaning guest rooms, and using paints and adhesives with low or no volatile organic compound (VOC) emissions. In addition, the Towns of Canmore and Banff, as well as the City of Calgary, have a no idling law, so The Fairmont Banff Springs personnel remind tour bus operators of this when they are waiting for guests if the bus is left running.

Business Case

Market Positioning and Consumer Response

The Fairmont Banff Springs is a AAA Four Diamond–rated hotel. There is a Fairmont corporate standard and mandate for environmental sensitivity. Owners buy into this philosophy when they contract with Fairmont as the management partner. While Fairmont has an environmental mandate as a company, the Fairmont brand stands for excellence in customer satisfaction and quality of product. The brand's slogan is "Turning Moments into Memories." The brand positioning is a luxury hotel chain and Fairmont believes that customers stay with the hotel chain for many reasons, with green features playing a part in their choice.

In the past, The Fairmont Banff Springs did not promote their green attributes on the website. Their most loyal customer group in the past has been the Baby Boomers who cared about affordability. However, the hotel is currently changing the website to highlight their green features as guest preferences change and green becomes trendy. While consumers are beginning to ask about green features, the hotel has not seen a significant shift from corporate guests. However, a Canadian government agency has asked about the hotel's practices for heating and cooling, lighting, and recycling.

Why High Performance Operations?

The hotel's green operations mesh with its national park location, Fairmont's corporate environmental mandate, and a desire to lower operational expenses. The hotel's foremost conservation efforts involve preserving wildlife habitats and conserving energy.

According to Parks Canada regulations, the hotel does not allow cross-country skiing on the golf course, and it removed fences that cut through an animal migratory path. Animals are welcome on the golf course. The hotel eliminated the use of chemical fertilizers and pest controls to protect animals that eat the grass. The hotel must comply with Parks Canada Agency regulations; the agency is very involved with preserving the natural habitat and wildlife. Fairmont's business interests coincide with preservation of the immense national park as well as the grounds immediately surrounding the hotel complex.

The hotel used creative financing to reduce energy consumption and signed a pay-for-performance contract with Honeywell to install an energy management system. Honeywell received payment after their system delivered the agreed-upon savings over a five-year period. The contract provisions meant Fairmont could forego any up-front capital investment as well as the risks associated with testing new technologies.

The hotel has received approval from the owners to implement a system to capture heat generated by the chillers. The following table describes the financials of the project. The calculations assume a $0.10 per kwh rate. The current price of electricity in Banff is $0.24 per kwh, so energy efficiency investments have a shorter payback period.

Table 2 **ENERGY REDUCTION TECHNOLOGY**

System	Cost	Payback
Heat capture system	$110,000	4.8 years

Fairmont brand standards dictate using non-toxic chemicals, recycling, and a linen reuse program. The owners agreed to these programs when they hired Fairmont to be the hotel management company. Fairmont's commitment to environmental issues may have helped to win the contract with the Parks Canada Agency.

Advantages of High Performance Construction and Operations

The Fairmont Banff Springs key impetus for green construction and operations is its location in a national park. Fairmont realizes that protecting the local environment is essential to attract tourists and maintain occupancy rates. Fairmont's environmental mandate and brand standards help employees innovate with environmental features. Lastly, as energy prices continue to increase, it becomes easier to justify capital investments in energy efficiency technologies that reduce operational expenses.

Table 3 is a summary of high performance hotel construction and operation advantages realized by the property oversight stakeholders – developer, owner, and management company.

Table 3 **STAKEHOLDER ADVANTAGES SUMMARY**		
Developer	**Owner**	**Management Company**
The hotel was developed in 1888 before green construction and operations concepts were formalized or discussed.	Contracts with the Parks Canada Agency mandate that the lessee comply with park conservation activities to continue operations.	The unspoiled natural setting and local wildlife attract guests. Maintaining the integrity of the site is important to maintaining a revenue stream.
The developers were able to sell the property because of its location in a natural landscape.	Establishing performance-based contracts with an energy efficiency contractor allowed testing new cost-saving technologies without initial capital expenditure.	Investing in green features helped reduce operational expenses and increase profit margins.
	Investing in green features helped reduce operational expenses and increase profit margins.	

Best Practices and Conclusions

This case features the benefits of a public/private partnership in pursuit of land conservation and historic landmark preservation while highlighting Fairmont's corporate leadership in sustainable operations.

The following programs implemented at The Fairmont Banff Springs are industry best practices for creating high performance hospitality operations:

- Green Team
- Community Outreach
- Wildlife Protection and Land Conservation
- Historic Landmark Preservation
- Public/Private Partnership
- Food Composting and Extensive Recycling Program
- Corporate Leadership and Leveraging Buying Power to Influence Shifts in Sustainable Products

Constantly reinvigorate staff about green initiatives to remain innovative.

The Fairmont Banff Springs is a leader in new and innovative environmental practices, and it communicates successful new programs internally to staff and externally to the community, so everyone can learn from the experience. When creative thinking stalls, new programs can infuse renewed passion by bringing the concept of sustainable operations back to the forefront.

Utilize trial and error to identify appropriate products and don't be intimidated by products that may not work.

The Fairmont Banff Springs works with the Jasper and Lake Louise properties to test alternative products and services from other vendors. The management team uses third-party expertise to sort through the plethora of product options available on the market. These three hotels, as part of the Fairmont portfolio, use their combined size to entice suppliers to meet environmental sustainability demands. As a result, the hotel is able to identify the most effective and efficient solutions for The Fairmont Banff Springs operations and the protection of the surrounding natural wilderness.

As the largest hotel in the area, and given the natural setting of the hotel, people look to The Fairmont Banff Springs to be a leader in the area of environmental sustainability. Internal and external stakeholders care about environmental metrics. Each year, travelers are increasingly asking for environmentally friendly features. Fairmont corporate standards guide the environmental innovation for the Banff Springs property, and the operational savings and public relations aspect make greening more attractive.

WALKING TOUR
The Fairmont Banff Springs

Site

- When driving to The Fairmont Banff Springs, you cannot help but see the majestic mountain peaks of the Canadian Rockies looming high above the hotel, or what appears to be a Scottish baronial castle complementing the evergreen trees that line the mountainside. Nestled at the convergence of the Bow and Spray Rivers, this hotel dates back to 1888 and has been declared a National Historic Landmark by the government of Canada.

- Feel free to hop aboard one of the hotel's shuttle vans that take guests to and from the golf clubhouse. These shuttle vans are fueled by locally purchased biodiesel. Once you arrive at the clubhouse, keep a lookout for elk, coyotes, cougars, bears, and other wildlife but do not get in their way! Even golfers have to circumnavigate the animals that decide to use the eighth hole as a resting stop. The hotel is situated on animal migratory paths so it is not uncommon to see golf course personnel close one hole and open another to respect the local inhabitants.

- After your visit to the golf course, feel free to hike on the many paths and trails around the hotel. Guests can also rent horses and go riding in the area.

Building Exterior/Entrance

- The Fairmont Banff Springs is protected by its landmark status. As a result, the exterior cannot be renovated and the original footprint cannot be expanded.

Dining Room

- Notice that only china dishware is used (no disposable products).

- The dining staff also make every effort to procure local produce, oftentimes from British Columbia's greenhouses and Alberta's meat suppliers. Food scraps are composted locally in the Town of Banff.

- If you are lucky enough to experience a wedding at The Fairmont Banff Springs, you might check to see if the flowers are organically grown, since the wedding party can request this service!

Guest Rooms

- Did you notice that your room was not the same temperature as when you left it? That is because the thermostats are equipped with occupancy sensors to determine if anyone is in the room. If there are long periods without motion, the thermostat will drop seven degrees. However, as soon as it senses motion, the thermostat will readjust to the previous setting.

- Also, note that all of the light bulbs in your room are compact fluorescent light bulbs that last longer than traditional incandescent bulbs and require less energy to operate.

- When entering the bathroom, notice that the toiletry amenities are stored in recyclable bottles. Also, look for the recycling bins located in each guest room for paper, cans, and bottles.

- Finally, please try to conserve water and energy by hanging up your towels in the bathroom after you use them. Housekeeping staff will not take them away for laundering after every use.

- Do not forget to fill out the guest comment card with additional ideas for improving the overall environmental sustainability of the property.

Property	The Ritz-Carlton, San Francisco
	600 Stockton Street at California Street, San Francisco, California 94108
	Branded, luxury hotel
Contact Information	http://www.ritzcarlton.com/en/Properties/SanFrancisco/Default.htm
	(415) 296-7465
Category	Five Star Mobil rating; Five Diamond AAA rating
Property Oversight	Developer: Waverly Partners
	Owner: Host Hotels & Resorts
	Management Company: The Ritz-Carlton Hotel Company, L.L.C.,
	a subsidiary of Marriott International, Inc.
Gross Square Feet (GSF)	440,000 GSF
	6 stories above grade
	3 stories below grade
Number of Guest Rooms	336 @ 1,310 GSF per room
Construction Type	Renovation
Date Completed	Ongoing; most recent project completed June 2006
Project Cost	$12.5 million for recent renovation
High Performance	• Site
	• Waste Management
	• Energy
	• Water
	• Indoor Environmental Quality
	• Education
	• Green Team
Awards and Certifications	Twice a recipient of the Malcolm Baldrige National Quality Award

San Francisco, California

The Ritz-Carlton, San Francisco

After four years of building renovation, The Ritz-Carlton, San Francisco opened its doors to guests on April 8, 1991. The hotel occupies a venerable San Francisco landmark (the Metropolitan Life building) and earns both the Mobil Five Star and the AAA Five Diamond ratings, which is a rare distinction reflecting the hotel's high level of luxurious guest services.

The commitment to environmentally sustainable operations is a top-down initiative that begins with corporate leadership and engages management and line staff. The Ritz-Carlton, San Francisco realizes this commitment through monthly meetings, daily line-ups, the ongoing measurement and analysis of key performance indicators, and innovative projects. For example, in 2007 the hotel allocated more than $0.5 million for energy conservation measures. The Ritz-Carlton, San Francisco is the world's first hotel to install the PureComfort® combined cooling, heating, and power (CCHP) solution – the latest in energy-efficient technology from UTC Power.

This case study is a premier example of how a luxury hotel can exceed guest expectations while balancing the demands of high performance environmentally sustainable operations and preserving an important historical landmark.

Background

The Ritz-Carlton, San Francisco occupies a building that was originally built in 1909 as the West Coast corporate headquarters of the Metropolitan Life Insurance Company. After five expansion projects over several decades, the building grew to encompass approximately 440,000 square feet. In 1984, the building was declared a San Francisco historic landmark as an architecturally significant structure designed by Napoleon LeBrun and Sons of New York. Waverly Partners purchased the building that same year.

After four years of renovation (in compliance with historic landmark limitations and requirements), The Ritz-Carlton, San Francisco opened its doors on April 8, 1991, with a new interior design enveloping the 1909 steel and concrete core and shell. Since 1991, the hotel has undergone several cosmetic renovations. The most recent was completed in June 2006.

The Ritz-Carlton, San Francisco property has the distinction of earning both the Mobil Five Star and the AAA Five Diamond ratings. Approximately twenty-five other hotels (out of 31,000 evaluated) in the United States share this recognition. The hotel's commitment to its guests is clear, and these ratings reflect the high level of luxury services offered by the hotel. As a result of this commitment to a luxurious guest experience, the hotel's management must ensure that all new initiatives (including environmentally sensitive projects) do not have a negative impact on the customer experience. Therefore, it is not surprising that most of the hotel's sustainable efforts are implemented in back-of-house operations.

In 2007, the hotel's ownership invested in a $500,000 energy conservation plan designed to reduce both demand and consumption. This program includes, among other projects, conversion to compact fluorescent light bulbs, installation of occupancy sensors, and procurement of variable frequency drives for the air handlers. The hotel also installed co-generation equipment on site to harness the waste heat emitted during the electricity generation process, specifically a PureComfort® combined cooling, heating, and power solution – the latest in energy-efficient technology from UTC Power.

The common denominator in each of these undertakings is the fact that a typical guest would never know these measures have been taken or that these features exist. This is exactly the outcome management was hoping for. In addition, when guests do inquire about the hotel's environmentally sustainable features, personnel are able to talk about the efforts that are "behind the scenes."

The commitment to environmentally sustainable operations is a top-down initiative that begins with corporate leadership and engages management and line staff. This commitment is realized, on the corporate side, through REACT (Ritz-Carlton Environmental Action Conservation Team), on the management side through monthly meetings, and on the line staff side through daily updates. The team also assesses ongoing measurements and analyzes key performance indicators.

This case study provides evidence of how a luxury hotel can exceed guest expectations while balancing the demands of high performance environmentally sustainable operations and preserving an important historical landmark.

Organization

Project Team

The project team consists of members from the property oversight group – in this case, the developer and management company led the high performance efforts.

Contact Information

Below is contact information for the project team.

Developer/General Contractor	Waverly Partners http://www.waverly-partners.com
Owner	Host Hotels & Resorts http://www.hosthotels.com/home.asp
Vice President and Area General Manager	Ed Mady The Ritz-Carlton, San Franscisco http://corporate.ritzcarlton.com
Director of Engineering	Paul Savarino The Ritz-Carlton, San Franscisco paul.savarino@ritzcarlton.com
Area Director of Human Resources	Milet D. Lukey The Ritz-Carlton, San Franscisco milet.lukey@ritzcarlton.com
Rooms Executive	Shaun O'Bryan shaun.obryan@ritzcarlton.com

Developer: Waverly Partners

High Performance Qualifications: The developer did not retrofit the hotel to be an environmentally sustainable property.

Manager: The Ritz-Carlton Hotel Company, L.L.C.; a subsidiary of Marriott International, Inc.

High Performance Qualifications: The management company's personnel are committed to expanding high performance knowledge and are interested in energy and water efficiency programs at the corporate level.

Managerial Structure

The Ritz-Carlton, San Francisco has approximately 513 employees. About half of the employees have been with the hotel for more than five years and 25% have been there more than ten years.

The hotel is managed by The Ritz-Carlton Hotel Company, L.L.C., a subsidiary of Marriott International. The management company espouses gold standards which include a high level of commitment to guest services that is articulated through its Credo.

Green Team

The Ritz-Carlton, San Francisco does not have a formalized Green Team but it convenes weekly meetings with representatives from several teams – including loss prevention, safety, recycling, and energy management. Discussions focus on injury, public safety, energy management, and recycling.

Staff at all levels, from line employees through managers, serve as members on each of the teams. Employees find these meetings both energizing and motivating. In addition, a voluntary group of managers and line staff meet monthly to discuss ways the hotel can achieve financial savings. The hotel also has initiated a daily lineup at the beginning of each shift to discuss repairs and/or high performance activities.

At the corporate level, The Ritz-Carlton Hotel Company has The Ritz-Carlton Environmental Action Conservation Team (REACT) program which addresses recycling and non-energy-related issues. This group is headed by the corporate Vice President of Engineering. The team conducts spending analyses and develops, across the hotel chain, opportunities for improving recycling in the dining and kitchen areas. Volunteers from many of the company's hotels participate in these meetings.

> *When you think of change, you must 1) create awareness, 2) roll out the new program, 3) get buy in, 4) implement and solicit feedback.*
>
> PAUL SAVARINO, *Director of Engineering*, The Ritz-Carlton, San Francisco

Staff Training and Compensation

The Ritz-Carlton, San Francisco has a strong training program that trains staff to understand customer preferences and ensure guest satisfaction. Each employee carries the company Credo card. Based on each employee's
job, staff members are trained in the hotel's recycling, composting, and energy management practices. The hotel
plans to create a "cheat sheet" to help employees answer guest questions about the hotel's greening efforts.

The hotel provides employees with incentives to bring forward innovative ideas through a "good ideas" program.
Employees submit ideas and receive a gift voucher if the idea succeeds through the first round of approvals.
The gift voucher increases if the idea succeeds through the second round of approvals. The hotel selects one
idea each month to receive the "good idea of the month" award, which translates into an additional monetary
award. Several ideas related to cost savings and sustainability have emerged from this program. According to
the management team, employees are always looking for opportunities to make improvements. Employees
suggest approximately 1,500 ideas annually at The Ritz-Carlton, San Francisco.

You either add revenue or save expenses with the Good Idea process.

Shaun O'Bryan, *Director of Rooms*, The Ritz-Carlton, San Francisco

Community Outreach and Education

The Ritz-Carlton Hotel Company promotes the "Community Footprints" program to encourage its hotels to give
back to the communities in which they operate. Through this program, each hotel sets targets for the hotel
generally and for each of its divisions. Department heads and team members set their individual goals to help
The Ritz-Carlton, San Francisco meet its Community Footprint targets. The hotel has been involved in a variety of
community projects, including volunteer work with local non-profits, product and in-kind donations, donating the
use of facilities, and sponsoring fundraising events. The company program focuses on these areas: community
partnership, employee involvement, product donations, signature fundraising, community career opportunities,
and environmental preservation.

The Ritz-Carlton, San Francisco serves on the advisory board of the San Francisco Unified School District
through the hospitality and tourism program. Students from these schools come to the hotel and shadow
the staff. This helps the students identify opportunities for future careers in the hospitality industry.

Currently, no educational material about the hotel's high performance efforts is found in the guest rooms.
However, the hotel is creating informational sheets for all employees so that they can more easily answer
guest questions about the hotel's greening efforts.

Construction and Operations

Table 1 highlights the high performance features of The Ritz-Carlton, San Francisco's construction and operations. The table reveals that the hotel favors operational efficiencies over construction opportunities. This is primarily due to the fact that the original structure was built in 1909. There are code restrictions attached to its historic landmark status, and it is situated in the heart of San Francisco where, as an urban adaptive reuse project, there are land constraints.

Table 1 HIGH PERFORMANCE CONSTRUCTION AND OPERATIONS HIGHLIGHTS	
1. Site	• The project is an example of urban infill development and historic site preservation. • Most parking is located underground. • One of the house vehicles is a luxury hybrid. • The property is accessible to public transportation.
2. Material and Resources, and Waste Management	• There is an extensive recycling program for guest rooms, common areas, and back-of-house operations. • The hotel minimizes the use of water bottles on site.
3. Energy	Features include: • On-site co-generation plant • Extensive energy management plan • Double-pane thermal glass • Energy recovery units capturing waste heat • Occupancy motion sensor technologies • Energy Star office equipment • Energy-efficient lighting programs utilizing compact fluorescent light (CFL) bulbs and light emitting diode (LED) night lights in guest rooms
4. Water	• Showerheads and faucets are equipped with low-flow hardware and aerators. • Washable linens and bedding do not require dry-cleaning.
5. Indoor Environmental Quality	• Adhesives, paints, and carpet systems have low volatile organic compound (VOC) emissions. • Operable windows and programmable thermostats permit individual thermal control in guest rooms. • The hotel has a smoke-free policy.

1. Site

The Ritz-Carlton, San Francisco is located in the heart of San Francisco with easy access to multiple public transportation lines. The hotel also has a hybrid sedan house car. The hotel's building originally was the West Coast headquarters for the Metropolitan Life Insurance Company, and served in that capacity until 1973 when it was sold to Cogswell College. The building then housed college classes until Waverly Partners bought it in 1984 and converted it into what it is today.

Construction

Waverly Partners took advantage of the building's urban location and transformed it into an adaptive reuse project. Adaptive reuse is the process of modifying old structures for new purposes. In this case, it meant renovating an old school and converting it into a hotel. Also in this case, the function would change but the architectural details would not. The project required the architectural team to preserve and retain the existing architectural details because the building was a unique historic landmark.

From an environmental standpoint, it is typically more efficient to redevelop older buildings closer to urban centers than it is to build new construction on distant green field sites. Not only does this conserve land, it also minimizes the effects of urban sprawl.

2. Materials and Resources, and Waste Management

Construction

The steel and concrete core and shell of the hotel's building date back to 1909. The interiors have been renovated several times (most recently in 1991) and cosmetic changes have been ongoing (the most recent in 2006).

Interior Design

The Ritz-Carlton, San Francisco installed recycled-tire flooring in the fitness center.

Operations

The hotel has developed an extensive recycling program that does not require any extra effort on the part of hotel guests. For typical rigid containers (plastic, metal, and glass), all of the waste is commingled, collected, and then sorted at the back of the house by housekeeping staff. If sorting is not obvious, off-site recycling collection facilities perform a more detailed separation. The hotel also has expanded the traditional definition of recyclables and now includes items such as furniture, linens and towels, and food waste in its recycling program.

The management team decided to pursue a substantial recycling program for several reasons. First, the City of San Francisco requires certain products, such as cooking oil, to be recycled. Second, in San Francisco the recycling infrastructure and market for recyclable materials is extremely advanced. And third, the hotel can reduce its landfill waste hauling by increasing the amount of on-site recyclables.

One of the challenges associated with the hotel's recycling program is the limited size of the loading dock. As a result, food waste and scraps are hauled away daily, as are the commingled recyclables. The hotel bales cardboard on site, using a baler that the City of San Francisco subsidizes. The cardboard bundles are removed every day.

Educating staff and guests about the commingling process has proven to be another challenge of the recycling program. Commingling requires all recyclables to be consolidated and then sorted off site, which is consistent with the municipal recycling process.

The Ritz-Carlton hotel must determine the best way to educate guests on the subject of recycling, and to let guests know that housekeeping staff will sort paper and bottles that are left behind. Newspapers also will be separated and placed in a different bag on the housekeeper's cart. All remaining recyclables will be sorted off site by Golden Gate Recycling, the disposal company hired by the hotel to haul recyclables.

Initially, it was just a simple matter of rolling it out, not a big deal at all.

Commingling makes it easier for both the guest and the employees because the recyclables are sorted off-site.

PAUL SAVARINO, *Director of Engineering*, The Ritz-Carlton, San Francisco

If The Ritz-Carlton, San Francisco does not reuse linens as rags, they donate old linens (in the 200–400 thread count range) to non-profit organizations such as Glide Memorial, to local animal shelters, or to the Society for the Prevention of Cruelty to Animals (SPCA) International. Old towels are cut, re-seamed, and transformed into rags by one of the two on-site seamstresses. The hotel sent discarded case goods resulting from the June 2006 renovation to a furniture liquidator who resold them on a secondary market. Another liquidator took the discarded carpet to be resold to smaller hotels. The hotel additionally recycles compact fluorescent light bulbs and used batteries.

In its back-of-house operations, The Ritz-Carlton, San Francisco recycles paper along with glass and water bottles. To minimize the use of water bottles on the property, the hotel provides employees with reusable glasses and a water station. The hotel also collects food scraps and waste for composting, and there are signs posted throughout the kitchen indicating that it is illegal to put grease down the drain. The hotel has found a company that processes the grease and reuses it for producing cosmetics and biodiesel fuel, among other uses.

A Bulgari bathroom amenities distributor ships guest bathroom amenities from New Jersey to The Ritz-Carlton, San Francisco. If shampoos and lotions are only partially used, and more than three-fourths of the bottle is full, housekeeping staff leave it for the guest to continue to use.

A discussion of this hotel's materials and resources must include mention of one additional operational feature. At The Ritz-Carlton, San Francisco, the dining room chef personally goes to the local markets every morning for the freshest ingredients, and the banquet staff tries to integrate organic produce into the menu.

3. Energy

Operations

As mentioned, the corporate Ritz-Carlton Environmental Action Conservation program conducts spending analyses and develops opportunities for new sustainable initiatives. Although the program originally focused on developing a corporate-wide strategy for reducing energy demand, it now also addresses recycling and non-energy-related issues. The Vice President of Engineering leads the program. Ideally, each hotel would have a different REACT and would own that hotel's sustainable initiatives, such as recycling and energy conservation. The program's ever-expanding scope notwithstanding, the corporate REACT program continues to set the pace for all other hotels in the chain.

Corporate Ritz-Carlton management also employs a third party, Servidyne Systems, for energy-audit assistance. One dedicated energy manager oversees all Ritz-Carlton properties to develop tools and perform a complete analysis of energy-saving opportunities throughout the portfolio. Management publishes an energy report each month to benchmark all Ritz-Carlton hotels. The Ritz-Carlton corporate goal is to reduce energy consumption by 3% each year for three consecutive years.

Following the corporate lead, The Ritz-Carlton, San Francisco has made significant investments in the area of energy conservation and the hotel's projects have been shared with and replicated by the rest of The Ritz-Carlton portfolio. These efforts generally reduce operating expenses, definitely align with the hotel's conservation efforts, and rarely impact the guest experience. In 2007, the hotel ownership approved more than $500,000 for phases one and two of a three-phase program. These phases ultimately include converting lighting to compact fluorescent light bulbs, installing occupancy sensors and programmable thermostats, and procuring variable frequency drives for the air handlers. In January 2006, the property also installed co-generation equipment on site. This was the PureComfort® combined cooling, heating, and power solution. At the time, this was the latest energy-efficient technology from UTC Power.

The effect of using an on-site co-generator is equivalent to eliminating the daily emissions of 250 motor vehicles, saving enough electricity to light 240 homes every day, or creating the same environmental advantages of planting 150 acres of forests. The direct advantage to the hotel is that The Ritz-Carlton achieves free cooling for the kitchen – an area that requires 12 to 15 hours of cooling every day. Other areas that require cooling throughout the year are the hotel's restaurants and meeting facilities. Waste heat from four gas-fired micro turbines flows into the absorption chiller where it is captured and cooled. The cooled water then passes through the hotel, cooling the areas where it is needed. Even though the turbines in the co-generator require energy to generate energy, the hotel still benefits from an overall reduction in energy consumption – 10% less than the energy consumed by the hotel's traditional cooling process.

Another energy-efficient project implemented at The Ritz-Carlton, San Francisco involved rebuilding the cooling towers and installing energy-efficient motors with variable frequency drives. The cooling tower dissipates heat from the hotel and the variable frequency drives on the main chiller adjust the motor frequency of the Carrier unit, depending on the time of day and the demand. The co-generator also enables the unit to hold a lower motor frequency. The unit's motors can decrease frequency from 60 Hz (hertz) to 42 Hz, thus requiring 100 amps (amperes) rather than 200 amps to run. This has resulted in a 50% reduction of consumed power.

In the guest rooms, the hotel installed LED nightlights and compact fluorescent bulbs (CFLs) in bathroom light fixtures and in table lamps. As a result, the team was able to reduce three 40-watt bulbs to one 20-watt compact fluorescent bulb. Ritz-Carlton corporate standards do not include CFLs, so The Ritz-Carlton, San Francisco converted T12 bulbs to T8 bulbs and 40-watt incandescent bulbs to 20-watt halogen bulbs. These typically are more expensive, but they last significantly longer. The utility company, Pacific Gas and Electric (PG&E), also offered rebates for the lighting conversion.

The Ritz-Carlton, San Francisco hotel also is a member of the San Francisco Load Curtailment Coalition (SFLCC), which includes twelve additional San Francisco hotels as members. In this program, the city calls on one of the hotel members each time the city needs to reduce energy loads, because of peak demand, extreme weather conditions, and/or other circumstances. In addition, each member of the SFLCC commits to curtailing a predefined amount of kilowatts of energy per day; The Ritz-Carlton, San Francisco has committed to curtailing 100 kilowatts of energy per day. For the hotel, some days are easier than others for honoring that commitment, depending on the events taking place on site.

Phase three of the energy conservation rollout plan includes occupancy sensors to detect motion in the guest rooms, as well as increased temperature control automation that allows staff to remotely set the guest room thermostats. At the present time, staff can remotely control temperature settings only in meeting rooms and common areas. These are the same locations that already have motion sensors. Window film that reduces heat and ultra violet (UV) transmission also is currently under review for phase three. This product prevents fading and discoloration (of fabric and furniture) and reduces the HVAC demand.

4. Water

Operations

In compliance with San Francisco code requirements, The Ritz-Carlton team installed low-flow hardware on showerheads (Kohler Rain with Restrictor) and aerators on faucets to reduce the amount of water consumed. The city provided the equipment and hardware for the faucets at no cost, and housekeeping staff have been trained not to run the water while cleaning the guest rooms.

The bedding, duvets, bedspreads, and linens were selected specifically for their low-maintenance laundering requirements. Everything can be cleaned on site so there is no need for dry-cleaning. This reduces the amount of chemicals entering the water supply. The management team currently is reviewing a water-reclamation project for the laundry facility – a project that will reclaim 90% of the used laundry water and will produce considerable savings in both water and sewage expenditures.

Owing to its urban location, The Ritz-Carlton, San Francisco has minimal landscaping. However, there is an elaborate courtyard fitted with a drip irrigation system, and both the fountain centerpiece in the courtyard and the swimming pool recycle water.

5. Indoor Environmental Quality

Operations

The hotel accomplishes a healthier indoor environment through a variety of actions. These include making The Ritz-Carlton, San Francisco a 100% smoke-free environment, using low volatile organic compounds (VOCs) in paints and adhesives for carpeting and wall-coverings, and providing guests with individual indoor environmental quality control (operable windows and programmable thermostats).

Business Case

> *The driving force is saving money, the environmental benefit is icing on the cake.*
>
> PAUL SAVARINO, *Director of Engineering*, The Ritz-Carlton, San Francisco

Market Positioning and Consumer Response

The Ritz-Carlton, San Francisco is the city's only Mobil Five Star and AAA Five Diamond hotel. The Ritz-Carlton Hotel Company focuses on exceeding customer expectations for service and quality, and is the only company to have won the Malcolm Baldrige National Quality Award twice. The Malcolm Baldrige Award is a federal government sponsored program that promotes quality improvement and customer satisfaction. Manufacturing companies usually win this award, since the human element that is integral to the hospitality industry makes consistency extremely difficult to achieve.

In order to exceed guest expectations consistently, the hotel uses the company's Guest Profile System (Mystique) to track guest preferences. The system tracks detailed information such as allergies, preferences for linen reuse, and for guest room cleaning products. This philosophy of personalized care helps to accommodate the environmentally sustainable preferences of guests. The hotel does not leverage high performance activities as a marketing tool, but it does make customers cognizant of what is being done.

Using surveys and focus groups, the hotel conducts studies in an attempt to understand guest demand for and response to high performance programs. Historically, feedback about a linen reuse program was not positive. At this stage, the hotel has decided not to pursue a linen reuse program that enables guests to choose when to have their linens and towels washed and replaced. While guests of The Ritz-Carlton, San Francisco are beginning to ask about the hotel's sustainability efforts, it appears that they are not yet willing to sacrifice any of the luxury services. In addition, in an effort to understand the importance of a hotel's environmentally sustainable efforts, some companies in the hospitality industry have begun to ask open-ended questions in their Request for Proposals (RFPs). The Ritz-Carlton, San Francisco hopes that the feedback from these surveys and inquiries will become an active element in the hotel's decision making.

The Ritz-Carlton, San Francisco is trying to balance high performance principles and guest satisfaction. The hotel has selected a Lexus hybrid to serve as a house car. This allows the hotel to transport guests in a luxury vehicle that is also eco-friendly. The hotel also hopes to address guest demand for environmental sustainability with projects (e.g., water reclamation) that reduce the hotel's environmental footprint without sacrificing the guest experience.

> *Even guests are inquiring about the "greenness." To them, it is important to know about what the hotel is doing so they continue to feel good about staying here.*
>
> PAUL SAVARINO, *Director of Engineering*, The Ritz-Carlton, San Francisco

Why High Performance Construction?

The hotel's building, originally built as the Metropolitan Life Insurance Company's West Coast headquarters, is a significant historic landmark. The property was converted to a hotel in 1991. The developers did not consider high performance construction elements in the construction and conversion phase.

Why High Performance Operations?

The hotel's environmentally sustainable operations primarily focus on back-of-house opportunities that minimize the impact on a guest's experience. For example, the hotel's energy conservation and waste reduction program is very strong. The hotel has also installed a UTC co-generation plant which generates electricity by using natural gas. Pacific Gas and Electric (PG&E) provided a rebate for this installation. The co-generation plant has helped the hotel to reduce key operating expenses in two ways: (1) by using the excess heat generated by the co-generation plant to cool the hotel, the system has reduced the hotel's electricity bill by 25%; and (2) at the current cost of natural gas, the electricity generated on site is 10% less expensive than electricity bought from PG&E. This unique project has also generated media interest for The Ritz-Carlton, San Francisco.

The Ritz-Carlton leveraged utility rebates to install energy-efficient chiller motors and to convert to CFL lighting. PG&E provided a 30% rebate to offset the initial cost of the high-efficiency motor used for the hotel's chiller and cooling towers. This motor is 50% more efficient than the original motor and it has helped the hotel further reduce energy costs. The hotel also leveraged PG&E rebates to convert all the guest rooms from incandescent to CFL lighting. This conversion cost $40,000, and PG&E paid $4,500 (approximately 11%) of the total cost. These rebates have helped to reduce the payback period for energy efficiency investments and to gain approval from the hotel's owners.

In the City of San Francisco, a consortium of local businesses (the San Francisco Load Curtailment Coalition) assists the city in its management of energy demand during peak periods. As a member of this consortium, The Ritz-Carlton, San Francisco received an incentive of $4,500 in 2007 as the hotel met its energy-reduction obligation. The hotel will receive additional incentives each year it meets its obligation to reduce energy usage. Reductions in energy consumption are much easier to achieve when the hotel is not fully occupied or is not hosting large conferences.

The hotel tries to save on waste collection fees through a strictly enforced recycling and composting program. The hotel pays approximately $1,800 per haul by a 25-yard waste compactor. Before implementing the recycling and composting program, the hotel required two or three garbage hauls each week. Now the hotel has only one haul each week and pays significantly lower fees for composting and recycling collection. Table 2 highlights the disposal costs for various materials.

Table 2 DISPOSAL COSTS		
Material	**Cost/Haul**	**Savings**
Garbage	$1,800	None
Recyclables	$ 900	50% savings over cost of garbage collection
Green Waste (compostable)	$ 450	25% savings over cost of garbage collection

The City of San Francisco tries to encourage water conservation in addition to reduced energy consumption. The city has provided low-flow faucets and aerators, free of charge, to The Ritz-Carlton. By installing the low-flow hardware, the hotel saves on the costs of both water and sewage, because the fees for water and sewage are linked. However, the financial advantages of this project have not been quantified.

Advantages of High Performance Construction and Operations

The Ritz-Carlton, San Francisco has focused on high performance operations primarily to reduce operational expenses. The hotel has leveraged utility rebates wherever possible to improve payback. The City of San Francisco's encouragement of sustainability efforts produces additional rebates for energy and water conservation, and strengthens the business case for environmentally sustainable operational improvements. The Ritz-Carlton, San Francisco has not identified opportunities for generating additional revenue through high performance efforts, but the hotel has begun to field guest questions about this topic. It is too soon, however, to know whether guests are willing purchase hotel rooms based on the hotel's high performance practices.

Table 3 is a summary of high performance hotel construction and operation advantages realized by the property oversight stakeholders – developer, owner, and management company.

Table 3 STAKEHOLDER ADVANTAGES SUMMARY		
Developer	Owner	Management Company
The building is a historic site and was converted in 1991 to function as a hotel. High performance features were not considered during the design phase of the hotel.	Supportive investing in energy-efficiency features (e.g., the co-generation plant), leveraging utility rebates for high-efficiency motors, and the purchase of CFL bulbs have reduced operational expenses and improved profit margins.	Supportive investing in energy-efficiency features (e.g., the co-generation plant), leveraging utility rebates for high-efficiency motors, and the purchase of CFL bulbs have reduced operational expenses and improved profit margins.
		The hotel executive team has shared what they have learned with the corporate brand group. There is now an opportunity to leverage best practices across The Ritz-Carlton brand and achieve operational expense savings.
		The "good ideas" program and green team meetings energize staff and have the potential to further boost morale and reduce turnover.

Best Practices and Conclusions

As mentioned above in the Case Overview, the case study of The Ritz-Carlton, San Francisco is a premier example of how a luxury operation can exceed guest expectations while balancing the demands of high performance environmentally sustainable operations and preserving an important historic landmark.

The following programs implemented at The Ritz-Carlton, San Francisco hotel have been identified as industry best practices for creating environmentally high performance hospitality operations:

• Energy Conservation Programs (e.g., the on-site co-generation plant)
• Extensive Recycling
• Minimal Guest Impact
• Green Team Morning Updates and Sharing Best Practices with Brand Management
• Business Priority Matrix and Senior Management Leadership
• Historic Landmark Preservation

> *With the proper incentive programs, employees can become partners in developing a hotel's sustainability initiatives.*
>
> MILET D. LUKEY, *Area Director of Human Resources*, The Ritz-Carlton, San Francisco

The Ritz-Carlton, San Francisco has implemented several energy and water conservation programs, and the hotel has been extremely innovative in its approach. However, one of the hotel's most useful practices to date has been the daily review of improvements at morning update meetings. These meetings sustain staff enthusiasm and are helpful for tracking potential problems. These regular meetings also communicate senior management's commitment. At the same time, problems do not linger and are addressed immediately.

> *Leverage consumer databases to gauge sustainability preferences and develop relevant programs that interface with customers.*
>
> MILET D. LUKEY, *Area Director of Human Resources*, The Ritz-Carlton, San Francisco

As a luxury hotel, The Ritz-Carlton, San Francisco strives to create memorable customer experiences. Many of the hotel's environmentally sustainable initiatives are implemented in back-of-house operations. Staff members are becoming aware of guest inquiries about the hotel's environmentally sustainable practices. However, these are the same guests who do not want to be "adversely" affected by environmentally sustainable practices. This has prompted the management team to track customer preferences in a guest database. Over time, the hotel will have accumulated enough data to identify trends. The team then can respond with the implementation of programs that meet guest expectations.

WALKING TOUR
The Ritz-Carlton, San Francisco

Building Entrance

- After disembarking from your BART subway, bus, trolley, taxi cab, or bicycle, look around and notice where you are. The center of San Francisco! Although this creates many limitations on land use, it also prohibits superfluous landscaping. For the foliage they do have, there is a corresponding drip irrigation system that can be manually or automatically controlled. A similar water system is located in the hotel's courtyard, which should be another destination on your tour. If you smoke, this is the only place on the property where you can have a cigarette.

- Finally, enter the lobby of The Ritz-Carlton, San Francisco hotel. Try to locate an employee and ask him or her about green operations. Most are knowledgeable about the latest conservation projects.

- Look around again and try to find recycling bins. Can you? Probably not. The hotel has hired Golden Gate Recycling to haul and sort all of the recyclables. That means that plastic, glass, metal, and paper are all commingled at the hotel and sorted at an off-site facility.

Dining Room

- Check out the daily menu and notice the local, fresh ingredients that are incorporated in the meals.

Meeting Rooms

- All lights in the back of the house are equipped with T8 bulbs and all meeting rooms are equipped with 25-watt halogen bulbs, as well as with motion detectors to minimize lighting vacant rooms.

- Also, you will find that most events are catered with water presented in pitchers and glasses. This minimizes the waste generated from disposable plastic bottles.

Guest Rooms

- You have control over the temperature in your room. Is it just right outside? If so, open your window and reduce the thermostat temperature setting.

- When returning to your room, enter the bathroom and notice that the amenities may not be completely full. If you left the room and the shampoo bottle was more than three-fourths full, then the housekeeping staff left it in the room for your continued use. And don't fret if you left a bottle that was less than three-fourths full. The housekeeping staff probably brought it to the staff locker room for employee use.

- Did you notice the nightlight in the bathroom? It uses an LED bulb which is even more efficient than the compact fluorescent bulbs that are in your guest room.

- Check out the fabric of the bedspread. The hotel can wash all the linens and bedspreads with a regular laundry process. Dry-cleaning is not necessary.

- Do not forget to fill out the guest comment card and applaud The Ritz-Carlton, San Francisco for the sustainable efforts. Be sure to jot down some improvement ideas of your own!

APPENDIX A
Advantages of High Performance Hotel Design, Construction, and Operations

A myriad of advantages exist for hotel industry stakeholders if hotels are designed, constructed, and operated sustainably. Opportunities still exist if one is implemented without the other, but the advantages are maximized if design/construction and operations work in tandem. For example, if a hotel's management performs a lighting retrofit by replacing all the incandescent bulbs with compact fluorescents, the facility will realize a considerable cost savings. However, if that same hotel management performs the retrofit after the developer has constructed the building with a tight envelope, efficient heating and cooling, occupancy sensors, and maximized daylighting, the overall savings will be compounded. Please see Table A-1 for a summary of the prevailing financial, environmental, and social advantages of high performance hotel design, construction, and operation.

A hotel realizes more value when environmental considerations are integrated into the design and construction process as early as possible. With integrated design, buildings perform better during their initial operation, and this performance continues over the life of the facility. This is the result of utilizing a "whole building" design approach. However, for integrated design to occur, it is critical to include input from hotel managers and owners during the design process. In addition, all property oversight stakeholders (developers, owners, and managers) must continue to communicate throughout the life of the project.

As of January 2008, there is broad consensus on the environmental and social benefits of high performance buildings. Additionally, a consensus also is emerging on the financial benefits of green buildings. Published studies emphasize that the capital costs for these buildings range from significantly less to slightly more than those of comparable buildings, with green buildings carrying an average premium of 2%.[1]

According to Davis Langdon, a green building scholar, many projects now are achieving LEED certification within budget and within the same cost range as non-LEED projects. Even though construction costs have increased sharply, projects continue to pursue LEED certification.[2]

High performance practices generally make economic sense if their evaluated costs are based on life-cycle cost analysis. This requires a long-term mindset, and it is not the most common method of cost analysis in the industry. Most hospitality decision makers still favor a short-term analysis that looks only at payback or initial cost.

The misconception that high performance buildings cost significantly more than traditional buildings is a result of the learning curve with regard to sustainable design and technologies, and to an imprecise definition of high performance buildings that regards green features as add-ons to the construction budget instead of considering them as essential components of the project.

Overall, it makes financial business sense to build and manage hotels with environmental considerations in mind. This fact is consistently evident in the hotel case studies presented in this report. What varies are the means by which developers, owners, and management companies achieve cost-effective projects, and the advantages they choose to target.

Financial Advantage #1

Properties can reduce the capital costs of hotel construction and equipment by reducing the size of required heating and cooling systems and stormwater capacity, and by reusing infrastructure and materials.

- Reducing the required size of a building's heating and cooling systems can be achieved with an energy-efficient building envelope.

- Employing natural stormwater retention and/or filtration can reduce the need for more expensive tanks and systems.

[1] Kats, Greg. 2003. *The Cost and Financial Benefits of Green Building: A Report to California's Sustainable Building Task Force.*
[2] Langdon, Davis. 2007. *Cost of Green Revisited: Reexamining the Feasibility and Cost Impact of Sustainable Design in the Light of Increased Market Adoption.* White Paper. July.

Table A-1 Financial, Environmental, and Social High Performance Hotel Advantages

	HIGH PERFORMANCE ADVANTAGES
Financial	• Reduced capital costs of hotel construction and equipment by reducing the size of heating and cooling system needed, stormwater capacity needed, and by reusing infrastructure and materials. • Reduced operating costs of hotel buildings and landscapes through energy and water efficiency measures, lower maintenance requirements, less waste produced, and having a "systems thinking" approach. • Market differentiation can create a competitive advantage that saves marketing dollars through free press, and increases guest occupancy rates. • Reduced liabilities and risks can be realized by building a healthier building that is ahead of regulation. • Improved health and higher productivity of workers can result from a more pleasant work environment, which leads to lower employee costs. • Municipal-based financial incentives such as fast-track permits, increased FAR, or tax incentives for sustainable construction and/or operations can be obtained. • In some markets, buyers will pay a premium to own or invest in a hotel that is built and/or constructed sustainably.
Environmental	• Lower energy and resource use, and fewer vehicle miles traveled, reduce overall CO_2 and greenhouse gas emissions. • Redevelopment of existing land (infill development) reduces the demand on greenfields and takes advantage of current transportation and stormwater infrastructures. • Sustainable construction methods can reduce the amount of material in landfills and minimize site disturbance. • The demand on natural resources can be reduced by selecting materials and products that have recycled content, are recyclable, and/or are rapidly renewable. • Natural stormwater filtration techniques improve stormwater quality and the flow of natural hydrology systems.
Social	• Sustainable hotel design, construction and operations can benefit the community through economic revitalization and by retaining business locally. • Sustainable hotel design, construction, and operations can benefit staff and guests through improved comfort, health, and productivity.

• Adapting an existing building or reusing building materials for a project can reduce up-front costs by minimizing the amount of new construction materials and reducing the amount of waste sent to the landfill.

• By creating an integrated planning and design team, and by utilizing whole systems thinking, overall capital construction costs can be reduced.

• Minimizing impervious surfaces reduces the required amount of stormwater infrastructure and the use of traditional paving materials.

• Recycling construction waste can minimize expenses because most landfill fees are higher than recycling charges, and leftover construction materials can be reused or resold.

Financial Advantage #2

Hotels can reduce the operating costs of buildings and landscapes through energy and water efficiency measures, lower maintenance requirements, less waste, and a "systems thinking" approach.

• Energy efficiency

- Any actions taken to make the hotel building envelope tighter will result in energy savings. This includes installing a reflective or vegetative roof, well-insulated walls, and low-emittance windows.

- Using occupancy sensors and installing compact fluorescent light bulbs all improve energy efficiency.

- Utilizing energy recovery units and carbon dioxide (CO_2) sensors creates energy savings by reducing demand on the heating and cooling systems.

- Installing energy-efficient equipment, such as heating and cooling systems, Energy Star equipment, and LED (light emitting diode) exit signs reduces energy consumption.

- Energy-efficient lighting can save 20–75 percent in lighting energy use, potentially saving the industry $133 to $777 million.

• Water efficiency

- Planting native, drought tolerant landscaping minimizes irrigation and potable water consumption.

- High efficiency water fixtures can cut water consumption levels. These fixtures include sink aerators, low-flow showerheads and toilets, dual-flush toilets, and waterless urinals.

- Recirculated water from showers, sinks, and fountains can be used for landscaping irrigation or for flushing toilets.

- Water-efficient fixtures can reduce water and sewer bills by 25–30 %.

• Lower maintenance requirements

- More efficient systems last longer and require less maintenance.

- Commissioning building systems, which is the process of ensuring that a building's systems are designed, installed, and tested to perform according to the design intent and operational needs, assures a more accurate and relevant performance.

- Some flooring material (e.g., wool carpeting) made from highly renewable resources is durable, long lasting, and requires minimal maintenance beyond cleaning.

- Natural ventilation, heating, and/or cooling cause less wear on building heating, cooling, and ventilation systems, which results in lower energy demand and equipment maintenance.

- Reduced operating waste can save money if the cost of recycling or composting is less than landfill waste fees.

- By creating an integrated planning and design team, and by utilizing "whole systems" thinking, operating costs can be reduced.

Financial Advantage #3

Market differentiation can create a competitive advantage that saves marketing dollars through free publicity and increases guest occupancy rates.

• Free publicity

- According to the Rocky Mountain Institute, The Inn of Anasazi in New Mexico received free and unsolicited coverage from major publications such as *Food & Wine*, *Traveler*, and *Travel + Leisure* magazines. This led to a 20% increase in business from guests and travel agencies (based on the Inn's projections).

• Product differentiation

- According to Cornell University, 58% of travelers indicate they would be willing to pay more for an allergen-free guest room.[3]

3 *Building Design + Construction*. 2006. "Green Buildings and the Bottom Line." White Paper. Pages 24–25. November.

Financial Advantage #4

Properties can reduce liabilities and risks by building healthier buildings that are ahead of regulation.

- Better ventilation and the use of non-toxic substances result in improved indoor air quality. This allows the hotel to mitigate liability and the risk of litigation from sick building syndrome. According to the Environmental Protection Agency (EPA), sick buildings are one of the top five environmental threats to human health.[4]

- Lower-risk buildings decrease insurance costs. Fireman's Fund Insurance, for example, now offers lower rates for LEED-certified buildings.[5]

- Sustainable hotel design, construction, and operations can help a hotel stay ahead of potential future resource or systems regulations. This is less costly than post-enactment compliance.

- Resource efficiency will be more important in the future when resources become even more scarce and costly.

Financial Advantage #5

A more pleasant and healthier work environment can result in the improved health and higher productivity of workers, and lead to lower employee costs.

- Workers are more comfortable in environmentally friendly surroundings, such as those produced by improved indoor ventilation, individualized temperature control, increased use of daylighting, a commitment to the use of low (or no) volatile organic compounds (VOCs), and green cleaning supplies. Studies indicate that employees are more productive and have higher morale in these environments.

- Staff who have healthier indoor environments experience less sick time.

Financial Advantage #6

Financial incentives for implementing high performance practices are available through government and local utility programs.[6]

- Municipalities promote green-building and renewable-energy practices with a variety of incentive programs. These include: fast-track site plan permits; grants for LEED certified projects or for projects built to LEED standards; low-interest loans; tax credits and fee reductions for different LEED certification levels; recognition programs; free training; and density bonuses.

- Under the Energy Policy Act of 2005, commercial building owners and developers can obtain tax "breaks" for energy conservation measures.

Financial Advantage #7

In some markets, buyers will pay a premium to own or invest in a hotel that is built and/or constructed sustainably, a phenomenon that is seen across other property types.

---

[4] U.S. EPA Indoor Air Quality website. Accessed November 2007. http://www.epa.gov/iaq/pubs/sbs.html
[5] Fireman's Fund Press Release. 2006.   *Fireman's Fund First to Introduce Green Building Coverage.* http://www.firemansfund.com/
[6] *Online Sources*
   1. Federal and State Incentives for Renewable Resources and Building Efficiency
   Visit DSIRE for a current list.
   Go to http://www.dsireusa.org/
   Click on your chosen state or on the federal incentives icon.
   2. Government LEED Incentives
   For a current list, use the following website commands:
   Go to http://www.usgbc.org/DisplayPage.aspx?CMSPageID=1780
   See LEED Initiatives in Governments and Schools.
   3. Tax Deductions for Commercial Buildings (from the Energy Policy Act of 2005)
   For information on tax deductions from Energy Star:
   Go to ENERGY STAR Brochure for Commercial Tax Deductions
   http://www.energystar.gov/index.cfm?c=products.pr_tax_credits
   4. Information on tax deductions from the United States Green Building Council:
   For current information, use the following website commands:
   Go to http://www.usgbc.org/DisplayPage.aspx?CMSPageID=1780
   See Energy Policy Act of 2005 analysis.

Environmental Advantage #1

Lower energy and resource use, and fewer vehicle miles traveled, reduce overall CO_2 and greenhouse gas emissions as a result of access to public transportation and locally sourced materials.

Environmental Advantage #2

Redevelopment of existing land (infill development) reduces the demand on greenfields and takes advantage of current transportation and stormwater infrastructures.

Environmental Advantage #3

Sustainable construction methods can reduce the amount of material in landfills and minimize site disturbance.

Environmental Advantage #4

The demand on natural resources can be reduced by selecting materials and products that have recycled content, are recyclable, and/or are rapidly renewable.

Environmental Advantage #5

Natural stormwater filtration techniques improve water quality and the flow of natural hydrology systems.

Social Advantage #1

Sustainable hotel design, construction, and operations can benefit the community through economic revitalization and by retaining local business.

- Hotel infill development prevents resources from leaving communities and economically revitalizes the area.

- Utilizing locally manufactured and extracted materials minimizes vehicle emissions, reduces transportation energy consumption and dependence on foreign oil, and retains financial profits within the community.

Social Advantage #2

Sustainable hotel design, construction, and operations can benefit staff and guests through improved comfort, health, and productivity.

- Improved indoor ventilation and individual temperature control, increased use of daylighting, and a commitment to the use of low (or no) volatile organic compounds and green cleaning supplies can result in the improved health, productivity, and morale of workers, as well as an enhanced guest experience.

Social Advantage #3

Sustainable hotel design, construction, and operations increases environmental awareness and encourages stakeholders to change their lifestyles.

- Hotel press releases, interior signage, and guided tours educate hotel guests, staff, and other stakeholders. The knowledge these individuals gain about a hotel's environmentally friendly practices can be applied to their personal, "at-home" lifestyles.

- Hotel developers, architects, contractors, management companies, owners, and other partners can share innovative practices with other portfolio facilities for implementation in future development and operations.

This report specifically emphasizes the financial advantages of high performance hotel design, construction, and operation. Our intent is to focus on the very real business opportunities that exist, without diminishing the importance of the environmental and social benefits that are realized as well.

APPENDIX B
Metrics and Key Performance Indicators

Measuring the performance of a hotel's operations is one of the key best practices identified by the case study hotels, especially those that have green teams. Measuring performance means that the hotel establishes a baseline measurement to determine how well or how poorly it is performing on a daily, weekly, monthly, and/or annual basis. The hotel determines progress by comparing its own performance to the baseline measurements, by benchmarking against other hotels in its portfolio, and/or benchmarking against an appropriate "comp set" – a comparative set of competitor hotels typically compiled by a third party. In addition to determining a baseline measurement, a hotel also may set targets and goals to motivate the management and operations team.

This section offers suggestions for implementing a robust measurement process and summarizes the metrics and key performance indicators that are relevant to measuring a hotel's progress toward environmentally sustainable operations.

Measurement Practices

1. Use the audit/criteria checklist from one of the hotel certification programs, even if there is no intent to apply for certification.

2. Hire a third-party consultant to assist with implementing an environmental operations reporting process.

3. Leverage third-party business partners to create usage reports (e.g., request summary reports from the waste hauler). Prepare a sample report to show the business partner what kind of information is being sought.

4. Leverage third-party business partners to perform annual energy audits.

5. Participate in a third-party survey, such as Smith Travel Research or Gallup, to benchmark against a hotel comp set.

6. Benchmark results with other hotels in the portfolio.

7. Regularly conduct room checks (once a month) specifically to evaluate environmentally sustainable attributes. Check whether or not the lights and the HVAC are turned off, all bulbs are compact fluorescent, and the environmental brochure is still in the room. One common approach is to check two rooms per floor, each at a different end of the floor.

8. Check utility meters daily for leaks and/or other problems. This includes gas, electric, water, and sewage.

9. Regularly (once a month) review and summarize utility bills – for energy, water, sewage, gas, and waste. Discuss energy consumption trends at staff meetings.

10. Implement an energy management system that is tied to the building systems and automatically generates monthly usage reports.

11. Implement an environmental management system to track all resource consumption, including water and energy resources.

12. Create a balanced scorecard by establishing baseline measurements and goals. Regularly monitor progress and adjust goals as needed. Incorporate relevant environmental feedback from guest satisfaction surveys.

APPENDIX C
Certification Programs for High Performance Hotels

Table C-1 Similarities and Differences of High Performance Hotel Third-Party Certifications

Similarities	Differences
• Voluntary enrollment by businesses	• First and third-party-certification
• Well-defined standards and criteria	• Process versus performance-based systems
• Assessment and auditing	• Multiple level versus pass/fail awards
• Recognition and use of a logo	
• Periodic follow-up audits to renew certification	
• Continual improvement	
• Transparency	
• Participatory mechanisms to define standards	

There are many different types of hotel certification programs. This section explains their similarities, differences, and benefits, as well as how to obtain additional information.

According to the Center for Ecotourism and Sustainable Development, in their report about certification programs, almost all such programs have similar components as well as differences.[1]

For a summary, please see Table C-1.

First-party certification occurs when a hotel self-reports measurements. Third-party certification requires an external entity to report the hotel's measurements.

Process-based systems are similar to ISO (International Standards Organization) standards in that they certify a hotel's established and documented processes. Performance-based systems certify results that comply with predetermined criteria.

Multiple-level certification programs are similar to a school grading system and allow hotels to participate even if they are not at the top of their class. Pass/fail certification programs only certify hotels that have achieved a specified grade.

Table C-2, on the following page, describes several well-known third-party certification programs in more detail.

[1] Center for Ecotourism and Sustainable Development. 3rd Edition. *A Simple User's Guide to Certification for Sustainable Tourism and Ecotourism.* Page 12.

Table C-2 Hotel Certifications and Rating Programs

Hotel Certification Programs

"Green" Hotels Association®

What is the initiative?
The purpose of the "Green" Hotels Association's is to bring together hotels that are interested in environmental issues. From adding "drinking water served on request only" to the menu, to installing new HVAC systems, and with every measure in between, the "Green" Hotels Association encourages, promotes, and supports the "greening" of the lodging industry.

What does it offer?
Hotel managers, chief engineers, and executive housekeepers do not have the time to search out all the water- and energy-saving ideas that apply to the hospitality industry. The "Green" Hotels Association has devoted itself to that purpose. On joining, members receive a comprehensive list of suggestions and ideas on how to reduce the hotel's impact on our environment.

How to find out more...
http://www.greenhotels.com

Green Seal – Environmental Standard for Lodging Properties

What is the initiative?
Green Seal is an independent, nonprofit organization dedicated to protecting the environment by promoting the manufacture and sale of environmentally responsible consumer products. Green Seal sets environmental standards and awards a "Green Seal of Approval" to products that cause less harm to the environment than other similar products.

What does it offer?
Green Seal has partnered with the lodging industry, the nation's second-largest employer, to support the notion of ecotourism. Green Seal's campaign to educate hotels and motels focuses on how environmental efforts improve the bottom line and benefit the environment. Green Seal also has initiated a certification program for lodging facilities that meet leadership standards in green management planning and practices.

How to find out more...
http://www.greenseal.org

Energy Star Program

What is the initiative?
Energy Star is a voluntary partnership between the United States Department of Energy, the EPA, product manufacturers, local utilities, and retailers. Partners help to promote efficient products by labeling them with the Energy Star logo and by educating consumers about the benefits of energy efficiency.

What does it offer?
The program includes initiatives for Energy Star Small Business, Energy Star Buildings and Greenlights, Methane Outreach, and Energy Star Labeling of Buildings.

How to find out more...
http://www.epa.gov/energystar

Adapted from http://www.epa.gov/oppt/greenmeetings/pubs/current_init.htm

Table C-2 Hotel Certifications and Rating Programs (continued)

WasteWise

What is the initiative?

WasteWise is a free, voluntary, EPA Office of Pollution Prevention program through which organizations eliminate costly municipal solid waste, benefiting their bottom line and the environment. WasteWise is a flexible program that allows partners to design their own solid waste reduction programs tailored to their needs.

What does it offer?

As a WasteWise partner, your organization can save thousands or millions of dollars by reducing, reusing, and recycling solid waste materials.

How to find out more...

http://www.epa.gov/wastewise

United States Green Building Council – LEED Certification

What is the initiative?

The Leadership in Energy and Environmental Design (LEED) Green Building Rating System™ is the nationally accepted benchmark for the design, construction, and operation of high performance green buildings. LEED gives building owners and operators the tools they need to have an immediate and measurable impact on building performance. LEED promotes a "whole building" approach to sustainability by recognizing performance in five key areas of human and environmental health: sustainable site development; water savings; energy efficiency; materials selection; and indoor environmental quality.

LEED provides a road map for measuring and documenting success for every building type and lifecycle phase.

How to find out more...

http://www.usgbc.org

Audubon Cooperative Sanctuary Program for Golf Courses

What is the initiative?

Audubon International awards certification to recognize golf courses that protect the environment, conserve natural resources, and provide wildlife habitats. Achieving certification demonstrates a course's leadership, commitment, and high standards of environmental management. Membership is open to national and international golf courses, including private clubs, public and municipal courses, PGA sites, nine-hole facilities, resort courses, and residential golf communities.

How to find out more...

http://www.auduboninti.org/programs/acss/golf.htm

Audubon Green Leaf Eco Rating Program

What is the initiative?

TerraChoice Environmental Marketing and Audubon International have partnered to present the Audubon Green Leaf™ Program. The Audubon Green Leaf Program is based on the premise that what is good for the environment can be good for business. By pursuing environmentally responsible practices in all areas of its operations, a hotel can reduce its costs, increase its market share, and protect our natural environment. The introductory level of commitment educates hotels on environmental and eco-efficiency issues. The second level provides hotels with a rating, a report that details how to get to the next level of performance, and an audit that verifies each property's eco-efficient functioning.

What does it offer?

Members receive a comprehensive tool kit that includes educational fact sheets and information on how to market the hotel as environmentally responsible. The program also provides sample news releases, sample radio public service announcements, sample guest room directory text, a list of "top ten" things to do, and background information for staff and guests.

How to find out more...

http://www.auduboninternational.org/programs/greenleaf

Table C-2 Hotel Certifications and Rating Programs (continued)

Hotel Association of Canada (HAC) Green Key ECO-Rating Program

What is the initiative?

Canada's Green Key ECO-Rating Program is a graduated rating system designed to recognize hotels, motels, and resorts that are committed to improving their fiscal and environmental performance. Based on the results of a comprehensive environmental audit, hoteliers are awarded a one-to-five Green Key rating and are offered guidance on how to "unlock" opportunities to reduce operating costs and environmental impacts through reduced utility consumption, employee training, and supply chain management. Members also benefit from powerful sales, marketing, public relations, and team-building opportunities, as well as positive feedback from guests. The HAC Green Key ECO-Rating Program is a voluntary program open to any lodging property in Canada, regardless of whether they are HAC members.

What does it offer?

ECO-rated hotels have access to the following unique tools and resources:

- Contact information for businesses and organizations seeking ECO-Rating

- ECO-Rating recognition in provincial accommodation guides

- Posting on the Federal Public Works/Environment Canada internal business travel directory

- Promotion on the ECO-Rating website with a direct link to the home page of the business

- Use of the HAC's ECO-Rating logo for collateral development

ECO-rated hotels can download press release templates tailored to their one-to-five key rating, and access sample key messages and media delivery information. The ECO-Rating program provides hoteliers with logos and an award plaque recognizing their performance. The program offers tips on promoting environmental awareness to guests without sacrificing service or satisfaction. The ECO-Rating audit also provides hoteliers with a property-specific action plan to focus employee resources and motivate behavioral changes.

How to find out more...

http://www.hacgreenhotels.com/site/about/index.htm

Green Globe

What is the initiative?

Green Globe is a worldwide benchmarking and certification program that facilitates sustainable travel and tourism for consumers, companies, and communities. The organization's website includes a list of participating hotels, resorts, and lodges. The Green Globe company standard is designed for organizations within the travel and tourism industry and sets out the criteria to attain certification. The program provides an environmental management framework for organizations to achieve sustainability. The Green Globe Benchmarking (Bronze) and Certification (Silver) processes focus on making operational improvements.

How to find out more...

http://www.ec3global.com/products-programs/green-globe

State Certification Programs

There are many state and municipal certification programs.
For more information, please go to the Web addresses listed below.

California
http://www.ciwmb.ca.gov/EPP/GreenLodging

California – San Francisco Green Business Program
http://www.abag.ca.gov/bayarea/enviro/gbus
http://www.sfenvironment.com/greenbiz

Florida
http://www.dep.state.fl.us/greenlodging

Georgia
http://www.gadnr.org/p2ad/Assets/Documents/ci_hospitality.html

Hawaii
http://www.hawaii.gov/dbedt/info/energy/resource

Maine
http://www.visitmaine.com/category/environmental_leaders.php

Michigan
http://www.michigan.gov/cis/0,1607,7-154-25676_25677_37026---,00.html

New Hampshire
http://www.nhslp.org

North Carolina
http://www.p2pays.org/hospitality

Pennsylvania
http://www.dep.state.pa.us/dep/deputate/pollprev/industry/hotels/default.htm

Vermont
http://www.vtgreenhotels.org

Virginia
http://www.deq.virginia.gov/p2/lodging/homepage.html

Wisconsin
http://www.travelgreenwisconsin.com/index.htm

APPENDIX D
Glossary

AAA Diamond The American Automobile Association hotel rating program that rates hotels from one to five diamonds.

acoustical ceiling tile Ceiling tile designed to improve sound quality and block noise transmission.

active solar heating Collection units absorb heat from the sun and transfer it through pumps or fans to a storage unit for later use, or directly to the building interior. The system requires controls to regulate its operation.

active solar water heater Collection units absorb heat from the sun and transfer it through pumps to a storage unit. The fluid in the storage unit conveys its heat to the domestic hot water of the building through a heat hanger. The system requires controls to regulate its operation.

aerator A device most installed on faucets to increase spray velocity, reduce splash, and save both water and energy.

air handling unit A heating and/or cooling distribution mechanism that channels warm or cool air to different parts of a building. The equipment includes a blower or fan, heating and/or cooling coils, as well as related controls, condensate drain pans, and air filters. The unit does not include ductwork, registers, grilles, boilers, or chillers.

albedo Also known as "solar reflectance," this is the ratio of reflected solar energy to incoming solar energy over wavelengths of approximately 0.3 to 2.5 micrometers.

alternative use license (AUL) In brownfield redevelopment, AUL refers to a district's capacity to be rezoned to an alternative acceptable use, taking into account the known contaminants of the site.

ambient air Open air, surrounding air, or outside air.

ASHRAE American Society of Heating, Refrigerating and Air-Conditioning Engineers.

ASHRAE 55-1992 ASHRAE standard: Thermal Environmental Conditions for Human Occupancy.

ASHRAE 62-1999 ASHRAE standard: Indoor Air Quality.

bamboo flooring Bamboo is a grass (not a wood) that annually produces new shoots. Individual stems are harvested from controlled forests every three to five years.

biodegradable Capable of decomposing naturally within a relatively short period of time.

broadloom Originally denoted carpet produced in widths wider than six feet. Today, carpet comes in 6-foot, 12-foot, and 15-foot widths.

brownfields Abandoned, idled, or under-used industrial and commercial facilities where expansion or redevelopment is complicated by real or perceived environmental contamination.

building automation system (BAS) A system that optimizes the start up and performance of HVAC equipment and alarm systems. A BAS system increases the interaction among the mechanical subsystems of a building, improves occupant comfort, lowers energy use, and allows off-site building control.

building related illness (BRI) BRI refers to a diagnosed illness of which the symptoms can be attributed directly to airborne building contaminants.

built environment Buildings and infrastructure constructed by human beings.

carbon dioxide (CO_2) A colorless, odorless, non-poisonous gas that exists in trace quantities (less than 400 parts per million) in ambient air. Carbon dioxide is a product of fossil fuel combustion. Although carbon dioxide does not directly impair human health, it is a greenhouse gas that traps terrestrial (i.e., infrared) radiation and contributes to the potential for global warming.

CERES A coalition of investors and environmentalists formerly known as the Coalition for Environmentally Responsible Economies.

chlorofluorocarbons (CFCs) A family of inert, nontoxic, and easily liquefied chemicals used in refrigeration, air conditioning, packaging, and insulation, or as solvents and aerosol propellants. Because CFCs are not destroyed in the lower atmosphere, they drift into the upper atmosphere, where their chlorine components destroy ozone.

CO_2 **sensor** A sensor for the measurement of gaseous carbon dioxide. Used in combination with energy-recovery units or demand-controlled ventilation to promote energy efficiency. Used to maintain appropriate indoor carbon dioxide levels.

cogeneration The generation of electricity and the capture and use of otherwise wasted heat energy byproducts. Also referred to as a combined heat and power (CHP) system.

combined heat and power (CHP) The generation of electricity and the capture and use of otherwise wasted heat energy by-products. Also referred to as cogeneration.

commissioning The process of ensuring that a building's complex array of systems is designed, installed, and tested to perform according to the design intent and the owner's operational needs. The commissioning of new buildings is most effective when considered throughout the planning stages, and as early as the schematic design phase.

compact fluorescent light (CFL) or lighting A type of fluorescent lamp. Compared to incandescent lamps of the same luminous flux, CFLs use less energy and have a longer life.

composite material Complex material made up of two or more complementary substances. Composite materials can be difficult to recycle (e.g., plastic laminates). They are best applied in situations where they can be removed for a reuse that does not require remanufacture.

composting A process whereby organic wastes, including food, paper, and yard wastes, decompose naturally and produce a material rich in minerals and ideal for gardening and farming as a soil conditioner or mulch, and for resurfacing or covering a landfill.

compressed natural gas (CNG) A substitute for gasoline (petrol) or diesel fuel. CNG is considered to be an environmentally "clean" alternative. It is made by compressing natural gas (which is composed mainly of methane [CH4]) in a percentage range of 70% to 98%.

daylighting A method of illuminating building interiors with natural light and reducing the use of artificial lighting. Common daylighting strategies include the proper orientation and placement of windows and the use of light wells or light shafts.

demand control ventilation (DCV) Ventilation provided in response to the actual number of occupants and to occupant activity.

demand control ventilation using carbon dioxide sensors A combination of two technologies: CO_2 sensors that monitor CO_2 levels in the air inside a building, and an air-handling system that uses data from the sensors to regulate the amount of air admitted.

density bonus A credit that allows developers to build more units than would normally be allowed in a certain zoning district by exchanging the excess units for other community benefits, such as affordable housing, historic preservation, and green building.

DEQ Department of Environmental Quality (usually at the state government level).

down-cycling The recycling of one material into another material of lesser quality. One example is the recycling of high-grade plastics into lower-grade plastics.

dual-flush toilet A toilet that has two buttons to allow appropriate water usage, typically ranging from one to two gallons

EA Energy and Atmosphere section of the LEED rating system.

emission The release of any gas, particle, or vapor into the environment from a commercial, industrial, or residential source, including smokestacks, chimneys, and motor vehicles.

emissivity The ratio of energy radiated by a specific material to the energy radiated by a black body at the same temperature. This is a measure of a material's ability to absorb and radiate energy.

energy modeling A computer model that analyzes a building's energy-related features in order to project the energy consumption of a given design.

energy recovery Obtaining energy from waste through a variety of processes (e.g., combustion).

energy recovery units Mechanisms that extract energy from the indoor air (warm air in winter, cool air in summer) and transfer it to the fresh incoming air.

Energy Star A United States government program that promotes energy-efficient consumer products.

environmental impact Any change to the environment, good or bad, that wholly or partially results from industrial manufacturing activities, products, or services.

EPA The United States Environmental Protection Agency, charged with setting and enforcing environmental regulations nationwide.

EPP Environmentally preferred product.

exposed aggregate The component pieces of a composite material used to resist compressive stress and visible in the end product.

fan coil unit (FCU) A small terminal HVAC unit often composed only of a blower and a heating and/or cooling coil (heat exchanger) and frequently used in hotels, condominiums, and apartments.

flashing A type of weatherproofing.

floor area ratio (FAR) The ratio of the total floor area of a building to the size of the land of its location, or the limit imposed on such a ratio.

fly ash The ash residue from high-temperature combustion processes. Electric motor plants using western coal produce a non-toxic fly ash that, because of its very high calcium content, can be a substitute for Portland cement (the common bonding material in concrete).

formaldehyde A colorless, pungent smelling, toxic material used as a component for the glues of many wood products. It can cause respiratory problems, cancer, and chemical sensitivity.

fossil fuels Fuels, such as coal, oil, and natural gas, produced by the decomposition of ancient (fossilized) plants and animals.

foundation mat slab Builders use mat-slab foundations to distribute heavy column and wall loads across an entire building area, and to lower the contact pressure as compared to conventional spread footings. Mat-slab foundations can be constructed near the ground surface, or at the bottom of basements. In high-rise buildings, mat-slab foundations can be several meters thick, with extensive reinforcement to ensure relatively uniform load transfer.

FSC products Forest Steward Council wood bearing the FSC logo guarantees that it was sustainably harvested from a certified, well-managed forest.

graywater Wastewater that does not contain sewage or fecal contamination and can be reused for irrigation after simple filtration.

green field A piece of undeveloped land.

Green Seal An environmental standard for hotel industry operations practices.

green team Interdisciplinary team comprised of representatives from various operating departments that is committed to improving the environmental sustainability of the property.

gross square feet (GSF) The total area occupied by a building when measured from exterior to exterior. This area includes all mechanical areas.

halons Synthetic substances (also known as bromofluorocarbons) that are chlorofluorocarbons containing bromine.

hardscape Paved areas such as streets and sidewalks, large business complexes and housing developments, and other industrial areas where the upper soil profile is no longer exposed to the actual surface of the Earth.

harvested rainwater Rain that falls on a roof and is channeled by gutters to a storage tank or cistern. The uses of this water depend on the existence and nature of pollutants that may have been picked up from the roof's surface.

heat island effect "Heat island" refers to urban air and surface temperatures that are higher than those of nearby rural areas. Many American cities and suburbs have air temperatures up to 10°F (5.6°C) warmer than their surrounding natural land cover.

heat recovery systems Building mechanical systems that capture waste heat from another system and use it to replace heat that would otherwise come from a primary energy source.

HVAC Heating, ventilating, and air conditioning equipment that controls the ambient environment (temperature, humidity, air flow, and air filtering) of a building. HVAC systems must be planned for and operated along with other data center components such as computing hardware, cabling, data storage, fire protection, physical security systems, and power.

HVAC&R Heating, ventilating, air conditioning, and refrigeration equipment.

hydrochlorofluorocarbons (HCFCs) Compounds containing carbon, hydrogen, chlorine, and fluorine. HCFCs originally were intended as replacements for CFCs, but they are only a temporary solution because they still contain chlorine and have the potential to destroy stratospheric ozone.

hydronic HVAC Water-based HVAC.

IACC International Association of Conference Centers.

IEEE Institute of Electrical and Electronics Engineers.

IEQ Indoor Environmental Quality section of the LEED rating system.

in situ remediation The cleanup or remediation of a polluted site, performed by using and simulating the natural processes in the soil, in contrast to ex situ remediation where contaminated soil is excavated and cleaned elsewhere off site.

incandescent light An electric lamp in which a filament is heated to produce artificial light. Incandescent lighting consumes more energy and is less efficient than CFLs or LEDs.

indoor air quality (IAQ) Pollution from gases or particles released into the air is the primary cause of indoor air quality problems. Inadequate ventilation can increase indoor pollutant levels by not bringing in enough outdoor air to dilute emissions.

infill development Real estate development that occurs in a previously built area.

integrated design Multi-disciplinary teams of building professionals work together from the pre-design phase through post-occupancy to optimize a building's environmental sustainability, performance, and cost savings.

irrigation Supplying water to grass, trees, and other plants.

ISO The International Standards Organization provides an internationally accepted specification for an Environmental Management System (EMS). The ISO specifies requirements for establishing an environmental policy, determining environmental aspects and impacts of products/activities/services, planning environmental objectives and measurable targets, the implementation and operation of programs to meet objectives and targets, checking and corrective action, and management review.

key card energy system An occupancy sensor system that uses an inserted computerized card to activate or deactivate equipment (e.g., heating, cooling, lighting).

kilowatt-hour (kwh) A unit of energy measured at 1,000 watt hours.

kilowatt peak (kWp) A measure of peak kilowatt output (e.g., of a photovoltaic system).

LCD Liquid crystal display.

LED Light-emitting diode.

LEED The Leadership in Energy and Environmental Design Green Building rating system. LEED is a voluntary, consensus-based, national standard for developing high-performance sustainable buildings.

LEED AP LEED accredited professional.

life cycle cost The amortized annual cost of a product, including capital costs and installation, operating, maintenance, and disposal costs discounted over the lifetime of the product.

low-e windows Low emissivity windows reflect heat, not light, keeping spaces warmer in winter and cooler in summer.

MERV The Minimum Efficiency Reporting Value for air filtration.

MR Materials and Resources section of the LEED rating system.

natural ventilation The process of supplying and removing air through an indoor space by natural means. There are two types of natural ventilation for buildings: wind-driven ventilation and stack ventilation.

net metering A method of crediting customers for electricity that they generate on site in excess of their purchased electricity consumption. Customers with their own generation offset the electricity they would have purchased from their utility. If such customers generate more than they use in a billing period, their electric meter turns backwards to indicate their net excess generation. Depending on individual state or utility rules, the net excess generation may be credited to the customer's account (in many cases at the retail price), carried over to a future billing period, or ignored.

NIMBY Not in my backyard.

occupancy sensors Mechanisms that automatically turn off lighting, HVAC, and/or electricity once a room is vacant.

on-site renewable energy generation Electricity generated by renewable resources using a system or device located at the site where the power is used. On-site generation is a form of distributed energy generation.

on-site sewage treatment Treating waste water where it is produced for reuse by technologies that require non-potable water at the same location.

ozone An unstable poisonous allotrope of oxygen (O_3) occurring in two forms. (1) Stratospheric ozone: In the stratosphere (the atmosphere layer beginning seven to ten miles above the earth), ozone is found naturally and provides a protective layer shielding the earth from ultraviolet radiation's harmful effects on humans and the environment. (2) Ground-level ozone: Ozone produced near the earth's surface through complex chemical reactions of nitrogen oxides, volatile organic compounds, and sunlight. Ground-level ozone is the primary component of smog and is harmful to humans and the environment.

PPM Parts per million.

packaged terminal air conditioner (PTAC) Equipment combining an air conditioner and a heater into a single, electrically powered unit typically installed through a wall and often found in hotels.

paspalum Tall American perennial grasses commonly known as paspalums, Bahiagrasses, or Dallis grasses. They are most diverse in subtropical and tropical regions.

passive cooling A building's structure (or an element of it) is designed to permit increased ventilation and retention of coolness with the intention of minimizing or eliminating the need for mechanical means of cooling.

passive design As applied to home construction, building design and placement permits the use of natural processes such as radiation, convection, absorption, and conduction to support comfort levels.

passive heating A building's structure (or an element of it) is designed to allow natural thermal energy flow, such as radiation, conduction, and convection generated by the sun, to provide heat. The home relies either solely or primarily on non-mechanical sources of heat.

passive solar water heater A water heating system that does not require mechanical pumps or controls to create hot water for domestic use.

passive ventilation The introduction and/or removal of air that uses both convective air flows resulting from the tendency of warm air to rise and cool air to sink, and takes advantage of prevailing winds. Many passive ventilation systems rely on building users to control their operation.

PERC The Property and Environment Research Center.

photo plastic laminate (P-Lam) A laminate is a material constructed by uniting (or bonding) two or more layers of material. Examples of laminate materials include Formica and plywood. Formica and similar plastic laminates (such as Pionite, Wilsonart or Centuryply Mica) often are referred to as High Pressure Decorative Laminate (HPDL) because they are created with heat and pressure that amounts to more than 5 lbf/in^2 (34 kPa).

photovoltaic (PV) A system that converts sunlight directly into electricity using cells made of silicon or other conductive material. When sunlight strikes the cells, a chemical reaction occurs, and this results in the release of electricity.

photovoltaic panels Devices using semiconductor material to directly convert sunlight into electricity. Power is produced when sunlight strikes the semiconductor material and creates an electrical current.

post-consumer recycled (PCR) content Material that has been recovered after its use as a consumer product. Examples include fleece clothing made from pop bottles and reclaimed carpet tiles used for new tile backing.

pre-consumer recycled content Material that is diverted from the waste stream following an industrial process. This excludes reutilization of materials such as rework, regrind, or scrap capable of being reclaimed within the same process.

recirculated water Rinse water that is reused before it is discarded, or water continually moving through a system, as in a fountain.

reclaimed water Wastewater (sewage) that has been treated and purified for reuse, rather than discharged into another body of water (e.g., a river).

recyclable content Materials that can be recovered or diverted from the waste stream for recycling and reuse.

recycled content The percentage of recycled materials in a product, generally determined by weight.

recycling The series of activities, including collection, separation, and processing, by which products or other materials are recovered from the solid waste stream for use in the form of raw materials for the manufacture of new products (other than fuel).

regulation A federal agency imposes a regulation; Congress enacts a law.

renewable energy Energy resources such as wind or solar power that produce indefinitely without being depleted.

renewable resources Resources that are created or produced at least as fast as they are consumed.

RFP Request for proposal.

R-value A measure of the thermal resistance of material, especially insulation.

SEER Seasonal Energy Efficiency Ratio, as defined by the Air Conditioning and Refrigeration Institute.

SF Square feet.

sick building syndrome A situation in which a building's occupants experience acute health conditions and/or levels of discomfort that appear to be linked to time spent in the building, but no specific illness or cause can be identified. Complaints may be localized to a particular room or zone.

SMACNA Sheet Metal and Air Conditioning Contractors' National Association.

smart growth A range of development and conservation strategies that help to protect our natural environment and make our communities more attractive, economically stronger, and more socially diverse.

sound attenuation A reduction in the intensity or pressure level of sound that is transmitted from one point to another.

SS Sustainable Sites section of the LEED rating system.

sustainability Meeting the needs of the present without compromising the ability of future generations to meet their needs.

toxic The attribute of any material or waste product that can produce injury and/or loss of life when inhaled, swallowed, or absorbed through the skin.

United States Green Building Council (USGBC) A national organization, founded in 1993, whose mission is to accelerate the adoption of green building practices, technologies, policies, and standards. USGBC established the LEED certification guidelines.

urban sprawl The unplanned, uncontrolled spreading of urban development into areas adjoining a city.

variable air volume (VAV) An HVAC system stategy through which the volume of air delivered to conditioned spaces is varied as a function of ventilating needs, energy needs, or both.

variable frequency drive (VFD) A specific type of adjustable speed drive that controls the rotational speed of an alternating current (AC) electric motor by controlling the frequency of the electric power supplied to the motor. VFDs also are known as adjustable frequency drives (AFD), variable speed drives (VSD), AC drives, or inverter drives.

vegetative roof/green roof A building roof that is partially or completely covered with vegetation and soil, or a growing medium, and planted over a waterproofing membrane.

veneers Thin slices of wood, usually thinner than 3.0 mm (1/8 inch), that are glued and pressed onto core panels (typically wood, particle board, or medium density fiberboard) to produce flat panels such as doors, tops and side panels for cabinets, parquet floors, and furniture elements.

volatile organic compounds (VOCs) Chemicals that contain carbon molecules and are volatile enough to evaporate from material surfaces into indoor air at normal room temperatures (referred to as off-gassing).

waterless urinals Units that resemble conventional fixtures, and easily replace them. The "waterless" units connect to the regular waste lines, but eliminate the flush water supply lines. This eliminates the flush valves, as well, and there are no handles to touch, no sensors, and no moving parts.

WE Water Efficiency section of the LEED rating system.

whole systems thinking A process through which the interconnections of systems are actively considered, and solutions are sought that address multiple problems at the same time.

zoning Legislative regulations by which a municipal government seeks to control the use of buildings and land within the municipality.

501(c)(3) Internal Revenue Service non-profit tax status designation.

APPENDIX E
Team Biography

Michele L. Diener is a dual-degree MBA/MS student at the Stephen M. Ross School of Business and the School of Natural Resources and Environment at the University of Michigan. Prior to pursuing graduate studies, Michele worked for Toyota Motor Sales, where she focused on sustainable construction, operations, and maintenance. As a summer associate at Sustainable Conservation, Michele identified and researched opportunities to promote sustainable business practices among California hotels. She emphasized increasing awareness of sustainable practices in hotel building design and construction, as well as in ongoing, daily operations. Upon completion of her graduate studies, Michele plans to work in the hospitality industry in a position that promotes environmental sustainability. Michele can be contacted at mldiener@umich.edu.

Amisha Parekh is a dual-degree MBA/MS student at the Stephen M. Ross School of Business and the School of Natural Resources and Environment at the University of Michigan. Prior to attending business school, she worked at Deloitte Consulting on marketing and governance-related projects in the financial services industry. She also spent six months with a non-governmental organization (NGO) in India working on wetland protection and air quality issues. Amisha interned with the marketing group at Procter & Gamble and with the sustainability strategy team at Wal-Mart, where she researched opportunities for promoting sustainable products in the mass market. Upon graduation she plans to work as a strategy consultant helping companies identify opportunities to improve environmental performance while addressing consumer needs. Amisha can be contacted at amishaa@umich.edu.

Jaclyn Pitera is a dual-degree MBA/MS student at the Stephen M. Ross School of Business and the School of Natural Resources and Environment at the University of Michigan. Jaclyn interned at The JBG Companies, a Washington, D.C. real estate developer, as an internal sustainable strategy consultant. After graduation, she plans to continue consulting for land-based organizations, advising them how to develop and operate sustainably. Jaclyn can be contacted at jpitera@umich.edu.

Faculty Advisor

Andrew J. Hoffman is the Holcim (US) Professor of Sustainable Enterprise, a joint appointment in the Stephen M. Ross School of Business and the School of Natural Resources and Environment at the University of Michigan. He also serves as Associate Director of the University's Frederick A. and Barbara M. Erb Institute for Global Sustainable Enterprise. Professor Hoffman's current research interests focus on the nature and dynamics of change within institutional and cultural systems. He applies this research toward an understanding of the cultural and managerial implications of environmental protection for industry. Professor Hoffman has published seven books and more than 50 articles on this subject. His published work includes *Climate Change: What's Your Business Strategy?* (2008); *Carbon Strategies: How Leading Companies Are Reducing Their Climate Change Footprint* (2007); *Getting Ahead of the Curve: Corporate Strategies that Address Climate Change* (2006); *Organizations, Policy, and the Natural Environment* (co-editor with Marc Ventresca, 2002); *From Heresy to Dogma: An Institutional History of Corporate Environmentalism (2001)*; *Competitive Environmental Strategy* (2000); and *Global Climate Change: A Senior-Level Debate at the Intersection of Economics, Strategy, Technology, Science, Politics, and International Negotiation* (editor, 1998). *From Heresy to Dogma* won the 2001 Rachel Carson Prize from the Society for Social Studies of Science. Professor Hoffman received the 2003 Faculty Pioneer Rising Star award from the World Resources Institute and the Aspen Institute.

Partnerships

This project would not have been possible without the generous financial support from the following organizations: